To

Tony and Caitlin

Contents

About the Contributors

Mary Cullen is a former Senior Lecturer in Modern History at NUI Maynooth. At present she is a Research Associate at the Centre for Gender and Women's Studies at Trinity College Dublin, where she teaches on the MPhil programme. Her current research interest is in the political thought of Irish feminism.

Angela Dowdell is a postgraduate student at the University of Michigan, Ann Arbor, Michigan. She is currently writing her dissertation entitled 'Real Men/Savage Nature: Big Game Hunting, Modernity, and the African Interior in fin-de-siècle Britain'. She anticipates completing her dissertation by April 2009.

Maureen Flanagan is a Professor of Urban History at Michigan State University, East Lansing, Michigan, USA. Among her more recent publications are *Seeing with Their Hearts: Chicago Women and the Vision of the Good City, 1871–1933* (Princeton, NJ: Princeton University Press, 2002) and 'The Workshop or the Home? Gender Visions in the History of Urban Built Environments: Canada and the United States', *London Journal of Canadian Studies* (2006/07). She is currently working on a book: *Consolidating the Patriarchal City: Gender Ideas and the Construction of the Built Environments of Chicago, Dublin, London, and Toronto, 1870s–1940s*.

Phil Kilroy is a Research Associate of the History Department, Trinity College Dublin. She has published *Protestant Dissent and Controversy in Ireland 1660–1714* (Cork: Cork University Press, 1994) and numerous articles on religious non-conformity in seventeenth-century Ireland. She is the author of *Madeleine Sophie Barat. A Life* (Cork: Cork University Press, 2nd impression, 2000), which has also appeared in Spanish (2000), French (2004) and Japanese (2008).

Mary McAuliffe holds a PhD in Medieval History from the Department of History, Trinity College Dublin. She lectures on Women in Irish History on the Women's Studies Programme, School of Social Justice, UCD. Her research interests include medieval Irish women and power, and female representations and identities in Irish History. She is currently secretary of the Women's History Association of Ireland.

Sandra McAvoy MA PhD co-ordinates and teaches Women's Studies at University College Cork. Her research interests include: the history of sexuality, with a focus on the experiences of women in Ireland in the twentieth century, the history and politics of reproductive rights issues, and women and politics.

Eve Morrison was born in the United States but has lived in Ireland for over twenty years. She is an Irish History student at Trinity College Dublin, where she held an IRCHSS postgraduate scholarship for three years. Her PhD is a thematic analysis of the Bureau of Military History collection under the supervision of Professor David Fitzpatrick.

Úna Ní Bhroiméil is a lecturer in the Department of History, Mary Immaculate College, University of Limerick. She is the author of *Building Irish Identity in America, 1870–1915 – The Gaelic Revival* (Dublin: Four Courts Press, 2003) and her publications include works on the Irish American press and on the gender construction of female teachers in late-nineteenth- and early twentieth-century Ireland.

Katherine O'Donnell lectures in Women's Studies in the School of Social Justice, University College Dublin. She has published widely on Irish literary history, the history of sexuality and specifically on the life and works of Edmund Burke.

Dónal O Donoghue is an Assistant Professor and Chair of Art Education at the University of British Columbia, Canada. His research addresses masculinity and schooling, art education and visual culture, and the intersections between educational research and art practice.

Mary O'Dowd is Professor of Gender History at Queen's University Belfast. Her most recent book is *A History of Women in Ireland,*

1500–1800 (Harlow: Longman Pearson, 2005). She is currently working on a history of the family in early modern Ireland.

Clíona Rattigan recently completed her PhD '"Dark Spots" in Irish Society: Unmarried Motherhood, Crime and Prosecution in Ireland, 1900–1950' in the Department of History, Trinity College Dublin where she held an IRCHSS postgraduate scholarship for three years. She is currently a teaching fellow at the University of Warwick.

Jennifer Redmond is a postgraduate student at the Centre for Gender and Women's Studies and a researcher in the Centre's Research Unit. She is completing her dissertation entitled 'Moving Histories: Discourses on Irish Women's Emigration to England, 1922–1948'. She is currently Treasurer of the Women's History Association, Ireland.

Maryann Gialanella Valiulis is the Director of the Centre for Gender and Women's Studies, Trinity College Dublin and a specialist in modern Irish History. She is in the process of completing a study of gender relations in Irish history entitled, 'Refashioning the Nation with Virtue: Gender Politics in the Irish Free State'. She is currently President of the Women's History Association, Ireland.

CHAPTER ONE

Introduction: Gender, Power and Patriarchy

MARYANN GIALANELLA VALIULIS

Gender makes power visible. Gender history makes power relations visible and allows us to explore the dynamic which privileges some at the expense of the many. Gender history allows us to isolate and highlight the ways in which power flows through society, charting how it operates, who it favours and how groups subvert and circumvent this power, exercising 'other' power in their own right. Or as Mary O'Dowd points out in her 'Madness of the Muses' piece, quoting Joan C. Scott, gender is 'a primary way of signifying relationships of power'. The essays in this collection can be read as making power visible in a particular historical context.

This collection grew out of a Women's History Association, Ireland (WHAI) conference held in Trinity College in November 2006. The theme of the conference was 'Doing Gender History: Methods and Modules'. The call for papers conceptualized gender as socially constructed and relational – the relation of men and women, of masculinities and femininities. The inspiration was from the work of the extraordinary historian, Gerda Lerner, who asked quite simply what gender history would look like. Our aim was to provide one answer to this question in an Irish context.[1]

Starting with this goal, we found that most of the participants at the conference seemed to think in terms of either women's history or the study of masculinities. Was this gender? Was women's history now simply renamed as gender history with masculinities and femininities added to the mix? A multiplicity of voices and views about gender history came from the open discussion we had at the conference. That diversity is replicated in the chapters in this collection.

However, there was a common theme: power. As the historian Joan Hoff points out, 'gender is, in fact, about the power of men over

women'.[2] Gender history is not simply about women, as important as this is, or femininities and masculinities, as important as they are. It is about society and the way it was governed, ruled, negotiated and understood. The actors may have been women but the stage was the larger society. Men were there, sometimes more visible, sometimes less visible. What we needed to do was to pull back the curtain and ask who had power in this particular historical situation.

Power is one of the keys to revealing what is happening in history: Who has it? Who wields it? Who disputes it? Where is its centre – is it the power of the monarch, the revolutionary movement, the Church, the State or the community? What we do know is that power privileges some, includes some, and defines the norms against which all of society is judged. Some are simply designated as more valuable than others.

In women's studies, we talk about patriarchy – 'a system of social structures and practices in which men dominate, oppress and exploit women'.[3] In women's history, this is a more contested term. I think it is an important concept because it provides us with a conceptual tool for understanding what is happening in a given society. There are, of course, caveats: the caveat that patriarchy be grounded in the particulars of the historical period we are analyzing; the caveat that we understand that not all men are part of the powerful elite although all men may profit from it in some way; and the caveat that some women not only collude but benefit from the hierarchies and distribution of power evident in patriarchy. However, thinking about patriarchy helps us to understand the organization, the structure, the dynamics of a given society. It helps us to see power.[4]

The ideological import of patriarchy also facilitates us moving from women's history to gender history. It makes us aware of the exercise of patriarchal power in the historical societies we are analyzing. Gender history is a means of thinking about power in society and we use gender analysis to explore these wider issues. This, to me, is a significant step. However, there is no denying that we needed/need a great deal of compensatory history. We needed/need to find women, to do the archival digging that would make women visible, to write women into the historical narrative. Phil Kilroy, in her essay in this volume, uses the metaphor of gardening and how gardening was necessary to make women's lives visible. It was and is an incredibly crucial task. However, as Kilroy also points out, this landscaping endeavour challenges 'long held vested interests and positions of power'.

Perhaps we need to stop thinking in a linear manner – as if it is a progression which starts with the history of women worthies and ends up with gender history, with all the steps in-between. Is it not a process which sometimes proceeds simultaneously? We need to find out what women did, thought, experienced as well as finding out what that tells us about the society of the time, about what was important, who was important, how power was exercised. Ultimately that may be the real challenge of gender history and its justification. Mary O'Dowd poses a very important question when she asks if Irish women's history has lost its ability to excite or stimulate passion. I would argue the passion, the madness comes with what we do with gender history – how we analyze, interpret and allow it to change our understanding of the working of a particular society or deepen our understanding of that society. That would enable us to rewrite history in a new and radical manner – an exciting prospect.

Using the theme of patriarchal power, the chapters in this volume cover a variety of time periods and topics, all of which highlight the use and misuse of power. We begin with the general, with Mary Cullen's chapter which, while specifically dealing with an analysis of enlightenment thinking, also deals more broadly with the potential of gender history. Cullen points out that Enlightenment egalitarianism had the potential to be truly revolutionary and recognize women as 'full human persons'. However, the intellectuals of the day shied away from the implications of their thinking and ignored the very forceful and ably argued claims of women. They were 'limited by the pervasive ideology of masculine superiority'. This leads Cullen to ask the more general question: what would have been the result if historians looked seriously at what feminists were saying? She calls for a major reassessment of traditional history to incorporate feminist scholarship:

> If gender analysis became a standard part of the historian's tool kit, it would undoubtedly lead to major reassessments across the board. One focus would be on the blindness of most 'mainstream' historians to the centrality of gender relationships in the history of human societies. A substantial body of feminist scholarship over several decades has documented and analysed the ideology of masculine superiority and dominance that pervades the history of Western philosophical, theological and political thought from Aristotle onwards, yet this has not been incorporated into general histories of political thought. Historians would have to face the question why this has been the case.

This theme of how gender history would change our understanding, alter our interpretations of the ideologies and societies under consideration permeates this volume. If we asked, as Mary Cullen does, who benefits, who holds the power and what does it mean, how would history be different?

We turn from this discussion of the potential of gender history to a more chronological framework. We begin with witch trials which are the subject of Mary McAuliffe's essay. She details how historians for a very long time ignored the gender dimension of these trials, despite the very obvious fact that the overwhelming majority of those who were accused of being witches were women. Instead, traditional historians spoke of interpersonal tensions between villagers, the existence of evil, economic and social pressures and the differences between the worthy and unworthy poor. Gender was not seen to be significant. It is only of late that the importance of gender is being acknowledged in the various case studies under consideration. McAuliffe notes the gradual change in historiography citing Clark who argues that 'gender analysis is a step forward in feminist history as it can make evident different forms of male power and it can incorporate sexuality and the body as a historical dynamic'. In addition to outlining the historiography of witchcraft, McAuliffe provides an Irish example of a witchcraft trial, the case of Florence Newton. Not only does it have the classic elements of a witchcraft trial but, significantly, it demonstrates that the ideas associated with witches – for example, the idea of women's weakness, or the diseased female bodies, or the polluting female touch – 'had some impact on the construct of femininity in early modern Irish societies'.

From the witches of the medieval period, we leap to the more contemporary period: the formation and reality of the Irish Free State. Eve Morrison examines the witness statements of women who were members of Cumann na mBan and fought in the Anglo-Irish war. These statements were taken under the auspices of the Bureau of Military History and, despite many difficulties, presented a golden opportunity to hear the voices of many of the women involved in the struggles. The picture that emerges is of the women of Cumann na mBan as active, courageous and valuable participants in the Irish struggle for independence. In her analysis of these witness statements, Morrison demonstrates how gender could be used to the advantage of nationalists because of stereotypes about women as passive, innocent and concerned only with domestic matters. Morrison concludes that while these women lacked official power, they certainly had unofficial power. Interestingly, while after the Anglo-Irish war, men, indeed heroes, like Michael Collins and Cathal Brugha recognized and praised the efforts of the women revolutionaries, subsequent popular and historical accounts of the period 'eclipse' women's roles.

The next three chapters deal with issues of, and discourse about, sexuality. Sandra McAvoy begins by examining the precedents for the Criminal Law Amendment Act of 1935. Drawing on evidence from the pre-Free State period, she convincingly demonstrates how the campaign to repeal legislation that reflected the sexual double standard began earlier and how feminists and moral purity campaigners: 'perceived the protection of women from sexual aggression as vital to female emancipation and ... explicitly challenged the myth underlying the acceptance of such standards: that as male sexual urges were uncontrollable, male sexual transgressions were excusable.' Her discussion of male sexual assaults on children in the context of a patriarchal judicial system is truly horrifying. In her chapter, she sets the context for the feminist campaign for the Criminal Law Amendment Act of 1935.

Valiulis continues the discussion of male power vis-à-vis sexuality in analyzing the discourse surrounding motherhood, sexuality and power. Her chapter focuses on the ways in which purity and virtue were critical to the Free State's definition of itself and its justification for independence. When it became evident that the morality of the Free State was not at the level its leaders proclaimed, the State intervened and legislated for morality. Birth control was forbidden, censorship was imposed and it was made clear that only 'virtuous mothers' were welcomed in the new State. State power over, and State control of, reproduction became an accepted fact of Irish life. As she notes: 'The control of Irish women's sexuality was too important to be left simply to women.'

Clíona Rattigan continues the analysis of sexuality in her discussion of abortion among Irish women in the twenty-six counties of the South and in Northern Ireland. She analyses the role of men and women in making this decision and concludes that both were usually active agents in deciding on abortion. She sees women as 'willing sexual partners', who did not necessarily want to marry – certainly not the judicial stereotype of hapless victims. Not surprisingly, those who were better educated, wealthier and more confident were quite forceful in determining their reproductive fate. What becomes apparent, however, are the difficulties, the trauma, of dealing with an unwanted pregnancy. Powders, potions or a trip to England were the options for those who wanted to terminate their pregnancies. As she notes: 'in most cases unmarried pregnant women were ... motivated to seek abortions because of the stigma associated with single motherhood, lack of financial resources and the lack of support from the man responsible for the pregnancy'.

Jennifer Redmond discusses this theme of sexuality and identity in the context of emigration. Women's emigration to England was condemned by priests, politicians and the media as having the potential for moral disaster as vulnerable women were seen to be at the mercy of a pagan, pleasure-loving society. Redmond argues that there were significant 'disjunctions between articulation of the lived experience of female emigrants and the rhetoric surrounding them'. Not only were these women morally suspect, but their motives were castigated as selfish, 'reflecting "uncontrollable fascination [with] ... garish distractions and ... the glamorous unreality of the films"'. No mention was made of the fact that there were no jobs for these women in Ireland and the decision to emigrate was most often based on the concrete realities of the day. Moreover, the lives of these Irish women in Britain revolved around parish clubs which provided for their social lives and through which they established social networks and clearly maintained a sense of 'Irishness'.

Úna Ní Bhroiméil and Dónal O Donoghue take us into the realm of visual history and the ways in which 'visual methodologies can be used in gender history research', to make power visible and to disrupt the linear narrative. Focusing on teacher training in single-sex institutions, both authors demonstrate the ways in which power is revealed through the visual. O Donoghue works with an installation in which he projects images and extracts from teaching practice reports on the screen. His aim in juxtaposing the two is to 'disrupt the linear narrative' and 'make visible tensions in representation and construction'. Úna Ní Bhroiméil focuses on uncovering feminizing practices and the social construction and regulation of femininities among teachers. She works with photographs and sees them as telling not one coherent narrative but many, 'a complex and multi-layered narrative'. From these photographs, she concludes that the women who were training to be teachers were being socialized into particular gender and class roles, roles which bespoke an 'air of gentility'. Both O Donoghue and Ní Bhroiméil invite us to 'look into rather than look at' these visual images.

Katherine O'Donnell's contribution brings us into the realm of masculinities and affect. As a literary scholar, she writes of women's history and gender history from a different perspective. She contends that women's history has difficulties dealing with lesbian relationships for a variety of reasons – the historians' dependence on documents, the reluctance to name a relationship lesbian and even possibly, she posits, the fear that the historian herself would be named as a lesbian. O'Donnell believes that gender history, 'that is history writing that focuses on the relations between masculinity and femininity', opens up the possibility for dealing with same sex relationships within the context of gender relations. Because she sees gender as relational, as fluid, as 'continually constructed, contested and negotiated in relation to each other', gender history, O'Donnell believes, is better able to deal with love, desire, affect and emotion.

With our last two chapters, we move toward comparative history to demonstrate how looking at gender in different contexts broadens our perspective. Angela Dowdell gives us a fascinating insight into big game hunting. Traditionally seen as a masculine preserve, and perhaps because it was so overwhelmingly classed, raced and gendered, it gave women big game hunters an opportunity for equality. Dowdell demonstrates that, defying both conventional norms and conventional wisdom, women big game hunters were able to go on safaris with only their African servants with no fear for their safety or reputation. Dowdell notes that this 'glimpse into the sexual politics of the safari is an eloquent example of the gaps that have been created in historiography' and the necessity for including the 'experiences, perspectives and contemporary reception of women hunters'. This chapter raises interesting questions about the intersection of issues such as class, race, gender and sexuality, about what constitutes civilization. It throws a 'masculine institution like big game hunting into relief' and asks 'what women's experiences and perspectives can tell us about the many notions bound up with safari hunting'.

Maureen Flanagan's chapter in urban history closes this volume. In her analysis of 'what a city ought to be and do', she looks at urban development in Chicago, Dublin and Toronto, cities which she sees as part of the Anglo-American urban tradition. Her argument is that overall there is a definite conflict between the male view of the purpose of the city as a commercial centre and the female view of the city as a living organism which encompasses both reproductive and productive elements. Flanagan states quite clearly that it is 'these gendered ideals that shaped the urban built environment', and that 'specifically gendered ideas about a city and life within it ... were intended to keep women under the control of men'.

Taken in total, these chapters, each in its own way, question the ways in which gender history throws into sharp relief the power structure of a particular society. From witches to witness statements, from motherhood to abortion, from cities to safaris, the exploration of gender leads to an examination of power in a more complex and exciting narrative – 'a kind of madness'.

For organizing the WHAI conference and the earliest stages of this volume, I would like to thank Aoife O'Driscoll, formerly a postgraduate student and researcher at the Centre for Gender and Women's Studies, Trinity College. I am indebted to Laura Carpenter, Catherine KilBride and Louise McCaul for their assistance in the production of this book and to my colleagues in the Centre for Gender and Women's Studies. I am grateful for the support of Trinity College. I would also like to thank my daughter, Caitlin Valiulis, for discussing with me the nature of gender in Irish history.

Maryann Gialanella Valiulis
Director, Centre for Gender and Women's Studies
Trinity College, Dublin
President of the Women's History Association, Ireland, 2008

NOTE

1. See, for example, Gerda Lerner, 'Reconceptualizing Differences Among Women', *Journal of Women's History* (Winter 1990), pp.106–19.
2. Joan Hoff, 'The Impact and Implications of Women's History', in Maryann Gialanella Valiulis and Mary O'Dowd (eds), *Women and Irish History. Essays in Honour of Margaret MacCurtain* (Dublin: Wolfhound Press, 1997), p.33.
3. Sylvia Walby, *Theorizing Patriarchy* (Oxford: Blackwell Press, 1990), p.20. I believe this discussion of patriarchy remains to this day one of the best and most inclusive. It documents the shift from private to public patriarchy and then looks at six aspects of society in which patriarchy manifests itself.
4. For a discussion of the use of the term patriarchy in women's history, see Judith M. Bennett, *History Matters: Patriarchy and the Challenge of Feminism* (Philadelphia: University of Pennsylvania Press, 2006). The 'Book Forum' of the *Journal of Women's History* (Summer, 2006), pp.130–154 provides an interesting response to Bennett's views.

CHAPTER TWO

Thoughts on Gender History

MARY O'DOWD AND PHIL KILROY

GENDER HISTORY, IRISH HISTORY AND THE MADNESS OF THE MUSES

> Fervent desire is a gift of the Muses, a kind of madness that takes over, igniting and transforming the subject. According to Plato, it 'seizes a tender, virgin soul and stimulates it to rapt passionate expression ... But if any man comes to the gates of poetry without the madness of the Muses, persuaded that skill alone will make him a good poet [we might substitute 'good historian by discipline'], then shall he and his works of sanity ... be brought to naught.'[1]

In her contribution to the 2004 debate on the future of women's history published in the *Journal of Women's History*, Joan Scott used the language of erotica to describe the desire for knowledge that is at the core of all intellectual investigation, including feminist criticism. She recalled the passion of the first generation of women historians in the United States as they pursued a desire to learn more concerning the history of women, a desire aroused as much by the search for knowledge about women as it was by the excitement of the intellectual enquiry involved. 'Passion', as Scott notes, 'thrives on the pursuit of the not-yet-known'.[2] To insist on a definition of women's history that focuses solely on women, Scott suggested, is to deny the intellectual passion, excitement and potential of feminist critique. Feminist history exists in a parasitical relationship with the discipline of history. It critiques history from the 'perspective of gender and power'.[3] It destabilizes or 'defamiliarizes' concepts and ideas hitherto taken for granted by historians. The form that the critique of feminist historians will take in the future depends, according to Scott, on the direction of the discipline. The priority is the desire and passion for knowledge, not the formation of boundaries or the conservation of what are currently established as traditional ways of writing women's and gender history.[4]

Coming almost ten years after her challenging article on using gender as a tool of analysis, Scott's summoning of the madness of the Muses, may, at first reading, induce despair rather than desire among historians of women.[5] Having struggled to come to terms with her advocacy in 1985 of post-structuralism, feminist historians were urged by Scott in 2004 to engage in a continuous process of thinking about the unthinkable: 'the passionate pursuit of the not-yet-known'. Gender, she acknowledges, is not the only category of analysis and is itself being 'defamiliarized' by a new generation of scholars interested in queer theory, ethnic and post-colonial studies.[6]

There are also, however, common themes that can be traced throughout Scott's writing in relation to feminism and feminist politics. In 1985 she presented gender analysis as a 'useful' or 'good way to think about history'.[7] In 2004, she urged feminist scholars to continue that quest to think about history in interesting ways. Scott's aim is not, however, to engage in a restless chase of new or innovative ideas for their own sake, or to reduce historical analysis to an intellectual game, but to develop methodologies that advance the feminist project. The goal is not just to destabilize interpretations of the past from the perspective of gender but ultimately to destabilize patriarchy in the present.[8]

In 1985 Scott had proposed gender analysis as a way around the continuing dilemma of women's history: how to widen the perspective of 'mainstream' history to incorporate the findings of the accumulated research on women's history. Scott defined gender as a social construct that can vary in different cultures, social groups and over time. She pointed to several ways in which thinking about gender could be useful to historians. The first involves comparing men's and women's experiences in the past, an approach that had led to the development of the field of men's studies and the history of masculinity but had not, in Scott's view, done much to change the way in which history was written. An alternative definition of gender defines it as an essential component in social relationships: a 'primary way of signifying relationships of power'.[9] Hierarchies of difference, subordination and dominance, exclusion and inclusion are frequently based on gender. Metaphorically and literally, gender is used to define difference and establish power relationships. The organization of society is often implicitly rooted in concepts of gender that are perceived as normative but, Scott notes, often vary over time and in different cultures. Used in this sense, gender as a category of analysis should form part of the critical apparatus of all historians and not just that of women. High politics, for example, is often dismissed as having little relevance for women's history because for much of historic time, women were excluded from participating in it. Scott's argument is, however, that the exclusion of women not only makes high politics a gendered concept but should lead the historian to query the implication of that notion. 'What is the relationship between laws about women and the power of the state?'[10] In modern states where universal suffrage has been achieved, gender remains central to the formation of political ideas and concepts. A classic example of this is the welfare state which was constructed around an image of the family in which the man was the head of household and wage earner and his wife, the child-carer and home-maker. Concepts of gender are also used metaphorically to legitimate political power and to describe relations between states.

Scott's 1985 article aroused considerable debate, partly because of its proposal that historians utilize theories of post-structuralism and partly because it implicitly suggested that gender analysis offered feminist historians a more sophisticated critical apparatus than focusing exclusively on the history of women. Despite the criticisms, however, Scott's advocacy of an innovative 'way to think about history' was timely. A younger generation of American scholars was attracted by the intellectual appeal of gender history, if not necessarily by Scott's wider feminist agenda, while some of the most influential of the first generation of academic women historians seem to have quietly agreed with Scott that women's history writing had lost its critical excitement: 'stories designed to celebrate women's agency began to seem predictable and repetitious, more information gathering to prove a point that has already been made ... the situation of women as wounded subjects does not inspire either creative politics or history'.[11] Many writers of women's history were clearly looking for new intellectual stimulation and found it in gender history. The 1990s and early 2000s have witnessed a steady accumulation of American history monographs that use gender as a core tool of analysis. Some studies integrate comparative studies of men and women while others, although focusing on women's experiences, use gender analysis to explore wider issues about the structure of political or economic organizations or to examine how gender metaphors are embedded in political, diplomatic and social discourse. As Kathryn Kish Sklar noted in 2003, the renewed vitality of American women's and gender history has meant that the boundary between women's history and wider interpretations of

American history are increasingly blurred. Gender analysis is now, for example, perceived as essential to understanding the history of the welfare state and the evolution of concepts of citizenship. Developing the metaphor of the 'mainstream', Kish Sklar suggests that 2001 was the 'moment when U.S. history jumped out of its old riverbed into a new one where it was reconfigured by U.S. women's history'.[12]

How do we apply this to Irish history? Has Irish women's history begun to reshape the narrative of Irish history? Where is the gift of the Muses in Irish historiography? A survey of the current state of research and writing on women's history in Ireland includes much to celebrate and welcome. Although operating in a much smaller academic community than in the US, the achievements have been, nonetheless, impressive. Since the publication in 1978 of *Women in Irish Society: The Historical Dimension*, edited by Margaret MacCurtain and Donnchadh Ó Corráin (Dublin: Women's Press, 1978) (usually recognized as the initiation of the academic study of Irish women's history), there has been a steady accumulation of articles and monographs on the activities of women in the Irish past. An academic infrastructure for the study of women's history has been created. An association of researchers with regular conferences, postgraduate seminars, large funded collaborative research projects, undergraduate courses, an MA programme, a small community of doctoral students and a reasonably high profile at international conferences are all indicators that the study of women in the past has been accepted into the Irish academy. The accumulated research on women's history has also made at least a limited impact on the writing of Irish history. Few general surveys of Irish history completely ignore women as was the case in the past, and some of the most recent overviews of twentieth-century Ireland give credit to women as agents of change.[13]

This steady trickle of research results into the 'mainstream' may be sufficient or all that can be expected given the small size of the university history community on the island of Ireland and the handful of historians of women in full-time academic employment. Yet, in terms of intellectual excitement, it could be argued that Irish women's history, like American women's history in the 1980s, has lost some of its ability to excite or stimulate passion. We can and should continue to accumulate information about women in the Irish past but should we also pause to ask to what purpose? The intellectual rationale for most studies of Irish women's history is the dearth of literature on the topic. It might legitimately be queried if this continues to be a sufficient reason? Is there a danger in this approach that we will begin to tell stories that 'seem predictable and repetitious – more information gathering to prove a point that has already been made'?[14]

Historians of women in Ireland have been slow to take up the challenge of Scott's advocacy of gender as a category of analysis. There are understandable reasons for this reluctance. Irish historiography, even more than its British counterpart with which it shares a common empirical emphasis, has always been suspicious of theoretical approaches. Scott's reliance on the difficult and, at times, inaccessible, language of post-structuralism did little to win her converts among Irish women historians. Moreover, her self-conscious political agenda as a 'feminist historian' sits uncomfortably in an historiographical tradition that was constructed in opposition to the labelling of historians as 'nationalist' or 'unionist'. In the 1980s and 1990s, historians of women in Ireland were enthused by the discovery of women in the Irish past and the application of the gender/women's history debate to an Irish context seemed, at best, premature and, at worst, part of the generational conflict among American women historians that had no direct parallel in Ireland.

Gender, of course, has not been totally ignored by Irish historians and a number of collections of essays have pointed to the potential of it as a category of analysis although the emphasis, as among British historians, has tended to be on examining the relative experiences of men and women with initial forays into the history of Irish masculinity.[15] There has, however, been no sustained debate on the value of gender as a category of analysis in Irish history. The conference call for papers for the 2006 Women's History Association of Ireland (WHAI) conference on gender history in Trinity College Dublin elicited a very limited response among the more traditional Irish historians. The papers presented to the conference did, however, underline the potential of gender history at an international level, as this volume indicates.

Compiling lists of topics to be researched can be a lazy way of analyzing the state of research in an academic field. Rather than lists of unresearched topics on Irish gender history what we perhaps need is the initiation of a discussion among historians of women in Ireland as to the value of gender as a category of analysis. Is it an 'interesting way' to look at Irish history? Many of the themes and issues that have benefited from gender analysis in US history also have a relevance for the study of Irish history. Republican ideology, the structure of the labour market, ideas about the family, concepts of masculinity and femininity are all perceived as more complex and more relevant by historians when they incorporate gender analysis into their writing.

Scott's thesis that political metaphors that are gender based reflect attitudes to gender in society also merits interrogation in an Irish context. This is not to suggest that we passively follow the American model but rather to debate if it is worth exploring some of the conceptual frameworks now being developed by American historians of women and gender within an Irish perspective. A possible forum for such a debate could be the new email list being developed by the WHAI.

Irish historians of women can bemoan the lack of gender awareness of a new generation of doctoral students (and often, their supervisors) but perhaps, too, we need to demonstrate more explicitly that gender analysis is among the gifts of the Muses and can be used to bring the 'kind of madness that takes over, igniting and transforming the subject' of Irish history.

Mary O'Dowd
Queen's University, Belfast

THE GENESIS OF WOMEN'S HISTORY/GENDER HISTORY

Discussing the genesis of the History of Women is rather like describing how over the centuries a world landscape or garden, or series of gardens, have been rendered visible. They were always there. Skilled and persistent gardening has enabled them to come into view. The landscape of a woman's life, of women's lives, the context of their lives, the history, geography, the society and culture in a given time and place, all serve to create the fuller picture. Whatever has emerged in the course of research is placed in a certain way, a certain place and space, in harmony or in polarity, to other plants and growths. Then the gardeners sit back and exchange commentaries and reflections, hear dialogues and reactions. New aspects of the landscape emerge and the process of gardening is enriched and expanded.

There was nothing idyllic in the creation of such gardens, such landscapes. Over centuries women have striven to find their space and growth in the cosmic garden, but it was barred to them (as it was to other disadvantaged groups of race, colour, class and creed) as by divine decree. Yet the conviction that the garden gates should be open to them was always alive, and over centuries grew, first in individuals, then groups of women, and finally they began to knock on the door of the Academy. Yet it is hardly more than a century since women were formally admitted to the garden of history, and Academy gardeners were challenged by the arrival of the women on their sacred soil.

On that land no History of Women existed on the curriculum, nor were there women on the gardening team. Changes in the wider field of history shook (de)fences and what had appeared as empty, as mere scrubland, and certainly of no interest to the Academy, proved to be an astonishingly rich land, awaiting discovery. Hardly knowing the extent of what they did, new methods of research were introduced, and these crossed the permissive frontier of history. Leading historians, women and men, shifted the focus of the past away from major figures in public life to determining influences on the actions and choices of individuals. Research was turned on the history of class and power structures in society, on occupational groups, on women, on ethnic, racial and religious minorities. Sometimes whole communities or societies, sometimes simply crowds, were the subject of enquiry.

So over the last hundred years, history broke its own boundaries and moved confidently into further areas of research, into social, economic, cultural and religious fields. Gradually a new consciousness emerged around the History of Women which led to centres for Women's Studies in Universities and an explosion of feminist studies at all levels and in all areas of life and history. This has reached all aspects of women's lives, past and present, in all countries and cultures, among all races and classes, in all religions, in all social and political contexts, including historical and current slavery. Arising from this focus on women, new and important studies of children emerged. Coupled with the Human Rights movement, the history of women has a powerful position from which to lobby the conscience of the world. First it was the History of Women in the First World, and then in recent decades the Global History of Women, and the inherent tensions within both fields, complex and demanding. So the garden has expanded, is expanding and new spaces are continually being plotted.

The results of careful gardening are elegant. But gardeners get their hands dirty. So the world of Women's History/Gender History has been achieved in the face of immense struggle and opposition from within the Academy, everywhere, evidenced in the struggle for space, funding and appointments. Dominant structures often see such developments as undermining long held vested interests and positions of power. Some gardeners have felt displaced, even cast out, and wish the new designers would go away.

Gardening is a very practical art. Gardeners can never not garden, otherwise the wilderness reappears. The ground needs continual turning, fertilizing and new planting. So in the field of history there are serious questions to address, beyond the metaphors. For example, in recent times many Centres for Women's Studies have been renamed Centres for Gender Studies/Equality Studies:

- Has this brought the issue and place of women in society more into public consciousness?
- Has it expanded the influence, skills and position of women in our world?
- Are such Centres better positioned to effect changes in attitudes between women and men in the Academy?
- Have in-depth studies of men and women led to radical, innovative changes in gender equality perceptions and actions?
- Has the change advanced the essential task of rigorous research and writing on women?
- Do such Centres consistently and critically address the basic question: why is the actual position of women in society, at all levels and in all fields, still so imbalanced?
- At present over 15,000 women are (December 2007)[16] enrolled in honours degree programmes in Ireland, compared with just 5,000 men. What models can Centres for Women's Studies/Gender Studies/Equality Studies offer these women so that they can take their place as our decision-makers in the near future?

By addressing such issues, new and different landscapes/gardens could emerge in the field of history, with truly pioneering and imaginative designs, with possibilities for growth now and in future generations.

Phil Kilroy
Trinity College Dublin

Notes

1. Joan W. Scott, 'Feminism's History', *Journal of Women's History*, 16, 2 (2004), p.15.
2. Ibid., pp.24, 26.
3. Ibid., p. 25.
4. Ibid., pp.23–7.
5. Joan W. Scott, 'Gender: A Useful Category of Historical Analysis', in Joan Wallach Scott, *Gender and the Politics of History* (New York: Columbia University Press, 1988), pp.28–50. The essay was originally presented as a paper to the American Historical Association in 1985 and published in *American Historical Review*, 91, 5 (1986). The article was revised for publication in the 1988 collection of essays by Scott.
6. Scott, 'Feminism's History', p.21.
7. Introduction to Scott, *Gender and the Politics of History*, p.10.
8. Scott, 'Feminism's History', pp.23–4.

9. Scott, 'Gender: A Useful Category of Historical Analysis', p.42.
10. Ibid., p.49.
11. Scott, 'Feminism's History', p.22.
12. Kathryn Kish Sklar's contribution to the debate in 'Considering the State of U.S. Women's History', *Journal of Women's History*, 15, 1 (2003), pp.147–51 (p.147). See also Kathi Kern, 'Productive Collaborations: the Benefits of Cultural Analysis to the Past, Present, and Future of Women's History', *Journal of Women's History*, 16, 4 (2004), pp.34–40.
13. Diarmaid Ferriter, *The Transformation of Ireland* (London: Profile Press, 2004); R.F. Foster, *Luck and the Irish: A Brief History of Change from 1970* (Oxford: Penguin Press, 2007).
14. Scott, 'Feminism's History', p.22.
15. See, for example, Margaret H. Kelleher and James H. Murphy (eds), *Gender Perspectives in 19th Century Ireland: Public and Private Spheres* (Dublin: Irish Academic Press, 1997); Anthony Bradley and Maryann Gialanella Valiulis (eds), *Gender and Sexuality in Modern Ireland* (Amherst, MA: University of Massachusetts Press, 1997); Nancy Curtin and Marilyn Cohen (eds), *Reclaiming Gender: Transgressive Identities in Modern Ireland* (New York: Macmillan Press, 1999). For more recent studies that incorporate gender in the relative and comparative sense see Mary E. Daly, *The Slow Failure. Population Decline and Independent Ireland* (Madison, WI: University of Wisconsin Press, 2006); Caitriona Clear's new book on *Social Change and Everyday Life in Ireland, 1850–1922* (Manchester: Manchester University Press, 2007) also incorporates a comparison of the lives of men and women.
16. Caroline Madden, 'Out of reach. Women in Business', *Irish Times*, Innovation, Dec. 2007, p.22.

CHAPTER THREE

The Potential of Gender History

MARY CULLEN

What do we mean by gender history? The definition used here developed during the upsurge of interest in women's history that was sparked off by second wave feminism in the mid-twentieth century. It became increasingly clear that many differences in the position of women and men in diverse societies could not be explained solely by biological determinism, and so 'gender' was drafted in to denote the entire range of social relations between the sexes. Gender analysis takes account of the political, social and economic consequences of being born a male or a female in a particular place at a particular time in history. It sees biological sex as one factor interacting with others, such as geographical location, race, colour, class, religion, education, wealth, age and many others in locating an individual in historical context. It follows that gender analysis cannot, explicitly or implicitly, treat the masculine role as the human norm.

However, the reality is that most history books *do* treat the masculine role as the human norm, presenting a past of male agency and leadership, and female passivity and dependency. When women as a group, or feminist activity, are discussed at all, it is almost invariably in terms of comparison with a taken-for-granted male norm, to which women can or, depending on the point of view, cannot hope to aspire. The books seldom, if ever, consider men as a group, or the advantaged position of males, socially, economically and politically, relative to females. And what history books tell us is central to our understanding of who we are and how we got to where we are.

This chapter considers one example of how gender analysis might help to develop a more inclusive and genuinely 'mainstream' history. It starts with the concept of citizenship expressed explicitly and implicitly by Irish feminist campaigners from the middle of the nineteenth century up to 1922 and the Constitution of the Irish Free State.[1] This provides the basis for a discussion of some aspects of the potential of gender history.

POLITICAL IDEOLOGIES AND THE EMERGENCE OF MODERN FEMINISM

Political thought is not static. It develops as individuals or groups respond to the issues and questions they see as most pressing in their own day. In doing this, they draw on the stock of political ideas and traditions in use in current political debate. This is inevitably a selective process as participants use or emphasize elements that appear relevant or favourable to their questions and aims, ignore or take issue with others, add new ideas and arguments, and so the stock develops and changes over time. Historians aim to locate the writings of individual thinkers and other expressions of political thought in historical context to help identify the major concerns of a period and the issues most important to different groups. They ask what the then prevailing ideologies were, how these were drawn on, to what extent protagonists tailored their objectives to what could be justified in their terms, and whether they added anything new to the body of political thought.

Republicanism was a dominant ideology in the eighteenth-century Western world.[2] Its origins (*res publica*, the 'public thing') go back to ancient Greece and Rome. Based on a holistic view of the good human life, republican thinking originally posited an independent city state and polity, the Greek *polis*, whose individually free (male) citizens shared responsibility for its survival and flourishing. Freedom and interdependence were interlocked and civic virtue required citizens to co-operate and be prepared to put the common good of all before individual interest when necessary to defend the State from both internal corruption and outside aggression. By the exercise of civic virtue citizens developed their individual human potential.[3]

Republican thinking was elitist in its origins, excluding women, slaves and foreigners from citizenship. In the city states of Renaissance Italy and during the revolutionary period in seventeenth-century England, it was drawn on and developed to answer questions of sovereignty, and the respective rights and duties of citizens and rulers. This reworking has been given the somewhat confusing name of 'classical' republicanism by political theorists. In the eighteenth century it was further democratized by Enlightenment, or Age of Reason, assertions of the basic equality of all rational human beings, and ideas of who could be a citizen broadened. In many countries, including Ireland, republicanism was a powerful contributor to arguments for reform of political systems, elimination of corruption and patronage in government and extension of political participation, as well as to the rebellion of the British colonies in North America in the 1770s, the French Revolution starting in 1789 and the 1798 rebellion in Ireland.

While few male thinkers applied their definitions of human rationality and equality to females, some radical women drew on the same body of ideas to challenge existing gender relations. Enlightenment egalitarianism could support their claims that women be recognized as full human persons. These claims defined full humanity in republican terminology and its concept of citizens as free individuals directing their own lives and sharing responsibility for the common good. One of the most influential expressions of Enlightenment and republican ideas applied to gender relationships was *A Vindication of the Rights of Woman* (1792) by the English radical thinker, Mary Wollstonecraft. Her basic argument was that denial of personal autonomy, of responsibility and of education aimed at developing rational judgement stunted women's development as human persons and corrupted their influence on family and society. 'Make women rational creatures and free citizens and they will quickly become good wives and mothers.'[4]

THE IRISH EMANCIPATION CAMPAIGNS

By the mid-nineteenth century when organized action for women's rights emerged in Ireland, republicanism was not as prominent among the ideologies drawn on in contemporary debate and campaigners did not employ its terminology. In response to political, social and economic change, liberalism, socialism and nationalism were coming to the fore, each emphasizing and developing different elements from the republican tradition. Liberalism prioritized individual freedom, making its protection from interference the primary role of government, and argued that this would, in practice, achieve the common good. It provided a tailor-made ideology for the rising commercial, business and financial interests. Socialism responded that unfettered pursuit of individual interest threatened the common good, and that real freedom and equality required control of the economy in the interests of the whole community. Meanwhile nationalism developed the republican emphasis on freedom from outside aggression or control.

Liberalism, dominant in mid-nineteenth century Ireland, had ambiguous messages for middle-class feminists. Its advocacy of individual liberty favoured claims for equality, though in practice liberal men gave them partial and ambiguous support. It also tended to support the ideology of separate private and public spheres, where women ruled in the home while men ran affairs in the public world. This justified the contraction of middle-class women's actual range of activity that resulted from the increasing separation of home and workplace. As commerce, bureaucracy and the professions expanded, the middle class grew in numbers and wealth, and middle-class men moved into political office and exercised political power. Some historians see the widening divide between the opportunities open to middle-class males and females as the driving force behind the women's movement.[5] While this argument obviously has some merit, feminist aims, as will be seen, went well beyond equality with men within existing political, economic and social structures.

Mid-nineteenth-century women's rights advocates could draw on a new ideology of a (limited) female superiority in the area of morals. This developed from the same matrix of eighteenth-century thinking. Enlightenment ideas of equality and their optimism that human reason could reform and improve human nature and society, and republican commitment to the common good, interacted with the challenges facing Christianity in a changing world to produce Evangelical religion, or revivalism. Emerging in the late eighteenth century within Protestantism, its influence spread across all denominations. It preached an individual life of active Christianity based on humility and self-sacrifice allied to a mission to regenerate a sinful world. Many of the virtues advocated were those seen as particularly 'female'. As a result Evangelicalism endorsed an enhanced role for women as guardians and promoters of moral standards within family and community, sanctioned their organized activity outside the home, and provided an ideology and normative language of female moral superiority.[6] Evangelicalism is seen as a major impetus behind the huge growth of philanthropy among middle- and upper-class Irish women from the late eighteenth century through the nineteenth. They developed an impressively wide range of services aimed at improving the moral and physical condition of the disadvantaged in society.[7]

The leading women's rights activists in mid-nineteenth century Ireland appear to have come from middle-class backgrounds in Protestant denominations and in philanthropy.[8] A radical minority emerged to openly challenge restrictions on women's autonomy and self-direction as well as their exclusion from political decision-making. Four main campaigns developed from the mid-century: 1) for married women's control of their own inherited or earned property; 2) for improved standards in female education, access to the universities and better employment opportunities; 3) for the repeal of the Contagious Diseases Acts passed in the 1860s to protect the health of the army and navy by subjecting women suspected of being prostitutes to compulsory medical examination and, if necessary, treatment for venereal disease; 4) for the parliamentary vote on the same terms as men.[9] As Ireland was part of the United Kingdom of Great Britain and Ireland, campaigns to change the law were aimed at the Westminster parliament. Action in Ireland was influenced by English developments and, in the cases of married women's property and the Contagious Diseases Acts, was essentially part of English-led campaigns.

Campaigners drew on Enlightenment egalitarianism, liberalism's stress on individual freedom, and Evangelical endorsement of women's moral mission, and argued that the good of society required moral standards in public life and political decision-making, standards which could only be achieved by women's participation. Also, however, and significantly for the discussion here, despite the fact that by this period republicanism was no longer so prominent among the ideologies drawn on in general political debate, the campaign objectives, separately and together, incorporated many basic elements of republican citizenship. Married women's control of their own property was essential for personal autonomy and freedom from domination, and it affected all women, single or married, and all social classes. Education for intellectual development was central to development of human potential and ability to reform society, as well as for employment, economic independence and autonomy. Repeal of the Contagious Diseases Acts challenged sexual double standards and aimed at the moral improvement of society. The parliamentary vote involved recognition as full human persons, free and self-determining, plus power to influence legislation.

Isabella Tod, a Presbyterian in Belfast, and a leading figure in all the Irish campaigns, was one of the most prominent and articulate advocates of the feminist agenda. In 1875, in what could be seen as an overall summary, she wrote that women were

> citizens of the state, inheritors with men of all the history which ennobles a nation, guardians with men of all the best life of the nation; bound as much as men are bound to consider the good

> of the whole; and justified as much as men are justified in sharing the good of the whole.[10]

Her speeches and writings constantly demonstrated how the different campaigns interacted. A 'wise and wide course of education ... enlarges and strengthens the mind ... to prepare it for all the contingencies of life'. If women had the vote they 'would be in all respects the better ... and ... the influence of women would be good at promoting all sorts of wise reforms, social and moral'. It would develop their individual potential and ability to contribute to the improvement of society. With it they could exercise 'moral responsibility and freedom of action'. The 'addition of women to the electorate would mean a far greater proportionate addition to the ranks of good'. The condition of women of 'the lower classes' might be greatly improved if 'not merely a few, but most of those in the classes above them have not only the will, but the power and the knowledge to help them'.[11]

For Tod, suffrage was 'not merely a claim of abstract right, but of necessary means for performing duties'.[12] It was 'the only practical means of redressing wrongs'.[13] This in turn was linked to women's particular contribution, which, she wrote, could be 'in the details of management of a workhouse (which needs an experience in house keeping) ... in the care of the sick, of the old, of the children, and the training of girls to earn their bread ... in the discrimination between honest poverty and imposture ... work that must be shared by women if it is to be done efficiently'.[14] It could also result from a greater commitment to the common good. Experience showed that women 'felt a deeper responsibility resting upon them, and ... attempted to carry their religious principles into the common things of life to a greater extent than men did'. Men were often drawn to politics 'from selfish motives' while women did not campaign 'only for themselves. They fight for others; and it is because we have so much work to do that we fight as hard as we do'.[15]

Women themselves, Tod argued, had a duty to make this contribution. They must demand the vote 'not only for the help which women must give to women, but even more, for the discharge of their special duty to the whole state, a duty which God has entrusted to them, and which no man can do'. They must 'feel it their task to uphold truth, purity and justice to all, in the legislation and administration of the realm'.[16]

THE IRISH CITIZEN 1912–20[17]

The same basic concepts of citizenship continued to inform Irish feminist thinking in the changing political context of the second decade of the twentieth century. The suffrage newspaper, the *Irish Citizen*, was founded in 1912 in association with the Irish Women's Franchise League (IWFL), a new suffrage association with nationalist sympathies though non-aligned politically. By this time substantial, though far from complete, advances had been achieved in most of the campaign objectives, with the parliamentary vote the major exception. Internationally, the suffrage movement had expanded dramatically. In Ireland, where the pioneering activists had been predominantly Protestant in religion and unionist in politics, now Catholics and nationalists were taking part in increasing numbers. The *Citizen* became the forum for a wide range of opinion and discussion. Contributors drew on socialism, nationalism and pacifism as well as liberalism and women's moral superiority and mission to reform society. A socialist voice emerged to challenge what it saw as middle-class feminists' maternalistic attitude towards poorer women. By this time also, for most Irish people, republicanism had come to mean complete separation from Britain. Nevertheless, the concept of citizenship as the interaction of freedom, self-determination, individual development and responsibility for the common good continued to inform the debates.

The paper's masthead carried its mission statement: 'For men and women equally the rights of citizenship: From men and women equally the duties of citizenship.' Individual development and the common good were generally accepted as its aims. The first editorial stated that it advocated the 'fullest development of a complete humanity' with no limitations on 'human freedom and human character'.[18] James Cousins[19] advocated 'adjustment between the needs of the individual and the needs of the community'.[20] Another editorial urged that women and men work together for a 'social organisation ... capable of giving the maximum opportunity of personal freedom to the maximum number of persons'.[21] The Irish Women's Reform League, whose objectives combined suffrage with working women's concerns, wrote of 'common needs and satisfactions ... the joy of one is a gain to all, and the suffering of one an injury to all'.[22]

There was wide agreement that women's participation was essential to achieve a better society for all. It was argued that women's values were different from men's, that women were sexually more chaste, more concerned with the common good, with 'true life-values' – concerning both the preservation and quality of life – and were more opposed to war and militarism. Whether these qualities were seen as biologically determined or arising from women's experience in maternal and domestic roles, it was seen as imperative to bring them into political decision-making. M. Alexander of the Irish Women's Suffrage Society, Belfast, wrote that women's value-system would 'ultimately lead to the spiritual regeneration of the race'.[23] Lucy Kingston of the IWFL believed that women would 'influence the trend of politics in favour of a respect for humanity'.[24] Louie Bennett, general secretary of the Irish Women Workers' Union, urged that to create a better society and a co-operative system the 'voice of woman's soul ... as distinct from man's', and women's 'greater sense of the sacredness of life', was needed.[25] Margaret McCoubrey, a socialist, claimed that when women gained equality, 'existing systems for maintenance of law and order, our gigantic farce called Courts of Justice' will go and there will be 'no need for charitable organisations, for prisons, or for rescue-homes'.[26]

At the same time reservations were voiced about women's preparedness to contribute this potential whether by direct political participation or as citizen-mothers educating future citizens. For both, development of potential and education for citizenship were essential. Mary Hayden, Professor of Modern Irish History at University College Dublin, deplored the general lack of a sense of 'social duty' among middle-class girls and women, and their slowness to volunteer for philanthropic work. She argued that education must go beyond the selfish interests of family, must include politics, economics, the place of the family in society, preparing a girl 'to do her duty efficiently' whether in the 'corporate life of her city or her country' or as a mother.[27] In similar vein 'Frances' wrote asking, in the name of citizenship, for volunteers for clubs for working girls in Belfast.[28] An Irish National Teacher argued that if teachers were to train their pupils to put 'principle before expediency and the good of the community before personal gain – in a word to be good citizens', then teachers themselves must be 'fearless and broadminded citizens' and not prohibited from political involvement.[29]

Socialist contributors, themselves almost all middle-class women, put forward the case for working-class women, essentially that the latter would and should achieve their own emancipation. Marion Duggan asked could 'wealthy or educated women ... be trusted to make laws for poor working women?' Should the latter be 'free and independent, or humbly receiving the legislative bounty of their better-off sisters?' Working women, she argued, needed to organize to combat bad working conditions, unequal pay and limited employment opportunities. They 'themselves must decide how best to get the vote, by full, frank, free discussion'.[30] Louie Bennett urged that women workers needed to raise their status, pay and working conditions to have 'that self-respect as a worker which gives a note of happiness to any toil', and then turn to civic reforms 'which only the workers themselves will ever achieve'.[31]

Middle-class women also faced obstacles to self-development. Margaret Connery of the IWFL deplored the contraction of their 'spheres of activity'. Suffrage was part of a broad movement towards the 'unity of humanity ... a universal brotherhood of man [*sic*]', a goal not achievable while half of humanity, women, were 'sunk in servitude and degradation'. She argued that 'new forms of labour and the right to labour' were essential, and that if woman 'may not grow and develop, and exercise all her powers of body and mind, she, and the race through her, are threatened with ultimate extinction'.[32] The growing numbers of university-educated women were frustrated by the obstacles to women entering the higher professions.[33] Law graduate Marion Duggan, urging that women lawyers were needed in the search for international peace, wrote that, while women were 'in some ways superior to men', they had 'failed to cultivate certain qualities which men have learned by experience', and wider opportunities, including the practice of law, 'may materially assist [their] moral development'.[34]

For socialist and trade-union feminists, international harmony, equality between the sexes and the common good depended on economic reform. Louie Bennett wrote that 'economic justice' was essential for feminism and a world 'safe for democracy'.[35] Tackling the exploitation of working women in conditions, unequal pay and limited employment opportunities involved tackling the co-existing exploitation of working men. As Bennett put it, 'the financial burden of keeping the home lies upon the male wage-earner, working under a system so heedless of human needs'. When 'co-operation has succeeded capitalism' the distribution of work could be 'completely readjusted'.[36] Cissie Cahalan of the Linen Drapers' Assistants' Association, while disagreeing with Bennett on the need for separate women's unions, shared her ultimate objective: men and women must work 'shoulder to shoulder' in mixed unions for the 'goal of Irish Labour – the Workers' Republic'.[37]

Regarding attitudes to war and militarism, the First World War from 1914–18, the 1916 Easter Rising, and the War of Independence from 1919–21 raised challenging questions for Irish feminists. Opinion expressed in the *Citizen* included support for Britain as engaged in a just war, support for Irish separatist rebellion as a just cause, and pacifism ranging from a total opposition to war to a general opposition allowing exceptions in a just cause. The issues and arguments were complex and nuanced. The Sheehy Skeffingtons provide one example of the complexities. On the eve of the world war an editorial by Francis, while accepting that not all suffragists opposed war, argued that war was a social evil 'based on a theory of society one-sidedly and arrogantly male'. It expressed confidence that 'the main current of the women's movement, in all countries, is definitely hostile to war and aims at its abolition'.[38] At roughly the same time Hanna wrote that she would support an Irish separatist rising that had a prospect of success, but 'still be radically opposed to war and militarism'.[39] Overall, it seems fair to see a general opposition to militarism and glorification of war per se, and a general agreement that women's values were basically anti-war.

GENDER AND POLITICAL THOUGHT

While the foregoing has been an extremely brief overview of developments that need in-depth exploration, enough has emerged to justify some tentative discussion. This will aim: i) to summarize the feminists' case; ii) to discuss their use of ideologies; iii) to assess some aspects of their contribution to political thought; iv) to ask what the result would be if historians took seriously what Irish feminists were saying.

The Feminists' Case

As has been seen, the feminists first asserted the equality of women and men as human beings. As such, women were entitled to be recognized and treated as autonomous, self-directing individuals. Restrictions imposed by marriage and property laws, exclusion from higher education, prestigious and well-paid employment, and from participation in public political life, were all inequitable and, it was believed, must be abolished. Women had both the right and the duty to be full citizens, sharing actively in the life of society, including political decision-making.

Next, feminists went beyond a claim simply for equality of rights within the existing system. They were highly critical of the results of exclusively male political decision-making. They argued that women had a contribution to make that was different from that of men, and one that was essential for the common good. This contribution comprised the values associated with women: purer moral standards, compassion, care for the poor and disadvantaged, aversion to war as the way to settle disputes. These values were all needed in public decision-making, and only the participation of women could ensure their inclusion. They further asserted that, to develop their potential to make that contribution, women needed education, wider opportunities and to shoulder their share of responsibility for society.

These arguments challenged realpolitik views that morality need not necessarily apply in political decision-making. They undermined justification of existing gender relationships by separate spheres ideology, and the stereotypes of male and female 'natures' underpinning that ideology. These stereotypes allocated some human characteristics to men and others to women in a division that posited some more-or-less mutually exclusive groups of characteristics grounded in biological sex. Feminist claims for women's values often appeared to accept that characteristics were divided to some extent into 'masculine' and 'feminine'. It is not always clear whether they saw the differences as originating in nature or nurture. However, there was broad agreement that women could and should display such 'masculine' attributes as independence, autonomy, rationality, judgement, suitability for political decision-making, while retaining 'feminine' caring, nurturing, chastity and moral virtue. At the same time 'masculine' aggression, dominance and militarism were rejected, as also 'feminine' dependence and subordination.

The new model of female 'nature' challenged the basis of the gender power allocation, and was deeply disturbing to many men. For example, Hanna Sheehy Skeffington recalled the words of the Home Rule MP, John Dillon, whom she described as a 'fine rebel on certain lines and up to a point'. In response to a feminist deputation he replied 'sadly: "Women's suffrage will, I believe, be the ruin of our Western civilisation. It will destroy the home, challenging the headship of man, laid down by God. It may come in your time I hope not in mine."'[40]

The Feminists' Use of Ideologies

a) Moral Superiority. In asserting women's full equality as human beings and citizens, feminists drew on Enlightenment equality and its optimism regarding the potential of education. However, its value for women was limited by the pervasive ideology of masculine superiority, which will be discussed later. For entry into public life, Evangelicalism was the only widely-accepted authoritative voice or ideology that, while not asserting complete equality, gave women a defined, if limited, area of expertise and authority that extended beyond the home, and could be used to support the need for women's values in political decision-making. The feminists exploited this to its full potential and undoubtedly far beyond the intentions of most male Evangelical leaders. And not only committed feminists did this. Rosemary Raughter sees eighteenth-century Irish female philanthropists offering a 'significant, if largely covert, challenge' to Establishment ideas of women's nature and role in society. For the nineteenth century, Maria Luddy makes a similar argument.[41]

So, how far was belief in women's moral superiority and mission a driving force on its own merits, and how far was its use a conscious strategy to exploit a useful ideology? It is entirely plausible that both operated and, for some people, both may well have operated at the same time. As has been seen, appeals to moral superiority went side by side with acknowledgement that women needed education and wider experience to develop themselves and their potential for contribution.

Nor was religious motivation incompatible with a rational critique of society. As noted above, Evangelical religion itself emerged from the matrix of eighteenth-century ideas. It was, according to one historian, 'permeated by Enlightenment influences', including scientific empiricism and inductive reasoning from perceived facts, and until well into the nineteenth century 'there was no hint of a clash between Evangelical religion and science'.[42] Inductive reasoning from perceived facts could well lead to the conclusion that the values associated with women were needed in political decision-making to create a fairer, more equitable and hence more stable, organization of society. It could lead women to conclude that confining themselves to narrow male-dictated spheres of human activity was itself irrational.

And there is evidence of women's interest in science. During the nineteenth century a number of Irish women made substantial contributions to scientific knowledge,[43] while many more women participated in the growth of popular interest in both the natural sciences and the application of scientific method to social and economic problems. Clara Cullen has shown that from early in the century women attended public lectures on scientific subjects in Dublin, Belfast and Cork. Also, between 1854 and 1867, the years when the pioneering colleges for the higher education of women were established, the

Museum of Irish Industry in Dublin ran popular courses on physics, chemistry, botany, zoology and geology, as well as 'systematic classes' leading to examinations and the award of certificates and prizes. Both were open to women and men, and the records show that women were well represented among the prize-winners and 'distinguished themselves in a high degree', according to the director, Sir Robert Kane.[44]

Mary E. Daly's work on the Statistical and Social Inquiry Society shows that women, who were eligible to be associate members, presented a number of papers, including three read by two of the most prominent feminist leaders. In 1875 Isabella Tod read a paper on the treatment of habitual drunkards, and in 1878 another on the boarding-out system for pauper children. In the 1879/80 session Anna Haslam read a paper on poor-law administration in workhouses.[45] Thomas Haslam, Anna's husband and co-feminist, was a long-time member and his 1865 pamphlet, *The Real Wants of the Irish People*, was published under the authorship of 'A Member of the Statistical and Social Inquiry Society of Ireland'. Carmel Quinlan's study of the Haslams[46] makes clear that he was actively involved in contemporary scientific debate on evolution, heredity, eugenics and methods of birth control, as well as the economic and social problems of contemporary Ireland. After his death, Anna corresponded with Marie Stopes, the birth-control pioneer, about Thomas's ideas and writings and about the Haslams' own contraceptive practice. Further research on women's intellectual interests should deepen our understanding of feminist thinking in nineteenth-century Ireland.

b) The Civic Republican Model. Whether or not campaigners consciously exploited moral superiority, it is significant that they used it to advocate a holistic model of society and polity, and to claim that certain specific values were needed in public life and political decision-making. That this model and these values continued to be widely promoted by participants in debate in the *Irish Citizen*, where contributors were drawn from a wide range of backgrounds, and included Catholics, Protestants, agnostics and atheists; nationalists and unionists; middle-class liberals, socialists and trade unionists, suggests a real and wide-spread commitment to the model and values promoted.

As has been argued, the model and values incorporated civic republican ideas. This has particular significance in light of the relative supersedence of civic republicanism in political debate during the nineteenth century. Iseult Honohan notes that republican 'ideas of widespread public participation in politics, of freedom as political activity and the importance of civic virtue' were declining by this time.[47] So, when feminists advocated what was essentially a feminist reworking of the republican concept of the good human life, where responsibility for the organization of society was not seen as separate from private life, where citizens co-operated to create the common good, and individual self-development was integrally related to political participation, they were not seeking endorsement from a widely-used political language and ideology calculated to win support. For the history of political thought this raises interesting lines of inquiry about the long-lasting persistence and attraction of the basic components of this concept, of their appeal for groups denied recognition, respect and participation in decision-making, as well as their potentially universal appeal to a rational self-interest that might see such a polity as the best guarantee for the well-being of all individuals and groups in the long run.

The issue of class in women's history opens a further dimension. The voice of working-class women appears largely absent from feminist debate in Ireland during the period considered here. Their case seems to have been generally argued by middle-class women. Helena Molony of the Irish Women Workers' Union, looking back in 1930, said the women's movement had 'passed over the head of the Irish working woman and left her untouched'.[48] Further research may reveal a more complex situation. Later, during the second wave of the women's movement, starting in Ireland around 1970, women's groups in working-class areas in Dublin and other urban centres developed a local politics that combined self-development programmes with campaigns for better community facilities and services. While they did not necessarily see themselves as feminists, the same combination of freedom, self-determination and active contribution to the common good informed their activities. Two recent studies of communities in nationalist West Belfast before and after the IRA ceasefire of 1994 show a similar pattern. For the earlier period Claire Hackett shows how the internment of men propelled women into new roles combining family and community survival with nationalist political activism, merging public and private spheres. Self-development programmes, growing feminist awareness and challenges to sexism, including domestic violence, within the nationalist community itself followed.[49] Callie Persic follows the transition of a women's group on a housing estate after 1994 from nationalist to community activism, pursuing better community conditions and futures for their children, but also their own self-development through education and new skills, and engaging in power struggles in the home. Here also, while many women were unwilling to call themselves feminists, domestic and political roles merged, and Persic suggests we may have to rethink the meaning of 'political'.[50]

The Feminist Contribution to Political Thought

The main points of this contribution, as they arise from the foregoing discussion, can be itemized as follows: firstly, feminists asserted the full humanity and equal citizenship of women; secondly, they asserted the need for 'women's values' in political decision-making to achieve the common good; thirdly, their challenge to male authority and privilege identified and made visible the ideology of male superiority and dominance that they saw as permeating both society and political debate. This ideology saw women as ineligible for citizenship for various reasons, God-ordained male authority and innate female irrationality among others. Feminists themselves were very much aware of its pervasiveness. Isabella Tod noted a 'tone of depreciation of women ... [in the 1860s] frightfully common, both in society and the press – whether it was an attitude of groundless or misplaced compliment, or of patronage, or of mockery or contempt'.[51] Margaret Cousins, co-founder of the IWFL, growing up in the 1880s became aware that '[b]oys were wanted and expected' in preference to girls and were given 'much more freedom of action, movement and friendship [and] more money', and that 'it was counted as a kind of curse ... to be born a girl'. She found it 'a joy later to find that such inequality and injustice and limitations were the result of circumstances which could and would be changed'.[52] Lucy Kingston, who joined the IWFL in 1912, began attending suffrage meetings in Dublin in 1911 and 'got sore, wrathful and with some cause ... [at] the condescending attitude of men towards our poor feeble wits'.[53] Hanna Sheehy Skeffington found that other Irish MPs, like John Dillon, 'good Irish rebels, many of them broken in to national revolt, ... at the whisper of Votes for Women ... changed to extreme Tories or time-servers who urged us women to wait till freedom for men was won. Curiously, too, these were joined by many Sinn Féiners.'[54] Mary Hayden, writing to the *Cork Examiner* in June 1937 on the draft new constitution, noted the repressive legislation passed by successive governments in the Irish Free State during the 1920s and 1930s, imposing restrictions on women's employment and in jury service,[55] and now, 'to crown all' the proposed constitution with 'its mixture of flattery and insult'.[56]

What if Historians Listened Seriously to what Feminists were Saying? If gender analysis became a standard part of the historian's tool-kit, it would undoubtedly lead to major reassessments across the board. One focus would be on the blindness of most 'mainstream' historians to the centrality of gender relationships in the history of human societies. A substantial body of feminist scholarship over several decades has documented and analyzed the ideology of masculine superiority and dominance that pervades the history of Western philosophical, theological and political thought from Aristotle onwards, yet this has not been incorporated into general histories of political thought. Historians would have to face the question why this has been the case. Their own value system would become part of that history and itself subject to scrutiny and critical analysis. Discussion of these developments lies outside the scope of this chapter. Here I want to consider some of the possible results if the history books in general use did include feminist political thought.

If the books included this thought, historians would have to consider to what extent political, social and economic relationships between the sexes resulted from human agency. The first question would be: *cui bono*? who benefits? For the period of the Irish emancipation campaigns, this would involve analysis of the privileged position of males in mid nineteenth-century Ireland, of how law, regulation and custom channelled social, economic and political power to males and away from females. If the focus narrowed to the objectives of the campaigns, historians would examine the consequences of the legal right of a husband to use and dispose of his wife's inherited and earned property, its benefits for men of all social classes, not least the lure of marriage to an heiress, and for women the loss of autonomy on marriage with its implications for young women's life options. They would consider the impact on each sex of the double standards in social attitude and legal response to sexual behaviour, as well as of the male monopoly of university education, degrees, entry to the 'higher' professions, and political power from the highest office to voting at elections.

Awareness of the feminist thinking of previous generations would empower societies to absorb it and build on it. New generations would be able first to *see* this thinking, to identify and analyze it, and then to locate it in the particular political, social and economic conditions, gender relationships and political ideologies within which feminists framed their questions and which in turn influenced their answers.

Locating ideas in historical context is crucial. Without context it is difficult to decide which elements we believe to have lasting value. It is equally important to be aware of our own historical context and the factors that influence our thinking as we pass judgement on the ideas of earlier generations. For example, it can be argued that critical analysis of middle-class nineteenth-century feminists' attitudes to social class contributes to our thinking today to the extent that we understand both their historical context and ours. Political, social and economic conditions change, and so do gender relationships and dominant ideologies. Trying to understand their world involves trying to understand our own.

This empowerment would encourage the envisioning of new models of human nature, both female and male. These issues are being tackled today in women's studies and masculinity studies, both still minority interests and on the periphery of 'mainstream' intellectual programmes, and so limited in their influence. Gender analysis demonstrates the centrality of gender relationships to the 'mainstream' of human thought, and hence the importance of critical analysis of dominant models of femininity and masculinity. Nor is today's generation the first to challenge the prevailing stereotypes. Earlier Irish feminists, among others, contested them, and put forward new and more inclusively human models. While they focused most attention on the female stereotype, feminists, men as well as women, also envisioned new masculine models. For example, Margaret and James Cousins were part of contemporary circles that did this, and an *Irish Citizen* editorial argued that the 'growing inter-relationship of the sexes in the affairs of life' required a new word the 'femaculine', to name 'the new sex, the community of sex in the hidden region of the soul of humanity'.[57] In this context Catherine Candy's work opens up a little-explored area of Irish feminist history where attitudes to sexuality and interest in the occult, theosophy and vegetarianism converge.[58]

Envisioning new models of human nature and 'natures' is as important for boys and men as it is for girls and women. Conventional history and conventional stereotypes combine in socializing males to conform to a model of masculinity based to a large extent on negative images: of not appearing weak, of not losing face, of not admitting mistakes or compromising, of not appearing like a woman or 'effeminate'. A history that includes gender analysis and feminist thought empowers men as well as women to analyze the role of stereotypes and the ideology of masculine superiority and dominance in human history, to make their own assessment of the damage these have done to individuals, men and women, to the organization of societies and to relations between societies, and opens both sexes to the possibility of developing new models.

Linked to this is the potential of the history of feminist thought to help in envisioning new models for the organization of society. In today's world of globalization, increasing inequality and threat to the environment, there is renewed interest in republicanism among political theorists looking for alternatives to the current dominant ideology of extreme neo-liberalism and its endorsement of a polity based on a competitive, profit-driven market economy. It appears to me that gender history has much to contribute to explorations of the potential of republicanism to answer today's questions. The history of Irish feminist thought provides one case study of how that potential was used and adapted by women to answer some of yesterday's questions. Basic concepts of republican citizenship continued to inform the political thought of the nineteenth-century middle-class feminists, that of the still largely middle-class contributors to the *Irish Citizen*, and that of the later working-class community groups, while they successively discarded its original sexism and elitism and developed more democratic and inclusive versions.

This is not to argue that feminist concepts of citizenship by themselves hold the key to a Utopia. Like all human thinking, feminist arguments are open to debate and challenge. Predictions that female suffrage would fundamentally change political decision-making for the better have yet to be fulfilled. Whether women as a group and men as a group hold different value-systems and, if so, why, is still a contested and unresolved question. Creating genuine participatory citizenship in democratic societies with large populations presents formidable challenges. Nor does either republicanism or feminism include a blueprint of policies designed to deliver the common good. Both will need to dialogue with ideologies such as socialism that do propose such policies. And there is little in human history to suggest that an ideal society will ever be achieved. However, the history of feminist concepts of citizenship suggests that efforts to put these into practice have intrinsic value for individual human development. They are also less prone to advocate rigid stereotypes, dichotomies of black versus white or male versus female, and hold out better prospects for creating societies that at least *try* to give every citizen the opportunity to develop and flourish than do the current ones. A history that incorporated gender analysis could help move today's debates away from models of perpetual adversarial struggle between opposing interests towards more inclusive, fluid and constructive dialogue, argument and debate.

NOTES

1. In a recent essay, 'Feminism, Citizenship and Suffrage: a Long Dialogue', in Louise Ryan and Margaret Ward (eds), *Irish Women and the Vote: Becoming Citizens* (Dublin: Irish Academic Press, 2007), pp.1–20, I discussed some of the issues raised in this chapter. I am grateful to the editors and publisher for agreeing to my drawing on some of its content here.
2. Gordon S. Wood, in his study of the origins of the United States of America, describes republicanism as 'the ideology of the Enlightenment': *The Creation of the American Republic 1776–1787* (Chapel Hill, NC and London: University of North Carolina Press, 1998), p.viii.
3. See Iseult Honohan, 'Freedom as Citizenship: the Republican Tradition in Political Theory', *The Republic: A Journal of Contemporary and Historical Debate*, 2 (Spring/Summer 2001), pp.7–24 and *Civic Republicanism* (London and New York: Routledge, 2002); John Morrow, *History of Political Thought: a Thematic Introduction* (Basingstoke and London: Macmillan, 1998), p.19.
4. Mary Wollstonecraft, *A Vindication of the Rights of Woman* (London: Dent, 1982), p.213. Wollstonecraft's writings were well known in Ireland. For the republican and feminist thinking of two United Irish women, Martha McTier and Mary Ann McCracken, see Mary Cullen, '"Rational Creatures and Free Citizens": Republicanism, Feminism and the Writing of History', *The Republic* 1 (June 2000), pp.60–70.
5. For example, Richard J. Evans, *The Feminists: Women's Emancipation Movements in Europe, America and Australasia 1840–1928* (London: Croom Helm, 1975).
6. Jane Rendall, *The Origins of Modern Feminism: Women in Britain, France, and the United States, 1780–1860* (Basingstoke and London: Macmillan, 1985), pp.73–107.
7. For these developments see Rosemary Raughter, 'A Natural Tenderness: the Ideal and the Reality of Eighteenth-Century Female Philanthropy', in Maryann G. Valiulis and Mary O'Dowd (eds), *Women and Irish History* (Dublin: Wolfhound, 1997), pp.7l–88; and Maria Luddy, *Women and Philanthropy in Nineteenth-Century Ireland* (Cambridge: Cambridge University Press, 1995).
8. Catholic women were also active in philanthropic work, but by the mid-nineteenth century the huge growth of female religious congregations had absorbed most Catholic philanthropists and few Catholic women appear to have become women's rights activists until the end of the century. See Cáitriona Clear, *Nuns in Nineteenth-Century Ireland* (Dublin: Gill and Macmillan, 1987) and 'The Limits of Female Autonomy: Nuns in Nineteenth-Century Ireland', in Maria Luddy and Clíona Murphy (eds), *Women Surviving: Studies in Irish Women's History in the 19th and 20th Centuries* (Dublin: Poolbeg, 1989), pp.15–50; Mary Peckham Magray, *The Transforming Power of Nuns: Women, Religion and Cultural Change in Ireland 1750–1900* (New York: Oxford University Press, 1998).
9. For a brief overview of these campaigns see Mary Cullen, 'Women, Emancipation and Politics 1860–1984', in J.R. Hill (ed.), *A New History of Ireland* Vol. VII (Oxford: Oxford University Press, 2003), pp.826–91. The property qualification for the male franchise meant that in the 1860s the vote on the same terms as men would in practice be votes for single or widowed middle-class women. This changed over time as married women gained control of their own property and the property qualification for the male franchise was reduced by successive acts of parliament until finally abolished in 1918.
10. Cited in Maria Luddy, 'Isabella M. Tod (1836–1896)', in Mary Cullen and Maria Luddy (eds), *Women, Power and Consciousness in Nineteenth-Century Ireland: Eight Biographical Studies* (Dublin: Attic Press, 1995), p.217.
11. Ibid., pp.205, 217, 219, 212, 205.
12. Helen Blackburn's obituary of Tod, *Englishwoman's Review*, 15 October 1897, p.60.
13. The Mayoress of Belfast at the unveiling of a memorial to Tod, *Englishwoman's Review*, 15 January 1898, p.53.

14. Luddy, 'Isabella M. Tod', p.216.
15. Ibid., pp.217–18.
16. Ibid., pp.215, 217.
17. For this section both Dana Hearne, 'The Development of Irish Feminist Thought; A Critical Historical Analysis of The Irish Citizen 1912–1920' (PhD thesis, University of Ontario, 1992) and Louise Ryan, *Irish Feminism and the Vote; an Anthology of the 'Irish Citizen' Newspaper 1912–1920* (Dublin: Folens, 1996) were very useful.
18. *Irish Citizen*, 25 May 1912, p.1.
19. While the majority of contributors to the *Citizen* were women, James Cousins and Francis Sheehy Skeffington, husbands respectively of Margaret Cousins and Hanna Sheehy Skeffington, founders of the Irish Women's Franchise League, were joint editors until the Cousinses left Ireland in 1913. The editors wrote unsigned editorial articles and notes and also individually signed articles. After Francis's death in 1916 Hanna took over the editorship, with Louie Bennett acting editor during her absence in the United States.
20. *Irish Citizen*, 17 May 1913, p.411.
21. *Irish Citizen*, 13 July 1912, p.60.
22. *Irish Citizen*, 2 August 1913, p.83.
23. *Irish Citizen*, 29 November 1913, p.225.
24. *Irish Citizen*, August 1917, p.373.
25. *Irish Citizen*, May 1917, p.260.
26. *Irish Citizen*, 27 February 1915, p.317.
27. *Irish Citizen*, 6 July 1912, p.51; 13 July 1912, p.59.
28. *Irish Citizen*, 13 July 1912, p.59.
29. *Irish Citizen*, 25 May 1912, p.19.
30. *Irish Citizen*, 8 August 1914, pp.93–4; 20 February 1915, p.307.
31. *Irish Citizen*, November 1919, p.44.
32. *Irish Citizen*, 28 December 1912, p.251; 4 January 1913, p.259. As noted above, the growing separation of home and work-place increasingly excluded women from their former participation in their husband's or family's occupation.
33. The reality of these obstacles was recognized by the passing of the Sex Disqualification (Removal) Act of December 1919 which made disqualification on grounds of sex or marriage for civil professions and jury service illegal.
34. *Irish Citizen*, 24 April 1915, p.381.
35. *Irish Citizen*, January 1918, pp.394–5.
36. *Irish Citizen*, November 1919, p.44.
37. *Irish Citizen*, December 1919, p.53.
38. *Irish Citizen*, 22 August 1914, p.108.
39. Cited in Margaret Ward, '"Rolling up the Map of Suffrage": Irish Suffrage and the First World War', in Ryan and Ward, *Irish Women and the Vote*, p.149. For further discussion of Irish feminists' definitions of pacifism, and their location in the context of international feminism, see also Margaret Ward, 'Nationalism, Pacifism, Internationalism: Louie Bennett, Hanna Sheehy Skeffington and the Problems of "Defining Feminism"', in Anthony Bradley and Maryann Gialanella Valiulis (eds), *Gender and Sexuality in Modern Ireland* (Amherst, MA: University of Massachusetts Press, 1997), pp.60–84; Rosemary Cullen Owens, 'Women and Pacifism in Ireland 1915–1932', in Valiulis and O'Dowd, *Women and Irish History*, pp.220–38.
40. Hanna Sheehy Skeffington, 'Reminiscences of an Irish Suffragette' (1941), in *Votes for Women: Irish Women's Struggle for the Vote* (Dublin: Andrée Sheehy Skeffington, and Rosemary Owens, 1975), p.18.
41. Raughter, 'A Natural Tenderness', p.72; Luddy, *Women and Philanthropy*, p.1.
42. D.W. Bebbington, *Evangelicalism in Modern Britain; a History from the 1730s to the 1980s* (London: Unwin Hyman, 1989), p.57.
43. See Mary Mulvihill and Patricia Deevy (eds), *Stars, Shells and Bluebells; Women Scientists and Pioneers* (Dublin: Women in Science and Technology, 1997); Susan McKenna-Lawlor, *Whatever Shines Should Be Observed: 'quicquid nitet notandum'* (Dublin: Royal Irish Academy, 2002).
44. Clara Cullen, 'Women, the Museum of Irish Industry and the Pursuit of Scientific Learning in Nineteenth-Century Dublin', in Ciara Meehan and Emma Lyons (eds), *History Matters 11* (Dublin: School of History and Archives, University College Dublin, 2006), pp.9–19.

45. Mary E. Daly, *The Spirit of Earnest Inquiry: The Statistical and Social Inquiry Society of Ireland 1847–1997* (Dublin: Statistical and Social Inquiry Society of Ireland, 1997), pp.73–4.
46. Carmel Quinlan, *Genteel Revolutionaries: Anna and Thomas Haslam and the Irish Women's Movement* (Cork: Cork University Press, 2002).
47. Honohan, *Civic Republicanism*, pp.113–14.
48. Cited in Rosemary Cullen Owens, *Smashing Times: A History of the Irish Women's Suffrage Movement 1876–1922* (Dublin: Attic Press, 1984), p.92.
49. Claire Hackett, 'Narrative of Political Activism from Women in West Belfast', in Louise Ryan and Margaret Ward (eds), *Irish Women and Nationalism; Soldiers, New Women and Wicked Hags* (Dublin: Irish Academic Press, 2004) pp.145–66.
50. Callie Persic, 'The Emergence of a Gender Consciousness: Women and Community Work in West Belfast', in Ryan and Ward (eds), *Irish Women and Nationalism*, pp.167–83.
51. Isabella Tod, cited in Helen Blackburn's obituary of Tod, *Englishwoman's Review*, 15 October 1898, p.59.
52. J.H. Cousins and M.E. Cousins, *We Two Together* (Madras: Ganesh and Co., 1950), pp.55, 128–30.
53. Daisy Lawrenson Swanton, *Emerging From The Shadow: the Lives of Sarah Anne Lawrenson and Lucy Olive Kingston* (Dublin: Attic Press, 1994), p.55.
54. Sheehy Skeffington, 'Reminiscences of an Irish Suffragette', pp.12–13.
55. For these developments see Maryann Gialanella Valiulis, 'Defining their Role in the New State: Irishwomen's Protest against the Juries Act of 1927', in *Canadian Journal of Irish Studies*, xviii, 1 (July 1992), pp.43–60; 'Power, Gender and Identity in the Irish Free State', in *Journal of Women's History*, vi, 4/vii, 1 (Winter/Spring 1995), pp.117–36; 'Engendering Citizenship: Women's Relation to the State in Ireland and the United States in the Post Suffrage Period', in Valiulis and O'Dowd, *Women and Irish History*, pp.159–72.
56. Cited in Joyce Padbury, 'Mary Hayden' (unpublished research).
57. *Irish Citizen*, 12 May 1912, p.12.
58. Catherine Candy, 'Margaret Cousins (1878–1954)', in Mary Cullen and Maria Luddy (eds), *Female Activists: Irish Women and Change 1900–1960* (Dublin: Woodfield Press, 2001), pp.113–40; and '"Untouchability", Vegetarianism and the Suffragist Ideology of Margaret Cousins', in Ryan and Ward, *Irish Women and the Vote*, pp.154–70.
59. See Honohan, *Civic Republicanism*, 'Part II: Contemporary Debates', for a wide-ranging discussion of these developments.

CHAPTER FOUR

Gender, History and Witchcraft in Early Modern Ireland: A Re-reading of the Florence Newton Trial

MARY McAULIFFE

The last decade of the twentieth century has seen an increase in scholarly research and publications in witchcraft studies, especially studies on the early modern period. A review of these works shows that there has been a paradigm shift among historians of witchcraft. This shift has seen the adoption of, as Bever states, 'anthropological and sociological methodologies, a greater attention to archival sources and an interest in focusing on "history from below". However, one area that remains problematic and controversial is the role of gender in the witchcraft discourse.'[1]

From the earliest investigations into the witch trials, historians had noted the associations between women and witchcraft. These associations could be seen as part of a general pattern of medieval misogyny that was evident from many of these original writings on witchcraft – especially from sources such as the *Malleus Maleficarum*.[2] This particular document, compiled by the Dominican inquisitor Heinrich Kramer, and first published in Germany in 1486, amply demonstrates the medieval belief that women were more inclined than men to be witches. Kramer held that it was the weakness of women's minds, their spiritual frailty, their vulnerability to demonic suggestion as well as their natural proclivity to evil, that caused women to become witches more easily than men. *Malleus Maleficarum* can be seen as representative of a long genealogy of misogynistic writings that were part of the Roman Christian tradition. These include Augustine (345–430) who wrote of Solomon being 'unable to resist the love of a woman drawing [him] into ... evil'[3] and St Thomas Aquinas (1225–74) writing of women as the 'inferior sex' and that 'women

[are] more bitter than death; she is a snare, her heart is a net, her arms are chains'.[4]

The precedents for these ideas about women found in *Malleus Maleficarum* can be found in the writings of the earlier Church fathers and in secular medieval society where, according to Balmires, 'a whole arsenal of miscellaneous proverbs ... reinforced misogyny', particularly around the voracious sexuality of women, one such example being 'one cockerel suffices fifteen hens, but fifteen men do not suffice one woman'.[5] Kramer included both the learned writings of the church fathers and the secular anti-women proverbs and sayings in his publication, all of which were used to prove the existence of witches and the very real danger they posed to the world. Along with most of his contemporaries, Kramer firmly believed that most of these witches were women. As he wrote:

> The wickedness of women is spoken of in *Ecclesiasticus* xxv: There is no head above the head of a serpent: and there is no wrath above the wrath of a woman. I had rather dwell with a lion and a dragon than to keep house with a wicked woman. All wickedness is but little to the wickedness of a woman ... What else is woman but a foe to friendship, an inescapable punishment, a necessary evil, a natural temptation, a desirable calamity, a domestic danger, a delectable detriment, an evil of nature, painted with fair colours.[6]

Other contemporaneous writings reveal an underlying belief in the vulnerability of the female mind to evil suggestion and satanic possession and extant records do show that women were the large majority of those accused as witches. Even as late as the sixteenth century, in England, a list of 'presumptions against witches' drawn up for Justices of the Peace in 1592 began with the first presumption that witches 'were most commonly weeke women'.[7]

However, until recent decades, scholarly works tended to underplay gender relations in their analyses. A quick overview of scholarly writing on witchcraft in medieval and early modern Europe shows that much of the research and writing has been, and is still, done by male academics. Many of these male-authored writings either ignore or dismiss the gendered context of witch accusations and trials. They argue that, rather than in gender relations, the origins of witchcraft accusations lie in village tensions and conflicts, or in the defence of power hierarchies from real/imagined enemies or in the very real fear of *maleficia*,[8] which is acknowledged to have been widespread among the peasant population of Europe.

In the 1970s the study of witchcraft, in particular in the English-speaking world, was revolutionized by the publication of two works, Alan Macfarlane's *Witchcraft in Tudor and Stuart England* (1970) and Keith Thomas' *Religion and the Decline of Magic* (1971). Using research methodologies influenced by those developed by social anthropologists, Thomas and Macfarlane concluded that accusations of witchcraft were not generally set in motion by judges or clergymen, but were attributable to interpersonal tensions between villagers, often brought to a head by the refusal of the more well-off to give to charity. Thomas and Macfarlane and the historians who followed in their footsteps saw witches as a product of the economic and social pressures on close knit communities, of anger aroused by giving to charity while seeing the 'undeserving' poor receive that charity.[9] They also held that the witch accusations occurred because of strongly held beliefs that '*maleficia*' or evil existed in the world and that those who were wrongdoers could be influenced by Satan. As Thomas stated, this *maleficia* was a way of making sense out of the misfortunes for which there was no other obvious cause.[10] While Thomas and Macfarlane could be seen as pioneers of social and micro histories, there is a general consensus that they neglected to include gender as a subject of consideration. As Keith Thomas stated, 'the idea that witch-prosecutions reflected a war between the sexes must be discounted, not least because the victims and witnesses were themselves as likely to be women as men'.[11]

Among some academics of witchcraft there was debate about some of the theories of Thomas and Macfarlane. Norman Cohn, in his work *Europe's Inner Demons* (1993), argued that the origins of witchcraft could be traced to the late Middle Ages. Cohn noted, in the extant legal and church records, in the fantastical accounts of witches' Sabbaths, in stories of night-flying and the compacts with the devil, in the holding of 'promiscuous and incestuous orgies' and the satanic killing of innocents, proof of a new understanding of witches as engaged in a conspiracy against the Christian Church. Believing in this conspiracy, an elite group of inquisitors, clergymen, bishops and lawyers used their power and position to conduct the witch-hunts against all opposition, real or imagined. Cohn therefore claims that the European witch-hunt had a strong political aspect to it, one where those in power used it as a weapon to destroy their enemies.[12]

Other theories on the origins of witchcraft, again, mainly from male historians, include Stuart Clarke's idea of 'inversion and misrule'. Clarke, in his work, *Thinking with Demons; The Idea of*

Witchcraft in Early Modern Europe (1997) argues that there is little need to search for explanations for the witch-hunt in changing social conditions, in power structures or as defence against enemies or in gender relations in the Middle Ages, rather he argues that

> witchcraft beliefs should not be understood as a substitute for or a symptom of something else, as the result of a failure to understand real causes and effects: people believed in witchcraft not because they didn't understand, but because that was how they understood.[13]

From this brief overview of male-authored scholarly works on witchcraft we can see that most, if not all, found that gender was not a significant aspect to understanding witchcraft accusations and trials. Even those who did include the issue in their work, such as James Sharpe in *Instruments of Darkness; Witchcraft in the Early New World* (1997), take issue with many of the debates put forward by women writers, particularly feminist academics and historians, on the witch-hunt. He argues that 'the simplistic connection between witchcraft accusations and male oppression collapses while, conversely, the impression that witchcraft accusations were somehow generated by disputes between women gains support'.[14] He sees validity for this argument in the fact that most accusations were of women by women, showing, as he states, that 'witchcraft tensions, witchcraft suspicions, and witchcraft accusations were frequently one of the ways in which disputes between women were resolved'.[15] He argues that the witches operated 'in a complex zone of female power' and 'within the female domain'[16] because witchcraft accusations were obviously 'a struggle between women for control of [this] female space'.[17] Basically women were doing it to themselves! Conversely we can see in Christina Larner's work a step towards opening up the gender debate, when she confronts the accusations of witchcraft in women by other women by arguing that women accused each other 'because women who conformed to the male image of them felt threatened by any identification with those who did not'.[18]

Most of these socio-economic analyses of witchcraft contain the arguments that women were accused as witches more frequently because of their economic marginality in society and, possibly, their threat to other women, and definitely not because they were women living in a patriarchal society. Contrary to this view, and with a few exceptions such as Larner, who while agreeing that the witch trials were sex related did not consider them sex specific, much of the early female authored and/or feminist writings on the medieval and early modern witchcraft were very definite in moving gender relations to the forefront of research in this area. Larner does, however, agree that 'witch hunting is women hunting or at least it is the hunting of women who do not fulfil the male view of how women ought to conduct themselves'.[19] It is Larner's more famous 'sex-related but not sex-specific'[20] quotation that has been much overused to position her with witchcraft scholars who deny the importance of gender. Many historians tend to use this quote (sex-related but not sex-specific) to undermine the argument that gender plays any major role in understanding the history of witchcraft. They also point to the oft-quoted statistic that 20 per cent of witches, accused and burned, were men, as if this number immediately removes the idea of a gender specific notion of witchcraft from the agenda. This counting of numbers can be misleading 'precisely because they [women] were accused of behaving as non-women, of failing to adhere to the social norm of femininity'.[21]

However, in many ways those who sought to introduce feminist theories of research to witchcraft studies were often derided both for their theories and their research methods. De Blécourt argues: 'The central aim of this research [feminist witchcraft research] is (or at least should be) to discover how the overall male hegemony and subsequent subordination of women in European and North American society was ... articulated through ... witchcraft'.[22] He outlines the problems faced by many feminist theorists and historians in getting their work accepted as valid by the Academy. De Blécourt notes that even feminist colleagues were critical of some of the early feminist works on witchcraft. For example, Olwen Hufton wrote 'much of the work has not relied on empirical evidence ... it is indeed frustrating to read Anne Barstow referring to having searched "the European records" when there is no evidence that she ever visited an archive'.[23] While feminist theories might provide the answer as to why so many women were accused, women writing on witchcraft were often accused of 'neglecting archival sources'.[24] In some cases these accusations clearly had weight.[25] Many of the early radical feminists writing on witches were obviously influenced by the writings of Margaret Murray.[26] Murray argued that the 'witch cult' suppressed in the sixteenth century was the remnant of a women-centred folk religion, based on fertility rites, widely practised in Europe. Murray's ideas of the survival of pre-Christian religious practices are now widely discounted, but were, and are still, referenced by some feminist writers on witchcraft. For example, feminist theologian and writer Mary Daly suggested that women had suffered through a virtual holocaust in the early modern period.[27] This so-called 'Burning Time' was when, she claims, anything upwards of three to four million women[28] were accused and burned in a 200–300 year period. The concept of the 'Burning Time' of the sixteenth and seventeenth centuries was a popularly successful attempt (especially on the Web, where it still holds sway) to show that these 'burnings' were a

> deliberate act in a campaign to get women to accept the domination of men in a gendered hierarchy and also to force women [and this explains why Daly and others felt it was mostly women healers and midwives who were burned] to renounce a more natural earth based spirituality attuned to the needs and possibilities of nature [the feminine quality] rather than faith and logic [the male qualities] which was seen as a threat to male hegemony and needed to be eliminated.[29]

These ideas were developed in the 1972 publication of Barbara Ehrenreich and Deirdre English's widely-read pamphlet *Witches, Midwives and Nurses: A History of Women Healers*[30] which was the first to present witches as midwives and healers burned by jealous men. Ehrenreich and English see the establishment of medicine as a profession as the beginning of the exclusion, and also the murder, of female midwives and healers. They saw a definite collusion between Church, State and the medical profession in the witch-hunts. Ehrenreich and English argue that, while the witch-hunts did not eliminate the woman healer totally from early modern society, they succeeded in branding her as dangerous, malevolent and possibly murderous.

Much of the writing done during the 1970s on witchcraft by feminists does not stand up to rigorous academic scrutiny, nor, it can be argued was it ever meant to. Many of these second wave feminist writers were seeing their own, often traumatic, attempts to theorize and create a new society with equality for women mirrored in the attempts of women to free themselves from a patriarchal structure, hundreds of years previously. As Daly wrote 'for women who are on a journey of radical be-ing, the lives of the witches, of the Great Hags of our hidden history are deeply entwined with our own process'.[31] However, as Katherine Hodgkin states in her article 'Historians and Witchcraft'[32] many of these feminist writers and thinkers in the late 1970s and early 1980s took these ideas of the burning times and the obliteration of the women healer, along with the deliberate destruction of a female-centred spirituality, for granted.

It is now accepted that most of the arguments put forward by Ehrenreich and English and others hold little academic validity. For example, historians such as David Harley, having examined all evidence available from court and church records, found that midwives, because of their status in their communities, were not likely to be accused of witchcraft.[33] Meanwhile, in more academically rigorous and archival-based works, the Thomas-Macfarlane model which effectively relegated gender to a matter of economics was predominant; women were more likely to be poor and marginal, therefore, more likely to be accused of witchcraft. Between the idea of witchcraft as nothing but a gendered discourse and the view of it as nothing of the kind, there seemed to be no intermediate possibilities. Indeed, as Hodgins argues, it seemed that women historians avoided any research in this area for fear of being associated with the 'lunatic fringe'.

To be interested in witchcraft, for feminist historians during the 1970s and 1980s, was (judging from my own experience) almost embarrassing. In trying to be serious scholars, and to avoid identification with what it was all too easy to regard as the lunatic fringe, going on about goddess-worship and the like, we somehow lost any position from which to explore gender. There seemed to be no way of reintroducing it into the debate without being – well, irrational. And to study witchcraft one had to be extremely rational to prove that one wasn't simply grinding axes.[34]

While there has been, more recently, an increase in feminist analyses of the witch hunt of the medieval and early modern period, many historians continue to see gender as having a minor role to play in an understanding of witchcraft persecutions. Mainstream historians of witchcraft have articulated interpretations of the witch hunt that have emphasized state-building, economic and social stresses, and the relationship of folk and elite culture with little regard for the role of gender in these processes. The study of gender and witchcraft has barely touched the surface of the research needed. The problem of gender has, as Sharpe noted 'only recently begun to attract the attention of historians of crime and of the law'.[35] Raymond Gillespie has argued that, in England, 'as gender tensions mounted ... so did persecutions of women for criminal and antisocial activities ... Perhaps the most dramatic example was the increase in prosecutions in early modern England and Scotland for the *crime most closely identified with women* [my emphasis], witchcraft.'[36] Weisner argues that the European elite, had, from two main bases, Aristotle and Christianity, developed the conflation of women and witchcraft.[37] Aristotelian belief in women as defective males and Christian belief in the sexual voraciousness of women, as well as a more general misogyny prevalent in the writings of the Church Fathers, constructed the general understanding of women as weak in body and spirit, vulnerable to sin and dangerous to society. As these ideas were developed and accepted by all sections of society, witchcraft was constructed as a crime seen to be particularly appropriate to women.

This new interest in feminist analysis and research by feminist witchcraft historians began to gain scholarly 'respectability' with the publication of Lyndal Roper's *Oedipus and the Devil* in 1994 which examined witch persecution as one aspect of gender history. With the works of Lyndal Roper, Anne Llewellyn Barstow's *'Witchcraze' A New History of the European Witch Hunts*, Deborah Willis' *Malevolent Nurture: Witch-hunting and Maternal Power* and Diane Purkiss' *The Witch in History*,[38] among others, we can see, as Hodgkin writes, that

> gender has re-entered the debate through an interest in the symbolic and psychic aspects of witchcraft, and in particular the relation to maternity: dead children, good and bad mothers/women, tension and hostility in the family as well as in the neighborhood, phantasy, fear and desire, have all become key interpretative elements in the study of witchcraft.[39]

These historians demonstrated the complexity of witchcraft accusations (not simply based on economics, power relations or belief in *maleficia*), of witch categories (not limited to those on the fringes of society) and of persecutors (not limited to men) while at the same time exploring early modern male discomfort with the female body, female sexuality and other, related tropes of misogyny. Roper, for example, contends that core anxieties behind witch persecution 'turned on motherhood, the bodies of ageing women, and fertility'.[40] The witch here is the inversion of the 'good woman and the good mother'. As Merry Weisner writes, she 'is argumentative, wilful, independent, aggressive and sexual, rather than chaste, pious, silent, obedient and married'.[41] It remains one of the main principles of feminist historiography to challenge the more traditional male-centred interpretations of history. This challenge provides all historians, not just those who work within a feminist methodology, with the opportunity to revaluate evidence and gain new insights – in this case into the lives, activities and experiences of early modern women.

Using the methodologies pioneered by these historians[42] and in particular their criticism of traditional historiography and its failure to engage with new sources, as well as its failure to deconstruct grand universalist theories and challenge assumed truths, I wish to look at the reporting of the story of Florence Newton of Youghal, a woman who is presumed to have been accused and tried as a witch in Cork in 1661. The extraordinary tale of Florence Newton and her doings forms the Seventh Relation in Glanvill's *Saducismus Triumphatus* (London, 1688).[43] It may also be found in Francis Bragge's *Witchcraft Further Displayed* (London, 1712). As Patrick E. Byrne states in his *Witchcraft in Ireland* 'there was a colony of Puritans in the town of Youghal where a famous witch trial took place in 1661'.[44] Mentioning that the witch accusations took place among the Puritans of Youghal immediately places the incident in a particular context.[45] In the more famous Puritan society (in New England, USA) where witchcraft accusations occurred later in the seventeenth century, historians have asked if there was something about Puritanism that linked women more closely with evil and deviancy. Elizabeth Reis in her work *Damned Women; Sinners and Witches in Puritan New England* argues that because women were regarded as weaker in body and soul they

> were in a double bind during the witchcraft episodes. Their souls, strictly speaking, were no more evil than men's, but the representation of the vulnerable, perpetually unsatisfied, and yearning female soul, passively waiting for Christ but always open to the devil as well, implicated corporeal women themselves ... A woman's feminine soul, jeopardized in a woman's feminine body, was frail, submissive, passive.[46]

In Youghal in 1661, Florence Newton was reportedly accused of bewitching Mary Longdon. The Florence Newton trial is interesting for many reasons. It shows that the witchcraft doctrine of the early modern period had finally reached Ireland.[47] This trial was a stereotypical witch trial. The accused was a single woman. The accuser was also a woman backed up by the local minister and elders. It is reported that the Mayor of the town committed Florence Newton to prison on 24 March 1661, for bewitching Mary Longdon, who gave evidence against her at the Cork Assizes (11 September 1661), as follows:

> Mary Longdon being sworn and examined what she could say against the said Florence Newton for any practice of Witchcraft upon her self, and being bidden to look on the Prisoner, her Countenance changed pale, and she was very fearful to look towards her, but at last she did. And being askt whether she knew her, she said she did, and wisht she never had.[48]

She stated that, at Christmas, Florence came to the house of John Pyne in Youghal, where Mary Longdon was a servant, and asked her [Mary] to give her [Florence] a piece of Beef. Mary refused to give away her Master's Beef, which made Florence angry and she went away mumbling 'Thou had'st as good give it me'.[49] It was also stated:

> That about a Week after, the Deponent being going to the Water with a Pail of Cloth on her head, she met her the said Florence Newton, who came full in her Face, and threw the Pail off her Head, and violently kist her, and said, Mary, I pray thee, let thee and I be Friends, for I bear thee no ill will, and I pray thee do thou bear me none.[50]

Within a month of the kiss at the well, Mary began to suffer violent fits and trances and 'three or four men could not hold her down'.[51] Mary's master, John Pyne and other men of the community, unable to understand these fits in terms of the natural, turned to supernatural explanations – as did Mary herself. She stated,

> That in her Fits she often saw this Florence Newton, and cryed out against her for tormenting of her, for she says, that she would several times stick Pins into her Arms, and some of them so fast, that a Man must pluck three or four times to get out the Pin, and they were stuck betwixt the skin and the flesh ... And being asked how she could think it was Florence Newton that did her this prejudice? she said, first because she threatned her, then because after she had kist her she fell into these Fits, and that she both saw and felt her tormenting.[52]

Florence was then committed for trial to Youghal Gaol, for harming Mary with the kiss, for, as Mary firmly believed, 'that with that kiss she bewitcht her'.[53] At the trial Florence stated that she had not bewitched her (Mary Longdon), but it may be she had overlooked her, and that there was a great difference between bewitching and overlooking,[54] and

> that she could not have done her any harm if she had not toucht her, and that therefore she had kist her. And she said, that what mischief she thought of at that time she kist her, that would fall upon her, and that she would not but confess she had wronged the Maid, and thereupon fell down upon her Knees, and prayed God to forgive her for wronging the poor Wench.[55]

In reporting the crime committed by Florence, Seymour (1913) presumes that Florence is an old woman: he calls her an 'unfortunate old woman'[56] and she herself is said to have stated in her replies during cross-examination that 'she was old and had a bad memory'.[57] The fact that Florence is constructed as old fits in with accepted wisdom on the gender (female) and age (old) of witches at the time. Through much of the early modern period it was presumed that 'witches be women which be commonly old'.[58] According to Levack it was 'believed older women were not as easily able to find sexual partners and were thus more susceptible to temptation by the sexual advances of the Devil'.[59] Lyndal Roper wrote that 'the witch hunt as it operated in the sixteenth and seventeenth centuries had offered a clear way of dealing with evil, by locating the source of evil in an old woman. Old women were disproportionately represented amongst the victims of the witch craze and the old woman was the abiding stereotypical witch.'[60]

Sona Rosa Burstein has suggested that old women accused of witchcraft, particularly if they were said to mumble incoherently and act aggressively towards others, were showing evidence of the onset of senility or dementia.[61] Older women were most likely to be without a male guardian – i.e. widows – or to be post-menopausal women who were regarded as unregulated and dangerous, therefore, the social containment of their touch/influence was all the more difficult. Edward Bever in his study of witchcraft argued that the stereotype of the older women which dominated in early modern Europe, the bawdy, aggressive and domineering woman, led to many accusations of witchcraft and in turn led to a change in behaviour patterns among older women – he suggests 'that the witch trials may have encouraged older women to act in a less "witch-like" fashion'.[62] However, most historians see age as only one part of the more complex explanations of witchcraft accusations. Age would matter in so far as a woman may have had time to build a reputation as a witch, or that older people, especially women who were single or widowed, were more vulnerable in a society which valued the male guardianship of women – especially as a control mechanism over their weak and susceptible bodies, minds and souls.

Another aspect of the accusations against Florence, which resonates with the general literature on witches, is the fact that she uses an intimate touch to bewitch. The 'violent' kiss Florence uses to bewitch Mary and, later as we are told, kill the children of three aldermen in Youghal[63] and one warden (David Jones)[64] in the jail, is mentioned in the text at least a dozen times. Again and again Mary and her allies all blame the kiss at the well for all her (Mary's) woes. Marianne Hester in *Lewd Women and Wicked Witches* suggests that many witches were accused of sexual deviance such as lewdness, fornication, orgies, bestiality, sex with the devil and lesbianism.[65] The female touch and, in particular, the kiss is often mentioned in medieval and early modern texts on demonology and witchcraft, as the avenue through which women bewitch. In the thirteenth-century text, *Dialogue on Miracles* by Caesarius of Heisterback, there is a tale of a Cistercian monk being bewitched by a devil in the shape of a Benedictine nun. As he lay asleep in bed 'she [the witch] placed her arms around the neck of the ... sleeping occupant, kissed him and then vanished ... The violated brother died within three days'.[66] From Early Christian times women were viewed as a source of contagion and defilement, as well as a conduit of demonic bewitchment in the battle between God and Satan for the souls of mankind. As Rosemary Radford Ruether writes, the female body was organized by 'the double definition of women as submissive body in the order of nature and the "revolting" body in the disorder of sin'.[67] Eve had, through her collusion with Satan, brought about the expulsion from Paradise and, henceforth, women were seen as susceptible to demonic influences and were, all, potential witches.

This is the effect of the 'diseased touch': the touch, as in the kiss from Florence, has 'knocked signifiers loose, ungrounded bodies, made them strange, provoked perceptual shifts and corporeal response in those touched'.[68] Mary and her master, the local preacher, are completely at a loss to explain this extreme shift in their ordered world – they cannot understand why Mary 'in her Fits she would be taken with Vomiting, and would vomit up Needles, Pins, Horsenails, Stubbs, Wooll, and Straw'.[69] Their world had been turned upside down, had been inverted and polluted by the 'violent kiss'. Further proof is offered to the poison and polluting effect of Florence Newton's touch/kiss, when it is stated that she bewitched one David Jones to death by kissing his hand through the Grate of the Prison: a witness, Francis Beasley, stated that she desired she might kiss his, Jones', hand 'whereupon he gave her his Hand through the Grate, and she kist it, and towards break of day, they went away and parted, and soon after the Deponent heard, that David Jones was ill'.[70] As Jones' wife stated in her deposition given after he died, Jones had stated before his death that

> she hath kist my Hand through the Grate, and ever since she kist my Hand, I have had a great pain, in that Arm, and I verily believe she hath bewitched me, if ever she bewitched any Man.

> To which she answered, the Lord forbid ... That all the Night, and continually from that time he was restless and ill, complaining exceedingly of a great pain in his Arm for seven days together, and at the seven days end he complained, that the pain was come from his Arm to his Heart, and then kept his Bed Night and day grievously afflicted and crying out against *Florence Newton*, and about fourteen days after he died.[71]

Interestingly Florence herself notes the importance of the kiss. She stated

> that she could not have done her (*Mary*) any harm if she had not toucht her, and that therefore she had kist her. And she said, that what mischief she thought of at that time she kist her, that would fall upon her.[72]

The above statement shows the deliberate intention to use the touch, the kiss, and through the violence of the kiss, to harm and destroy. Women as well as men had been socialized to accept the diseased nature of the unregulated touch, especially the uncontained female touch. Florence knew what she was doing to Mary, and had even reason to believe that her kiss would cause Mary harm. The polluting effect of the touch of an uncontrolled/unregulated woman was held to kill indiscriminately – men and women. During the court case Florence continues to make violent motions at Mary; she was seen 'lifting up both her hands together, as they were manacled, cast them in an angry violent kind of motion (as was seen and observed by *W. Aston*) towards the said *Mary*, as if she intended to strike at her if she could have reacht her'.[73] Was Florence still trying to 'touch' Mary, to continue the bewitchment? Mary Longdon, David Jones and his wife (in common with the whole neighbourhood) truly believed in the existence of a witch in their community, in her ability to bewitch and in the polluting, poisonous effect of her touch. The effect of the violence of her kiss (and her subsequent hand motions) on Mary is extraordinary: as soon as Florence shook her manacled hands at Mary, 'the Maid fell suddenly down to the ground like a stone, and fell into a most violent Fit'.[74]

Women were not supposed to be active players in any situation, erotic or otherwise. That Florence, a poor woman, managed to bewitch a young Maid shows the frightening, unnatural ability of older, possibly widowed or single, women; women who were often living on the social and economic fringes of their society. The acceptance of a gendered understanding of religion and religious ideology that left women particularly vulnerable to accusations of witchcraft was very important in the construction of the stereotypical witch. Added to this was a fear of the single or widowed woman (who usually were without direct male guardianship or control) and the construct of the dangerous old hag makes some sense. Other elements, which included a fear of female sexuality and a fear of female access to both social and economic power, leaves one with a potent mix. These beliefs often endangered women whose actions, imagined or otherwise, placed them outside of the accepted norms of behaviour and left them open to accusations of witchcraft. As de Blécourt argues, a witchcraft accusation 'articulated the crossing of male-designed boundaries'[75] by women who were perceived to be unregulated and uncontrolled.

In *The Devil in the Shape of a Woman; Witchcraft in Colonial New England*,[76] Carol Karlsen focuses on the position of accused witches as, mainly, females placed in precarious social and economic positions, whose actions, presence, bodies and beliefs threatened an established, but precarious, social order. With Florence Newton and her 'kiss' we have an illuminating example of how the female body was seen to be a danger to the very society in which she lived and, like all pollutants, that body has to be excised for the common good. The society could then proceed to the restoration of the natural order of things. Therefore, while the records do not note it, it is presumed that Florence was executed. Certainly in the details recorded by Seymour in his *Irish Demonology and Witchcraft* she was subjected to torture and the amateur witch-finders of Youghal threatened her with the 'water test'.[77] Interestingly Florence does admit to being a witch: after torture she confessed to 'overlooking'[78] Mary Longdon.

In both the accusations of witchcraft and confessions/or refusal to confess on the part of the women, feminist historians also find the gendered analysis of women's position in early modern society at play. Elizabeth Reis in *Damned Women: Sinners and Witches in Puritan New England* clearly lays out the impossible situation that many of the accused women found themselves in as the refusal to accept guilt was seen as further proof of that guilt: 'It was the women who denied any collusion with Satan ... [who] displayed a measure of independence in the face of authority'.[79] This apparent independence was contrary to Puritan expectations of female behaviour while 'a confessing woman was the model of Puritan womanhood, even though she was admitting to the worst of sins, for she confirmed her society's belief in both God and the Devil'.[80] Florence Newton, in initially denying the accusation and then admitting to it, conforms to this image of the transgressing and ultimately repentant Puritan woman. Newton crossed the boundaries of accepted societal norms when she kissed and bewitched Mary Longdon, she behaved contrary to the acceptable construct of femininity in her community, was accused and tried, and finally vindicated the taboos and regulations of a Christian and moral society by accepting her own guilt and punishment.

There is another aspect of the Newton case in which we see a commonality with many of the Early Modern witchcraft trials. In common with these trials, Florence was accused and borne witness against by another woman. As well as seeing women as the primary victims of the witch hunt we can also see them as actors in the drama – being accusers, giving evidence against other women, upholding the social and economical hierarchies and believing the '*malefica*'. This is one of the areas that have proved problematic for feminist historians of witchcraft. Many [mostly male] historians have argued that the presence of female accusers lessened the likelihood that the witch persecutions were a 'battle between the sexes'.[81] However, feminist historiography and the use of gender 'as a category of analysis'[82] can affect, change and alter our reading of early modern sexuality, power relations, social controls, religious ideology and what constituted 'otherness' in certain societies. Anna Clark argues that gender analysis is a step forward in feminist history as it can make evident different forms of male power and it can incorporate sexuality and the body as a historical dynamic. In allowing the historian to 'illuminate different forms of male power' we can come close to 'the fundamental question as to why women's subordination [has] lasted so long'.[83] However she also argues that rather than writing of the 'discourse' of a subject area (she was discussing class, but this also applies to gender), one should use the term 'rhetoric' for, as she states, 'discourse evokes the image of ... [construction of] the identity of passive subjects, while rhetoric implies a political *dialogue* [her emphasis] that intends to persuade its audience and pressure its opponents. And women were part of the audience who needed to be persuaded.'[84]

The idea of a rhetoric of witchcraft which seeks to persuade its audience of the existence of witches, and the harmful effects of demonic control on people, particularly women, does make sense in light of our understanding of the construction of women as weak, vulnerable and malleable in an inherently misogynistic society. This rhetoric developed over the centuries sought to persuade its audience, both male and female, of the validity of its argument. Having women believe in witchcraft and in the susceptibility of themselves and other women to evil and diabolic persuasion, as well as positioning women as both victims and accusers in witch persecutions, points not to the absence of gender as a key category of analysis but rather to the success of the misogynist rhetoric of witchcraft. As Clive Holmes has shown in his analyses of women witnesses and witchcraft trials in Early Modern England,

> all witnesses, but particularly those girls who described their possession and the matrons who discovered the genital marks, ratified the misogynous rationalizations proffered by the divines to explain the preponderant numbers of women accused of witchcraft. Their testimony apparently confirmed that women were the weaker sex ... but the machinery in which they became involved, often at the instigation of men, was created, controlled and ultimately discarded by the magisterial and clerical elite.[85]

These women, victims and witnesses, were involved in a rhetoric created, controlled and eventually repudiated in more 'rational' times by men, and more particularly, by the male secular and clerical elite. This rhetoric of witchcraft demonstrates where law, religion, sexuality and gender intersect with the exercise of power in a patriarchal society. The fact that those accused of witchcraft and the accusers were as Larner states 'overwhelmingly female, should form a major part of any analysis'.[86] Using a gendered rhetoric we can see how, in the Florence Newton witchcraft trial, women could be both victim and accuser, while the conduct of the trial itself was under male control. As with many witchcraft trials, we see in the Newton case how the accusations did not stop with Florence; Florence herself names Goody Half-penny and Goody Dod who 'could do these things as well as she', however Mary Longdon denies that Half-penny and Dod were witches.[87] Mary's denial of their guilt may have come too late for these women as the trial judges had a boat brought and are 'thought to have tried the Water Experiment on them all three'.[88] Whether they actually used the water experiment or not the judges did in fact torture a confession out of Florence using an awl.[89] The famous Valentine Greatrakes[90] was one of the main actors in the trial as judge, amateur torturer, witch finder and jury. In his 'Advertisement' for his 'Authentick Record' of the trial of Florence Newton, Glanvill mentions that he had 'heard Mr Greatrix [sic] speak of her at my Lord Conway's at Ragley'.[91] Here Glanvill uses his close proximity with one of the main, male players in the trial to authenticate his tale of

Florence Newton. Interestingly Greatrakes was also renowned for his 'touch', although in his case it was seen as a magical, healing touch as opposed to the 'veneficae or magical venom' emitted by the touch of Florence, which bewitched and killed rather than healed.[92]

The Florence Newton trial demonstrates that religious belief in '*maleficia*', in the weakness of women, in diseased female bodies and the polluting female touch all show the rhetoric of misogyny at work. Although this is one of the few witchtrials ever held in Ireland, it does demonstrate that these deas had some impact on the construction of femininity in early modern Irish societies. This and other trials demonstrate that witches in most European and Early American cultures were very successfully gendered as women. As Stuart Clark, so often dismissive of feminist interpretations of witchcraft, wrote, 'we should ask not why women were associated with witchcraft but why contemporaries associated witchcraft with women'.[93]

NOTES

1. Edward Bever, 'Witchcraft, Female Aggression and Power in the Early Modern Community', *Journal of Social History* (Summer 2002), p.1.
2. *Malleus Maleficarum* (The Hammer of Witches), written by Heinrich Kramer and first published in 1486, served as a guidebook for inquisitors during the Inquisition, and was designed to aid them in the identification, prosecution and dispatching of witches.
3. Alcuin Blamires (ed.), *Women Defamed and Women Defended; An Anthology of Medieval Texts* (Oxford: Oxford University Press, 1992), p.81.
4. Ibid., p.90.
5. Ibid., p.8.
6. Kramer, *Malleus Maleficarum*, Part 1, question 2.
7. Darren Oldridge (ed.), *The Witchcraft Reader* (London: Routledge, 2006), p.268.
8. Maleficia/Maleficarum – occult means of doing evil or harm – usually harm done by women. Using Maleficarum (the feminine form of the Latin noun maleficus or malefica) immediately implies that the witches are women.
9. In the Thomas-Macfarlane model the poor were the most likely to be accused of witchcraft, as they were the most likely to need the charity of their neighbours. Therefore the fact that it was mostly women accused of witchcraft was a matter of economics rather than gender – women were much more likely to be poor and in need of charity than men.
10. Alan Macfarlane, *Witchcraft in Tudor and Stuart England* (London: Harper & Row, 1970), pp.111–12 and Keith Thomas, *Religion and the Decline of Magic* (London: Weinfield & Nicholson, 1971), Ch.17.
11. Thomas, *Religion and the Decline of Magic*, p.568.
12. Norman Cohn, *Europe's Inner Demons: The Demonization of Christians in Medieval Christendom,* rev. edn (Chicago: University of Chicago Press, 2000).
13. Stuart Clarke quoted in Katherine Hodgkin, 'Historians and Witchcraft', *History Workshop Journal*, 45 (Spring 1998), pp.271–8; p.276.
14. James Sharpe, *Instruments of Darkness; Witchcraft in the Early New World* (Philadelphia, PA: University of Pennsylvania, 1997), p.178.
15. Ibid., p.177.
16. James Sharpe, 'Witchcraft and Women in Seventeenth-Century England; Some Northern Evidence', *Continuity and Change*, 6, 2 (1991), pp.179–99.
17. Sharpe, *Instruments of Darkness*, p.185.
18. Christina Larner, *Enemies of God; The Witch Hunt in Scotland* (London: Chatto &

Windus, 1981), p.92.
19. Ibid., p.83.
20. Christina Larner, *Witchcraft and Religion, The Politics of Popular Belief* (Oxford and New York: Basil Blackwell, 1984). Larner argues that any attempt to see the witch hunts as the oppression of women by men distracts from the wider social and religious implications of the persecutions. While she saw that the stereotype of the witch was based mainly on femaleness, she stated that witches were hunted primarily because they were witches, not because they were women. Concentrating on the gender aspects, she felt, could distract from the fact that people actually believed in the existence of witches and the evil (*maleficia*) they created.
21. Willem de Blécourt, 'The Making of the Female Witch', *Gender and History*, 12, 2 (July 2000), p.293.
22. Ibid., p.289.
23. Olwen Hufton, *The Prospect Before Her; A History of Women in Western Europe* (London: Harper Collins, 1996), p.336 as quoted in de Blécourt, 'The Making of the Female Witch', p.291.
24. De Blécourt, 'The Making of the Female Witch', p.291.
25. Ibid. He mentions, among others, that Diane Purkiss 'scorns serial research', while Marianne Hester's work is based on 'published source material'.
26. Margaret Murray, *The Witch Cult in Western Europe* (Oxford: Clarendon, 1921).
27. Mary Daly, *Gyn/Ecology: The Meta-Ethics of Radical Feminism* (Boston, MA: Beacon Press, 1978).
28. Or nine million according to the nineteenth-century suffragette Matilda Joslyn Gage in *Woman, Church and State: An Historical Account of the Status of Women through the Christian Ages: With Reminiscences of the Matriarchate* (New York: The Truth Seeker Company, 1893).
29. See Part 1, 'A Holocaust of One's Own; The Myth of the Burning Times', in Diane Purkiss, *The Witch in History: Early Modern and Twentieth-Century Representations* (London: Routledge, 1996), pp.7–30 in which Purkiss shows that Daly and others dismissed evidence that their figures of three to four million were flawed. The view of these radical feminists of witchcraft as a successful campaign by men to get women to accept the dominance of men is soundly dismissed by Purkiss.
30. Barbara Ehrenreich and Deirdre English, *Witches, Midwives and Nurses: A History of Women Healers* (New York: Feminist Press, 1972).
31. Daly, *Gyn/Ecology*, p.15.
32. Hodgkin, 'Historians and Witchcraft', *History Workshop Journal*, 45 (Spring 1998), pp.271–7.
33. David Harley, 'Historians as Demonologists: The Myth of the Midwife-Witch', *Social History of Medicine*, 3, 1 (1990), pp.1–26.
34. Ibid., p.274.
35. James Sharpe, 'Women, Witchcraft and the Legal Process', in Darren Oldridge (ed.), *The Witchcraft Reader* (London: Routledge, 2001), p.289.
36. Raymond Gillespie, 'Women and Crime in Seventeenth-Century Ireland', in Margaret MacCurtain and Mary O'Dowd (eds), *Women in Early Modern Ireland* (Dublin: Wolfhound Press, 1991), p.45.
37. Merry E. Weisner, *Women and Gender in Early Modern Europe* (Cambridge, Cambridge University Press, 2000, 2nd edn), p.272.
38. Lyndal Roper, *Oedipus and the Devil; Witchcraft, Religion and Sexuality in Early Modern Europe* (London: Routledge, 1994); Anne Llewellyn Barstow, *'Witchcraze' A New History of the European Witch Hunts* (London: Pandora, 1994); Deborah Willis, *Malevolent Nurture: Witch-hunting and Maternal Power* (Ithaca, NY: Cornell University Press, 1995); Diane Purkiss, *The Witch in History* (London: Routledge, 1996).
39. Hodgkin, 'Historians and Witchcraft', p.275.
40. Lyndal Roper, *Witch Craze: Terror and Fantasy in Baroque Germany* (New Haven, CT: Yale University Press, 2004), p.7.
41. Weisner, *Women and Gender in Early Modern Europe*, p.276.
42. A number of whom self-identify as feminist historians – Roper and Willes being examples.
43. Joseph Glanvill, *Saducismus Triumphatus: OR, Full and Plain Evidence Concerning Witches and Apparitions. In Two Parts. The First treating of their Possibility; The Second of their Real*

Existence. The Third Edition. The Advantages whereof above the former, the Reader may understand out of Dr H. More's Account prefixed thereunto. With two Authentick, but wonderful Stories of certain Swedish Witches; done into English by Anth, Norneck, D.D. London (Printed for S. Lownds at his Shoppe by the Savoy-Gate, 1688). Cornell University Library Witchcraft Collection <http://racerel.library.cornell.edu:8090/Dienst/UI/1.0/Display/cul.witch/053>. Accessed 23 July 2007.

44. Patrick E. Byrne, *Witchcraft in Ireland* (Cork: Mercier Press, 1967), p.28. Byrne outlines most of the cases of witchcraft accusation that occurred in Ireland, from the first in 1324, of Alice Kyteler in Kilkenny, to the last trial of seven accused women at Island Magee, Co Antrim in the early eighteenth century. In total only about a dozen cases were recorded in over 400 years.
45. It was Samuel Hayman who first mentioned that it was among a Puritan colony in Youghal that the Newton incident occurred in his *The New Hand-book for Youghal: containing notes and records of the ancient religious foundations, and the historical annals of the town* (Cork: 1855).
46. Elizabeth Reis, *Damned Women; Sinners and Witches in Puritan New England* (Ithaca, NY: Cornell University Press, 1997), p.94.
47. There had been some, albeit very few, earlier witch accusations and trials in Ireland, the most famous being the accusation of witchcraft levelled at Dame Alice Kyteler in Kilkenny in 1324.
48. Glanvill, *Saducismus Triumphatus*, p.365.
49. Ibid.
50. Ibid.
51. Ibid., p.366.
52. Ibid., pp.366–7.
53. Ibid., p.367.
54. When Florence Newton mentions that she 'overlooked' Mary she draws a distinction between 'overlooking' and 'bewitching'. When a victim is overlooked, it means to be given the evil eye, to be bewitched by being looked upon. However, Florence also admits she could not have hurt Mary without kissing her, therefore she was doing more than simply 'giving her the evil eye' or overlooking her. Mary herself claims bewitchment. By drawing a distinction between 'overlooking' and 'bewitching', Florence may have been trying to admit that she was angry with Mary, and had cast an evil eye at her/overlooked her, but deny that she was trying to undertake the more heinous crime of bewitchment. Her attempt fails as the judges at the trial believe this to be a case of witchcraft.
55. Glanvill, *Saducismus Triumphatus*, p.371.
56. St. John D. Seymour, *Irish Witchcraft and Demonology* (Dublin: Hodges, Figgis & Co., 1913) p.106.
57. Glanvill, *Saducismus Triumphatus*, p.369.
58. R. Scot, *The Discoverie of Witchcraft* (London: William Brome, 1584), p.5.
59. Brian Levack, *The Witch-Hunt in Early Modern Europe* (London: Longman, 1995, 2nd edn), p.143, supra note 8.
60. Lyndal Roper, 'Evil Imaginings and Fantasies; Child Witches and the End of the Witch Craze', *Past and Present*, 167 (May 2000), p.123.
61. Sona Rosa Burstein, 'Aspects of Psychopathology of Old Age Revealed in Witchcraft Cases of the Sixteenth and Seventeenth Centuries', *British Medical Bulletin*, 6. 1–2 (1949), pp.63–71.
62. Edward Bever, 'Witchcraft, Female Aggression, and Power in the Early Modern Community', *Journal of Social History*, 35, 4 (2002), p.974.
63. When he was deposed to give evidence at the trial, Richard Mayre, Mayor of Youghal, stated that three Aldermen in Youghal said Newton had kissed their children and that all three children died soon after. See Glanvill, *Saducismus Triumphatus*, p.375.
64. Glanvill, *Saducismus Triumphatus*, p.376.
65. Marianne Hester, *Lewd Women and Wicked Witches; A Study of the Dynamics of Male Domination* (London: Routledge, 1992), p.181.
66. Dyan Elliott, *Fallen Bodies; Pollution, Sexuality & Demonology in the Middle Ages* (Philadelphia, PA: University of Pennsylvania Press, 1999), p.31.
67. Rosemary Radford Ruether, *Religion and Sexism; Images of Women in the Jewish and Christian Tradition* (New York: Simon & Schuster. 1974), p.157.

68. Carolyn Dinshaw, *Getting Medieval; Sexualities and Communities, Pre and Postmodern* (Durham, NC and London: Duke University Press, 1999), p.151.
69. Glanvill, *Saducismus Triumphatus*, p.366.
70. Ibid., p.377.
71. Ibid., pp.376–7.
72. Ibid., p.371.
73. Ibid., p.367.
74. Ibid., p.365.
75. De Blécourt, 'The Making of the Female Witch', p.303.
76. Carol F. Karlsen, *The Devil in the Shape of a Woman; Witchcraft in Colonial New England* (London: Norton, 1987, 1998).
77. Seymour, *Irish Witchcraft and Demonology*.
78. See note 53.
79. Reis, *Damned Women; Sinners and Witches in Puritan New England*, p.141.
80. Ibid., p.136.
81. Oldridge (ed.), *The Witchcraft Reader*, p.303.
82. Joan Wallach Scott, 'Gender; A Useful Category of Historical Analysis', *American Historical Review*, 91, 5 (December 1986), pp.1053–75.
83. Anna Clark, 'Comment', in Sue Morgan (ed.), *The Feminist History Reader* (London: Routledge, 2006), p.168.
84. Ibid., p.170.
85. Clive Holmes, 'Women; Witches and Witnesses', in Oldridge (ed.), *The Witchcraft Reader*, p.319.
86. Larner, *Enemies of God: The Witch-Hunt in Scotland*, p.3.
87. Glanvill, *Saducismus Triumphatus*, pp.371, 375.
88. Ibid., p.375. As St John D. Seymour says of this experiment in his book *Irish Witchcraft and Demonology*: 'The suspected witch is taken, her right thumb tied to her left great toe, and *vice versa*. She is then thrown into the water: if she *sinks* (and drowns, by any chance!) her innocence is conclusively established; if, on the other hand, she *floats*, her witchcraft is proven, for water, as being the element in Baptism, refuses to receive such a sinner in its bosom' (pp.106–7). If this experiment actually took place Florence Newton and the other two women did survive it. However as survival would have proved Florence guilty it is likely that the experiment was threatened and did not take place. It is the word of Mary Longdon that seems to have condemned Florence and released the other two women.
89. Glanvill, *Saducismus Triumphatus*, pp.372–3. The judges made Florence sit on a stool and tried then to stick an awl through the stool but could not. When they pulled her off the stool they found that the blade of the awl was shorter by an inch but could find no place of entry on Florence's body for the missing piece. Then they made Mary hold the awl and got her to run violently at Florence but could not stick her – in fact the awl was so bent by this that it could not be straightened. Then they lanced her hand an inch long and an inch deep but it didn't bleed, however when they lanced the other hand, both hands bled.
90. Valentine Greatrakes (1628–82), a healer, born in Affane, Co. Waterford was thought to have a divine ability to heal. He was know as a 'stroker' because of his method of stroking people with his hands in order to cure them. In 1666 he published an account of his life and his cures. He was living in Youghal when Florence Newton was accused of witchcraft and he got involved in the trial. He and the other judges carried out a series of tests on Newton (lancing her skin and sticking awls into her body) to prove she was a witch.
91. Glanvill, *Saducismus Triumphatus*, p.378. Glanvill may also have had access to the notes taken by Sir William Ashton, who is purported to have taken verbatim notes of the trial. These notes are now destroyed or missing, but it is possible that Glanvill saw them and based his description of the trial on these.
92. Ibid.
93. Stuart Clark, *Thinking with Demons* (Oxford: Clarendon Press, 1997), p.110.

CHAPTER FIVE

The Bureau of Military History and Female Republican Activism, 1913–23

EVE MORRISON

In March 2003 the 1,773 oral testimonies known as witness statements, contemporary documents, photographs and voice recordings collected by the Bureau of Military History (BMH) between 1947 and 1959 were finally released to the public after decades of controversy and delay. The statements are the most comprehensive single assemblage of individual accounts by Republicans active during Ireland's revolutionary decade of 1913–23 currently available to historians, a status they will most likely retain until the military service pension files are released. If interrogated carefully and in conjunction with other primary sources, they yield much welcome detail about the overall structure and day-to-day workings of Irish separatist organisations, though the lapse of over three decades between the events described and the recording of the testimonies sometimes weighed heavily on their contents. The interviewees were of advanced age, had almost always read other versions of the events recalled and frequently confused dates and details. Inevitably, as a government-funded project carried out under the auspices of the Department of Defence, the Bureau was also influenced by the prevailing political climate. The result was that the material it amassed was often as reflective of the period in which it operated as the one witnesses were being asked to remember. This chapter will explore how its contents were shaped on a number of different levels by the gendered divisions of Irish politics and society in both periods, concentrating in particular on the 146 witness statements and over thirty collections of original documents and photographs collected from a total of 153 women.[1]

In the first two decades of the twentieth century nationalist women seeking to access mainstream political life faced a number of obstacles. The Irish Parliamentary Party would not allow women into most of its organizations or include provisions for their suffrage in home rule legislation.[2] Female nationalists also remained outside the ranks and excluded from the decision-making of the Irish Republican Brotherhood and the Irish Volunteers.[3] The Citizen Army founded by socialist James Connolly supplied fifteen or so women combatants to the ranks of the Easter rebels in 1916 but this practice was not emulated by the Volunteers. As the organization's most recent historian has noted, Cumann na mBan, the Volunteers' female auxiliary founded in April 1914, had participated in but not led the Irish revolution.[4] The 1916 Rising was planned, the War of Independence (1919–21) fought and the Civil War ended in May 1923 without the Republican leadership ever consulting the women's organization.[5] Even within Sinn Féin (an organization they were formally allowed to join on an equal basis with men), though women were well represented among the leadership at regional and local level, they faced widespread resistance and suspicion of their involvement in the 'man's world' of politics.[6] Cumann na mBan organizers such as Bureau witness Bridget O'Mullane regularly encountered such attitudes when they began organizing branches around the country in 1918:

> I had a good deal of prejudice to overcome on the part of the parents, who did not mind their boys taking part in a military movement, but who had never heard of, and were reluctant to accept, the idea of a body of gun-women. It was, of course, a rather startling innovation and, in that way, Cumann na mBan can claim to have been the pioneers in establishing what was undoubtedly a women's auxiliary of an army. I fully understood this attitude and eventually, in most cases, succeeded in overcoming this prejudice.[7]

Organisations of the cultural revival such as the Irish Agricultural Organisation Society and the Gaelic League as well as Protestant and Catholic churches actively promoted the idea that women's primary role was in the domestic sphere.[8] Likewise, in Republican propaganda throughout the revolutionary period, women were most commonly portrayed as keepers of the hearth, instillers of the faith, willing to sacrifice their livelihood, their husbands and their sons in the cause of Irish freedom[9] and this was reflected in the gender-based division of labour that operated in the organizations of Republican militarism. A great deal of female activists' time was spent cooking, making tea, washing clothes, sewing haversacks, learning first aid, providing safe houses, typing, raising funds, handing out leaflets and visiting Republican prisoners. Kerry Volunteer Daniel Mulvihill's glowing tribute to his female relatives gives a good description of the infrastructure for the Republican military campaign provided by Irish nationalist women without which it was unlikely to have succeeded:

> I would say that my mother (RIP) was one of the greatest Irishwomen I ever knew. She never spared anything during the Tan time and Civil War. She knew more about Irish history than anyone I have ever met since. The house was always full, both during the Tan time and Civil War and even though it was a marked spot in the Civil War, the boys stayed there the whole time through ... My two sisters were in the Cumann na mBan and did a lot of work in the line despatches. I think it took most of the time of my mother and sisters, cooking for and feeding the lads from the summer of 1920 to the spring of 1924. I don't think in all that period – the Truce included – that the house had one night that there was not some stranger in it.[10]

However, evidence in the statements tends to confirm the findings of historians such as Marie Coleman, who argue that the role of Cumann na mBan (and women activists generally) underwent a significant transformation with the onset of guerrilla war in 1919.[11] As early as 1917 in Cork and most other places over 1919–20 Cumann na mBan was restructured along military lines with each branch assigned to an Irish Volunteer company.[12] Women were increasingly involved in intelligence work, scouting, the procurement and transfer of arms and communications that contributed directly to military successes in the field.[13] The most detailed descriptions of these activities are found in the women's testimonies and the pithy, if sometimes patronizing, comments of former Irish Volunteers are almost always positive and generally confirm what the women say: 'The Cumann na mBan, led by Miss Mary K. Sheedy of Ballingaddy, Mai Moloney of Lackelly, Lizzie Hogan of Tankardstown and others, used a rifle and kept the kettles boiling as occasion demanded.'[14]

The escalation of the guerrilla war and the onset of serious coercion following the introduction of the Restoration of Order in Ireland Act in August 1920 made women increasingly valuable assets. The dominant assumptions of gender were an essential element in female activists' success. Central to women's usefulness was that they were much less likely to be suspected by the authorities, their activities masked by the daily routines and assumptions of ordinary life. Women used their babies' prams and their long skirts to transport arms, accompanied male Volunteers to pose as courting couples when selecting ambush sites and lured unsuspecting soldiers to the docks to be disarmed by waiting Volunteers.[15] Women were sent where men could not go and into situations where they would not be suspected. One Westmeath Volunteer remembered: 'The Cumann na mBan had a branch of their organisation in Summerhill which co-operated with us in many ways ... They often carried dispatches for us and were able to get through hold-ups and cordons of the enemy where a man would not have a chance of doing so.'[16]

Some female Republican activists operated outside of the formal command structures of Cumann na mBan. Nan Nolan in Carlow seems to have worked mostly with her brother who was an officer in the Ballon Irish Volunteers. Mary Flannery Woods and Moira Kennedy O'Byrne were specifically asked by Michael Collins to leave Cumann na mBan to transport arms and find safe houses for the IRA.[17] Catherine Rooney smuggled arms and gelignite from Glasgow and was utilized by members of the Squad to carry out various activities:

> The Cumann na mBan knew nothing about all these activities of mine, as I did them on instructions from the boys with whom I was in touch. That is why I got no help from the Organisation when I came to apply for my pension. They would not even certify my claim for 1916 as they did not see me in the GPO. Fortunately, I was able to get certificates from the different fellows that knew of my work.[18]

The invisibility of women created by dominant perceptions of gender allowed Josephine Browne in Cork City,[19] Siobhan Creedon and Annie Barrett in Mallow Post Office[20] and Lily Mernin in Dublin[21] to carry out intelligence activities that were as vital as any performed during the War of Independence.[22] Barrett kept the 5th Battalion, Cork II Brigade reliably informed and delayed communications between British forces at crucial moments throughout the War of Independence and Civil War period while maintaining outwardly friendly relations with her Post Office superiors. She played an instrumental part in the successful raid on Mallow Barracks carried out by Cork II Brigade in 1920:

> On this occasion, although all telephone wires in the area were supposed to have been cut, the wire connecting the barracks to

> the Post Office was left intact through some mischance. As the attack on the post was opened the operator then 'phoned the Post Office, 'Get me Buttevant quick also Fermoy. We are being raided.' I took the message and replied 'I can't hear you' ... When the raid was over the military came to the Post Office and with Post Office engineers had the lines repaired. When the lines were again in order the British were sending urgent messages to Fermoy, Buttevant, Ballyvonare and Cork, but I delayed the messages giving the excuse, 'the lines must be faulty'. In this way I helped to delay the arrival of enemy forces and so helped the IRA to get away with the captured arms.[23]

Her predecessor, Siobhan Creedon, was dismissed under suspicion in 1920 but Barrett never seems to have been suspected. This was confirmed by a message received in the Post Office shortly after she had successfully helped a Cork flying column evade capture in the Spring of 1921: 'Following this incident there was a telephone message from Mallow to Cork Headquarters, "Birds have flown". During the course of this conversation it was stated, "Moylan must have tapped the lines".'[24]

In 1922, Michael Collins, Cathal Brugha and several other leaders of the Republican movement publicly commended Cumann na mBan for services rendered and that same year the right to vote was extended to all Irish citizens over the age of 21 in the Free State constitution.[25] However, the gendered roles that had been so skilfully employed by female activists to the advantage of the Republican campaign during the fight were turned against them in the harsh climate of civil war, economic downturn and political retrenchment that followed the War of Independence. Cumann na mBan voted overwhelmingly against the terms of the Anglo-Irish Treaty in February 1922. During the Civil War when popular support for the anti-treaty side fell drastically, the women's assistance became even more crucial. Many of their former allies, however, were in government and the mantle of invisibility that had allowed them to slip through police cordons was gone. Only about fifty women had been arrested during the War of Independence, but over 400 were imprisoned and held without trial under the Emergency Powers Resolution enacted in September 1922.[26] The widespread arrest and detention of women by the pro-treaty side during the Civil War was an implicit recognition of their military value and was an important factor leading to the defeat of the Republican side.[27] Like their male compatriots, they were incarcerated without trial and went on hunger strike, though on their release the women faced the special indignity of finding that their families were often ashamed of the fact that they had been in prison.[28] The invocations of the dead by the widows and relations of Republican martyrs that had been encouraged by Sinn Féin during the Anglo-Irish War and had long been a part of traditional Irish culture were depicted as examples of female irrationality in the women who opposed the Treaty.[29] Those who took the Republican side in the Civil War were vilified by supporters of the Free State and condemned by the Catholic hierarchy.[30]

The pall cast by the Civil War over political life had particularly negative consequences for women involved in the Irish separatist organizations. Successive governments proved reluctant to accord Cumann na mBan the military status that many of its members felt it deserved. It was excluded altogether from the terms of the Military Service Pension Act introduced by the Cumann na nGaedheal government in 1924, a measure from which anti-Treatyites were effectively excluded.[31] Eventually, after the intervention of Senator Michael Staines, the organization was included in the 1934 pension bill enabling those who had taken the Republican side to apply for pensions, though only at the lowest grades.[32] The portrayal of Cumann na mBan as a 'Sinn Féin women's club' was greatly resented by its members.[33] In 1939, a perceived attempt to ignore the pension claims of the Longford contingent provoked furious reactions:

> You have no idea what some of these ladies can say when they get going on the question of neglect of our claim. I quite understand that the matter was taken out of the hands of the Brigade staff yet I would suggest they making [*sic*] an effort to have the matter attended to soon or we may have another Civil War.[34]

The staunch and uncompromising Republicanism of the women themselves also isolated them from the political mainstream. In 1923, four of the five women elected to the Dáil opposed the Treaty and refused to take their seats.[35] Many other women were embittered by their experiences and dropped out of politics altogether or remained in Sinn Féin after the formation of Fianna Fáil in May 1926.[36]

The position of women in the 1940s stood in considerable contrast to the first decades of the twentieth century when Ireland had been home to a vibrant and successful feminist movement. Ireland was just one of several European countries to prioritize the return of women to their traditional domestic roles as a means of restoring order and normalcy in the inter-war period.[37] Although formal political equality was retained, the participation of women in public life and employment was significantly curtailed by a series of legislative measures.[38] The contribution of female Republicans to the campaign for independence suffered a similar eclipse in popular and historical accounts of the period. Even Dorothy Macardle's history *The Irish Republic* underplayed the role of female Republicans.[39] In some instances the explanation for their omission may lie in the covert nature of their activities rather than deliberate attempts to exclude them. This may be part of the reason, for instance, why there is no mention of Annie Barrett in the *Capuchin Annual's* commemorative edition of the year 1920 or in other Bureau witnesses' accounts of the Mallow barracks attack.[40]

Yet many of the questionnaires and letters collected at different times over the years from former members of Cumann na mBan by Eithne Coyle, Sighle Humphries and Bridget O'Mullane (in the hope that an account might be written) bear painful testimony to the lack of effort made to acknowledge women in the memorials and commemorations of Independent Ireland.[41] Coyle, who remained in Cumann na mBan until 1941, felt that 'it would be a crime against history if the often brave, and often hidden actions of the women's sections were not recorded for posterity'.[42] It was a legitimate concern. When the Bureau began its work in January 1947, women's involvement and contributions were generally subject to little more than a brief acknowledgement in a paragraph or a page at the end of a 'fighting story'.

The Bureau's decision to concentrate on collecting material from surviving officers of the Irish Volunteers who had seen active service in the field[43] ensured that former members of other organizations and individuals who had participated in, but not led, the military campaign, or had been involved in the political and cultural side of the movement, were interviewed in significantly smaller numbers. Of the various ancillary organizations represented in the collection, the highest number of statements was taken from Cumann na mBan. Although female contributors account for less than 10 per cent of the collection overall, it is worth pointing out that this was a considerably higher proportion of women than were approached by Ernie O'Malley, Father Louis O'Kane or the three priests in Monaghan who assembled the material in the Marron papers in the 1960s.[44]

To a large extent the BMH seems to have adhered to the gender segregation that was common practice in oral history and still the social norm in 1940s Ireland.[45] Of the 146 statements from women, ninety-seven were taken by the Bureau's only female investigator, Jane Kissane.[46] More than half of the women had been Dublin-based activists and most of her interviewees were resident in Dublin or Wicklow. Almost all testimonies from outside Dublin were done by the twenty-nine male investigators and the highest number of interviews taken by any one of them was eight.[47] The working notes of investigator John Grace provide some interesting insights into the Bureau's attitude towards collecting statements from women. Original lists of officers to target for interview were assembled by the BMH from files relating to 1924 and 1934 military service pension applications.[48] It is significant that while Grace's papers contain lists of the brigade and battalion officers for the Irish Volunteers, there are no corresponding lists for Cumann na mBan, suggesting that he had not intended to collect statements from women. Grace interviewed just two, both in Tipperary, and seems to have done so at the request of their husbands with whom he had actually come to speak.[49]

More than 60 per cent of the women interviewed were former members of Cumann na mBan. Over half of them were officers and twenty-five served on the organization's Executive or were full time organizers.[50] The Irish Citizen Army, Inghinidhe na h-Éireann, Sinn Fein, the Gaelic League and women who had held administrative positions in the Dáil were represented in smaller numbers.[51] Both male and female veterans of the 1916 Rising were accorded an elite status within the Republican movement and this is reflected in the collection.[52] Over fifty of the women interviewed had taken an active part in the Easter Rising and almost one third of all the statements given by women end in 1916. As it has been estimated that something fewer than 200 women were involved in the rebellion, women associated with the Rising were well represented. Almost all of the female witnesses had close relatives who were active in advanced nationalist organizations. Like Irish separatists in general, their political motivations were often closely intertwined with their family histories and local traditions[53] and their political activity was an extension of familial and communal loyalties.

Familial or other connections to well-known male Republicans seem to have played a significant role in the Bureau's choice of female interviewees. Thirty-two women were the widows or relations of famous Republican martyrs or well-known personages, with almost half of the women devoting most and sometimes all of their statements to recounting the activities of their male relatives. The tendency to devote significant sections and sometimes all of their statements to the activities of others is much more common in the testimonies of female than male activists. Several of the anti-treaty women who discuss the experiences of their male relatives only (such as Cait O'Callaghan, Kathleen O'Donovan, Katherine Barry Moloney) may have been motivated more by their unwillingness to co-operate fully with the Bureau than a demure acceptance of their secondary role. Yet, whether taking a stand against a project funded by a state that had betrayed their martyred relatives, or simply paying tribute to the lives lost, in accepting the status of speakers for the dead it had much the same effect; both contributed to the absence of women from accounts of the period. It is frustrating to discover, for instance, that although Una Stack was imprisoned in Kilmainham Gaol during the Civil War and 'battered and bruised' by military police with blackened faces when she was forcibly transferred to North Dublin Union in April 1923, the contents of both her Bureau statements are devoted entirely to the activities of her husband, Austin.[54]

Over sixty of the female contributors opposed the Treaty. Although officially the Bureau guidelines excluded discussion of the Civil War, in practice they were frequently ignored, and no-one seems to have been prevented from talking about events after the July 1921 Truce if they wished to do so.[55] The majority of women interviewed chose to adhere to the official remit, but about a quarter of the statements from female activists discuss the Truce and Civil War in varying degrees of detail. Overall the number of individuals who refused to give statements seems to have been relatively small,[56] though members of Cumann na mBan were among them. Pauline Keating, a veteran of the Four Courts garrison in Easter 1916 recalled in her statement that:

> I met some of the Cumann na mBan at the reunions and they were discussing the work being done by the Bureau and many of them surprised me by their attitude towards it. They seemed to think that the inquiries being made by the Bureau were stimulated by mere curiosity and some of them said they would rather burn anything they had than give it to the Bureau ... I could not understand their point of view. I suggested that the information might be of interest to future generations, but I did not succeed in convincing them.[57]

Several well-known Republican women, like Mary Alden Childers, Mary Colum, Maura Comerford and Sighle Humphries, declined to give statements but submitted collections of documents, as did Jane

Kissane. It is probably significant that several of the more prominent Republican women who did give statements had either dropped out of politics or come to some accommodation with the Irish State by the time they did so. Nora Connolly O'Brien, Kathleen Lynn and Cait O'Callaghan were no longer actively political. Eithne Coyle had secured a job with Irish Hospital Sweepstakes. Leslie Price was heavily involved in the provision of international humanitarian aid.[58] Honorary Secretaries of the Association of Old Cumann na mBan, Bridget O'Mullane and Molly Reynolds, had assisted their members in applying for Military Service pensions in the 1930s and 1940s.[59] Dorothy Macardle and Linda Kearns were both members of Fianna Fáil's first Executive.[60]

The tendency to select for interview former officers of the Dublin-based leadership of Cumann na mBan and the reluctance of some of the women to give statements (or to talk about their own activities if they did) had a negative impact on the representation of female Republican activism. The lack of accounts from provincial nationalist women is probably the collection's most significant limitation in its representation of female activists. While the overall regional spread of former Irish Volunteers broadly corresponds with areas that experienced the highest levels of activity during the War of Independence (Dublin and Munster)[61] and Cumann na mBan tended to be most active and organized in the same areas, the numbers of women interviewed in any particular county do not follow this pattern. For instance, in 1921 the Munster organization had 375 branches and the highest membership in the country.[62] Yet only ten statements discuss the activities of female Republicans in Cork and Kerry where they had worked very closely with the flying columns.[63] Cait O'Callaghan and Mary Clancy speak only about the murder of their husbands in March 1921, leaving Madge Daly's two statements to cover the activities of Limerick Cumann na mBan. In Tipperary, most of Mrs M.A. McGrath's statement concerns the activities of her brother and other local IRA men for whom her home was a meeting place and despatch centre. Other statements cover only the period up to 1916, so that just twelve female Republicans from the province where they were most active deal with their own activities in the years 1917–21.

Munster was the Civil War's Republican heartland and it is possible that many women would not co-operate with the Bureau. However, if this was a major factor in determining numbers of statements taken from women, then the failure to collect more than one in Longford where most of Cumann na mBan had supported the Treaty and over 100 female activists applied for military service pensions seems an odd omission.[64] It is particularly strange in light of the fact that in his statement the former OC North Longford Flying Column, Seán MacEoin, whose wife and two sisters had been in Cumann na mBan, went out of his way to list the organization's most prominent members, and stated that it was mobilized for every engagement and said that he wished to 'leave it to these ladies to tell of their own activities'.[65] Dissatisfaction with, or refusal of, pension claims was the most common reasons given by individuals who declined to speak to the Bureau and this may explain the dearth of statements from Longford Cumann na mBan.[66] The combined effect of these factors is that the Bureau collection considerably under-represented Cumann na mBan in several areas where they were most organized and in periods when women's activity was most vital.

That said, despite the fact that many of the interviewees were drawn from the relatively small pool of leading women activists based in Dublin, their statements contain a considerable range of opinion, experience, motivation and self-perception. In common with most Bureau witnesses, the majority of women simply state what they did without obvious political intent. However a minority of women, almost all of them associated with the Irish Citizen Army, openly express dissatisfaction at the misrepresentation and subordination of female Republican activists in their statements. Probably the most overtly 'feminist' passage in all of the collection is Helena Molony's withering attack on Seán O'Faoláin's characterization of Countess Markievicz as 'intuitive' rather than rational in his patronising but influential biography[67] published in 1934:

> It is a curious thing that many men seem to be unable to believe that any woman can embrace an ideal – accept it intellectually, feel it as a profound emotion, and then calmly decide to make a vocation of working for its realisation, they give themselves endless pains to prove that every serious thing a woman does (outside nursing babies or washing pots) is the result of being in love with some man, or looking for excitement, or limelight, or indulging their vanity. You do not seem to have escaped from the limitations of your sex, therefore you describe Madame as being "caught up" by or rallying to the side of Connolly, Larkin, or some man or other, whereas the simple fact is that she was working, as a man might have worked, for the freedom of Ireland.[68]

Molony was particularly annoyed as he had consulted her while writing it and thanks her in the acknowledgements where, to add further insult to injury, he misspelled her name 'Moloney'.[69] Similarly, Ernie O'Malley does not escape the censure of Maureen McGavock for his failure to credit the aid rendered to him by Josephine Aherne in his memoirs. She ends her statement with this subtle expression of dissatisfaction at the lot of Cumann na mBan in general: 'These are a few incidents that occur to me as being characteristic of the type of work that fell to the lot of us members of Cumann na mBan. It is not necessary to multiply examples.'[70]

'Poetess of the revolution' Maeve Cavanagh was equally unhappy with the activities allotted to the women's organization: 'I was in Cumann na mBan, being Secretary for a time. I think it was at Harcourt Street the Branch met. I got tired of that, as they were only collecting money and like activities. I went to Liberty Hall for good and took part in all the activities of the Citizen Army.'[71] She was one of several female witnesses[72] interviewed who had couriered Patrick Pearse's remobilization orders to various parts of the country after Eoin MacNeill's famous countermanding order. The first part of the statement covers some of the same ground as R.M. Fox's profile of her in *Rebel Women*, including the story of a rebel leader who had burst into tears in front of her when she asked to speak to the men under his command after he refused to announce Pearse's instruction. Though the name of the man in question (Ginger O'Connell) was withheld by Fox, in her account to the Bureau Cavanagh names and shames him for his attempt to undermine her credibility after the fact:

> Afterwards at a meeting at Gould's Cross someone who was in gaol with O'Connell told me that he – O'Connell – wondered why they kept sending these hysterical women after him. I was amazed because if anyone was hysterical it was certainly not I. I had formed a conviction that day that he was not a revolutionary.[73]

In joining Cumann na mBan female Republican activists chose to prioritize the independence struggle over their own civic and political rights, though many still aspired to and expected equality in the republic they hoped to create. The Republican movement drew some of its most active and talented female activists from the ranks like the bourgeoning and successful feminist and labour movements of the time.[74] Even Mary McSwiney, who would become one of the staunchest and most uncompromising Republicans in the Treaty debates in December 1922, had her initial political experience as a member of the Munster Women's Franchise League.[75]

For many women it was not a question of if they would achieve equality but how and when. The Gaelic past (of which very little was actually known) served as the inspiration for their aspirations. It was widely propagated by both Irish suffragists and nationalist women's organizations that the subordination of women was the product of British rule and that by participating in the national struggle, they were reclaiming the rights held by women before Ireland's colonization.[76] Although on its inception the stated goals of Cumann na mBan had been simply to further the cause of Irish liberty and to assist in arming the Volunteers, it emerged from the 1916 Rising a significantly more assertive and confident organization. From 1917 onwards, its constitutional objectives included the preparation of Irish women to take up their 'proper position in the life of the Nation'.[77] It is important not to underestimate the significance of the 1916 Proclamation and women's participation in the Easter rebellion in providing female Republicans with the means to demand parity of esteem. The Proclamation gave nationalist women a language to assert their equality not previously available to them. In Ernie O'Malley's Civil War memoir, *The Singing Flame*, he remembered how in July 1922 the women in Dublin refused to leave Cathal Brugha when he remained to cover the retreat of anti-treaty forces from O'Connell Street after the buildings had been set alight by the Free State army:

> They recited the proclamation of Easter Week: 'The Irish Republic is entitled to, and hereby claims, the allegiance of every Irishman and Irishwoman. The Republic guarantees religious and civil liberty, equal rights and equal opportunities to all its citizens...' Why, if the men remained, should women leave? The question was debated with heat in rooms of burning buildings, under the noise of shells and the spatter of machine guns. Cathal Brugha had to exert his personal influence to make them go.[78]

Though often implied rather than openly stated, the Easter Rebellion serves the same legitimizing function in some of the Bureau statements. James Connolly's feminism was a touchstone for the small number of Republican socialist political women to give statements such as Helena Molony and his daughters, Ina Heron and Nora Connolly O'Brien.[79] In later years Connolly's legacy was often invoked by them to impart legitimacy to the specifically Republican, militaristic demand for women's equality legitimized by the Easter Proclamation and secured by their active participation in the independence struggle.[80] The influence of militarism on their feminist beliefs is obvious in their statements. Helena Molony was herself a combatant (the only female with this status in the collection) while Ina Heron, Nora Connolly O'Brien and other members of Belfast Cumann na mBan refer to having received arms training and being willing to fight.[81] In 1954 the Bureau received an account of the 1916 Rising from a female participant in the week's events accompanied by a note from Ina Heron:

> Miss Mary McLoughlin has been a friend of mine since 1916. Sometime ago she took ill and has been confined to bed for the last 12 months. She often told me of her experiences of Easter Week and I took down her statement for the Military Bureau about six weeks ago. When I returned with the statement to have it signed I was told she had been anointed and was unable to see anyone. She had just been given a morphine injection. Under the circumstances, I think there is very little chance of getting her to sign.[82]

Mary McLoughlin had been a 15-year-old member of the Hibernian Rifles' auxiliary for girls *Clann na nGael* in April 1916 who had couriered despatches, food and ammunition between the various rebel garrisons. Her brother Seán, just one year older than Mary in April 1916, had been a courier for Seán Heuston in the Mendicity Institute until the building was surrendered on the Wednesday. His role in the retreat from the GPO down Moore Street was the subject of much controversy in later years and he had been interviewed by the Bureau in 1949.[83] Very little else is known about Seán McLoughlin's younger sister, though two Cumann na mBan members attached for the week to the Irish Citizen Army, Julia Grennan and Elizabeth Farrell, never forgot the small girl[84] who slipped through cordons of soldiers and delivered despatches with a discarded revolver found in Abbey Street slung in her belt. Her memories of Easter Week retained the sensibilities of the very young girl who had taken part in the events recalled, the child-like quality of her story rendered even more poignant in knowing that it was probably the very last time she told it. Yet in some respects, McLoughlin's recollections belie their apparent innocence in a way that might explain Heron's persistent efforts to ensure that her friend's experiences be recorded. A salient political point was being made in her opening paragraph's reminder that although *Fianna Éireann* in Dublin would not allow girls, in Belfast she might have joined the Betsy Gray sluagh captained by James Connolly's daughter, Nora. McLoughlin's recollection that Connolly, lying wounded on a stretcher in the GPO had refused Tom Clarke's request to take her revolver saying 'the gun could not have been in better hands' was equally resonant.

Martial references and imagery are also an important element in the statements of some former members of Cumann na mBan who had taken the Republican side in the Civil War. Witness Máire Fitzpatrick from Enniscorthy, whose entire family were issued service medals for their activities from 1916–23, says at one point: 'I knew what I had to do when the real fighting started. I had a first aid certificate, but it's the rifle I would have preferred.'[85] Bridget O'Mullane's description of Cumann na mBan as a 'body of gunwomen' (quoted earlier) had similar implications. In the 1930s the IRA advised members and supporters not to vote in the referendum to ratify the 1937 Constitution. Cumann na mBan accepted the policy of non-co-operation with the State and was not involved in the campaigns organized against the successive curtailments of women's rights brought in by Irish governments in this period.[86] However, in May 1937 O'Mullane, in her official capacity as secretary of the Association of Old Cumann na mBan, wrote a letter of protest to Éamon de Valera in response to the recently published draft of the proposed constitution that was obviously informed by her experiences during the revolutionary period:

> this clause about the inadequate strength of women is ... particularly hurtful to us who in the various phases of the struggle for National Independence, were so frequently called on by the IRA Army, both in the Anglo-Irish and Civil wars to undertake tasks entailing heavy muscular toil, with the added risk of discovery and capture by the enemy. One of our proudest achievements is that we conveyed safely from place to place machine guns, heavy explosives and rifles, not to mention smaller arms, without any loss or capture of same in transit.[87]

Article 45.4.2 was eventually rephrased and the 'inadequate strength of women' removed from the final version of the 1937 Constitution. Several incidents recalled by O'Mullane in her Bureau statements underline how galling the offending passage must have been for her. In 1921 she had almost been shot as a spy by local Volunteers in Naas who had not realized she was a Cumann na mBan organizer. In July 1922 during the Civil War she was fired on by Free State troops while carrying dispatches and with Sighle Humphries had fought female searchers hand to hand in a Dublin street to protect Cathal Brugha's papers. O'Mullane later successfully removed a machine gun and rifles from an abandoned Republican outpost and came near to being shot once again when, in 1923, Paudeen O'Keefe, the Deputy Governor of Mountjoy prison during the Civil War, stuck his revolver through the spy hole of her prison cell and fired. The militarized imagery employed by O'Mullane and others in the statements highlights the extent to which their aspirations to Republican citizenship were grounded in Cumann na mBan's martial status.

It was probably no accident that prominent pro-treatyite Ernest Blythe attempted to undermine Republican women's credibility in the statement on just these grounds. In 1927, as Minister for Finance, he flatly denied that Cumann na mBan qualified as a military organization during the debate following the introduction of the bill extending the terms of 'wound pensions' despite Labour TD Thomas Johnson's protestations to the contrary.[88] The casual misogyny displayed in his testimony has obvious political overtones. Blythe takes a more subtle tack than P.S. O'Hegarty and his 'irrational holders of death and destruction'.[89] Women's participation in the Independence struggle, indeed their access to the public sphere in any manifestation, is ridiculed and belittled rather than portrayed as a serious threat to the social order. Blythe described the girl's sluagh of *Fianna Éireann* in Belfast as a 'terrible thorn in the side of the boys', he refused to read books written by women while in Brixton prison in 1916 and he mocked Cumann na mBan:

> one of the things that plagued the Volunteers in Bantry most was that the Cumann na mBan insisted on trailing after them whenever they went on a route march, a proceeding which subjected them to a certain amount of derision from the rural population. I remember conspiring with the local Captain of the Volunteers in several schemes to outwit the Cumann na mBan and leave them behind.[90]

Likewise, he says very little about women during the Treaty debates apart from the odd swipe at Mary MacSwiney:

> when the plenipotentiaries were being nominated, she made a speech in which she declared that they were being sent to England for one sole purpose – to obtain British recognition of the Irish Republic. She wound up pointing her finger directly at me and saying: 'If anyone here has a contrary opinion, let him speak now or be forever silent.' I only laughed at her.[91]

His negative comments about women who attempted to intrude into the macho world of the Volunteers are in considerable contrast to the long descriptions of the practical jokes and mock secret societies with names like the 'Rough and Toughs' and the 'Ku Klux Klan' formed by the men in prison. He clearly enjoyed the camaraderie and male bonding that existed among the prisoners and was anxious to maintain his political life as a male preserve. Even under duress, when several ministers moved into government buildings for safety accompanied by their wives during the Civil War, they were uncomfortable enough with the presence of their womenfolk to promptly ban them from the dining area:

> This applied both to wives living in and those who might call. We made a rule that the wives would be served with breakfast in their own rooms and that they should go outside for their meals. Actually, some little stresses did arise and I am satisfied that it was a wise regulation, although all of them resented it and probably would have it upset only that Mr Cosgrave was very firm about it.[92]

The nature of his comments suggests that the conditions of Civil War did less to create male chauvinists than provide the ones who took power in 1922 with an opportunity to vent their spleen.[93] However the point should not be pushed too far. Ernest Blythe's views may have been typical of Free State ministers like Kevin O'Higgins and William Cosgrave but not necessarily of pro-Treaty men in general. It is worth noting that Blythe's most extensive contact with the women's organization was limited to the period when he worked as an organizer for the Volunteers in 1914–16. He did not take part in the Easter Rising and as a Dáil Minister of Trade and Commerce during the War of Independence was not directly involved in the military campaign.[94] Prominent military leaders who supported the Treaty and had worked with Cumann na mBan on the ground (and were therefore in a better position to judge their usefulness) such as East Clare Commandant Michael Brennan and North Longford OC Seán MacEoin praised the women highly.[95] As we have seen, Blythe's attitude to the women's organization was also out of step with the opinions expressed by the vast majority of Irish Volunteers in the Bureau collection. The statements are mostly free of the rhetorical excesses heaped on Republican women during the Civil War by the press and government ministers. Women's role in the conflict is even explicitly defended in the statement of anti-treaty Republican Séan Prendergast when recalling reports of the fighting he received while interned in Gormanstown:

> Cases were even cited where some women kept cooler heads than the men in the face of impending or actual shooting or when an ambush was carried off. Then they would sally off carrying the guns and sometimes guiding the men to safety. We were informed that many a man owed his life and his liberty to the presence of mind and valuable assistance of 'the weaker sex', on many such dangerous occasions and missions. If the women earned and deserved the approbation of the IRA outside they in an opposite sense were dubbed by the Free Staters as 'these wild women.' Yet they were not as wild as they were computed to be; their wildness actually sprang from a desire to help the IRA cause, a wildness that was none the less characteristic then as during the previous regime.[96]

Most of the specifically gendered abuse is reserved for the notorious 'separation women', soldiers' wives in receipt of government allowances for the duration of their husbands' army service during the First World War. A constant source of opposition to the Republican movement throughout the period, they were almost universally (though unfairly) reviled by both male and female witnesses alike as violent, drunken 'amazons' and 'French Revolution Furies'.[97]

There is, however, no strong correlation between opposition to the Treaty and a more feminist standpoint in the statements. 'Heroic subordinate' would be a most unsuitable description of Nancy Wyse-Power or Bridget Lyons Thornton, the woman who went on to become the first female commissioned officer in the Free State Army.[98] Yet, the markedly deferential tone adopted by some of the women closely associated with prominent pro-Treaty men suggest that they may have been making a conscious attempt to dissociate themselves from the political stance of Republican women. The statements of Mrs Batt O'Connor and Maude Griffith reflect the extent to which attitudes toward Irish women's participation in politics had become closely intertwined with the positions taken by the opposing sides in the Civil War. Mrs O'Connor was the wife of a close associate of Michael Collins and Cumann naGael TD for South Dublin. She joined the Gaelic League but was not otherwise involved in politics saying, 'It gives me great solace to remember that I had the privilege of cooking, washing for and putting up all those great men who sacrificed themselves for Ireland and I would be very happy to do it all over again.'[99]

The attitudes displayed by Maude Griffith, the widow of Dáil TD and Sinn Féin's founder Arthur Griffith, are more complex but just as telling. She also professes to have no interest in discussing politics in her statement. While it is the case that she had no significant involvement in the Republican movement, the circumstances surrounding her rebuke of the noted feminist and anti-Treaty Republican Hanna Sheehy Skeffington for saying that her husband 'always kept me at home and gave me a bad time'[100] provides a good example of the way the politics of the Civil War complicated the issue of women's political agency. Sheehy Skeffington was a suffrage campaigner who had joined Sinn Féin and Griffith, although always putting the achievement of self rule first, had supported votes for women. They were not always in agreement, but in 1912 he had publicly objected to Sheehy Skeffington's dismissal from her teaching post for suffrage activities. Moreover, much to Labour leader Jim Larkin's irritation, she had lauded Griffith in her lecture tours in the USA after her husband Francis Sheehy Skeffington's murder by a mentally unbalanced British officer during the Easter Rising.[101]

However, Sheehy Skeffington opposed the Treaty and when she and other suffragists took part in a deputation to the Dáil asking that the electoral registers be updated before the election to allow young Irish women to express their views, the two clashed bitterly.[102] The denouement of the relationship between two long standing supporters of women's suffrage in Irish politics involved political reversals for both parties. In the *Irish World* feminist Sheehy Skeffington attacked Maude Griffith and other women ('the wives of famous Irish men') who joined Cumann na Saoirse in order to express their support for the government while Griffith, who had once claimed to have been happy to live in a 'gynocracy' denied Irish women a chance to vote on the Treaty he had negotiated.[103] Sheehy Skeffington had been dead three years when Maude Griffith made her statement and Arthur Griffith had died of a brain haemorrhage in 1922. Mrs Griffith was a lonely figure in the Free State, embittered that the country for whose independence her husband had given his life had forgotten him, and isolated from those on both sides of the political division that had undoubtedly been a significant contributory factor in his untimely death.[104]

The Bureau of Military History collection illustrates well the complexity of the relationship between nationalist women and prevailing notions of gender in Ireland's revolutionary period and after. Republican political and military activity during the Easter Rising of April 1916, the Anglo-Irish conflict and Civil War was largely segregated. Women and men were allocated different activities, operated in separate organizations and were ideologically assigned roles and values according to what was deemed appropriate for their sex. Women had to overcome or work around widespread prejudices against their involvement in politics. Yet the Republican military campaign made the very gender constraints under which they laboured an essential cloak for their activities. Most women who gave statements to the Bureau were content to leave for posterity a record of their contribution to the struggle for independence. However, as has been demonstrated, the political context in which the Bureau of Military History operated shaped both its administrative decisions and the attitudes of contributors. In particular, the political fallout from the Civil War had considerable impact on the way the BMH gathered material from and about female activists, affecting as well the way women represented themselves and were portrayed by others. Some statements demonstrate the extent to which attitudes toward Irish women's participation in politics had become closely intertwined with the positions taken by the opposing sides in the conflict as the battles of the past continued to be fought in deliberately constructed narratives of a still contested history.

NOTES

1. In total 1,726 men and women and 121 anonymous donors and organisations made contributions to the Bureau, 1,618 people and two organisations contributed 1,773 statements and an additional 126 individuals or organizations submitted other material. Interviewees sometimes either gave more than one statement or submitted a single statement as a group which resulted in a discrepancy between the number of statements and individuals interviewed.
2. B. McKillen, 'Irish Feminism and National Separatism, 1914–23', *Éire-Ireland*, XVIII, 3, (1982), p.52.
3. A. Sheehan, 'Cumann na mBan: Policies and Activities', in D. Fitzpatrick (ed.), *Revolution? Ireland 1917–1923* (Dublin: Trinity History Workshop, 1990), p.90.
4. C. McCarthy, *Cumann na mBan and the Irish Revolution* (Cork: The Collins Press, 2007), p.1.
5. S. McCoole, *No Ordinary Women: Irish Female Activists in the Revolutionary Years 1900–1923* (Dublin: The O'Brien Press, 2003), p.32; and Oonagh Walsh, 'Testimony from Imprisoned Women', in D. Fitzpatrick (ed.), *Revolution? Ireland 1917–1923*, p.84.
6. M. Laffan, *The Resurrection of Ireland: The Sinn Féin Party, 1916–1923* (Cambridge: Cambridge University Press, 1999), pp.210–14.
7. Bureau of Military History Witness Statement [BMH WS] 450 (Bridget O'Mullane), pp.2–3. O'Mullane gave a second statement to the Bureau giving an account of the Truce and Civil War: WS 485.
8. Frank A. Biletz, 'Women and Irish-Ireland: The Domestic Nationalism of Mary Butler', *New Hibernia Review*, 6, 1 (Spring 2002), pp.60–1; and James MacPherson, 'Ireland Begins in the Home: Women, Irish National Identity and the Domestic Sphere in the Irish Homestead, 1896–1912', *Éire-Ireland* (Fall/Winter 2001), pp.31–2.
9. Maryann GialanellaValiulis, 'Neither Feminist nor Flapper: the Ecclesiastical Construction of the Ideal Irish Woman', in Mary O'Dowd and Sabine Wichert (eds), *Chattel, Servant or Citizen: Women's Status in Church, State and Society* (Belfast: Institute of Irish Studies,

Queen's University, 1995), pp.169–70.

10. WS 938 (Daniel Mulvihill), p.1. See also WS 1163 (Patrick McCarthy), p.1 and WS 618 (Sean M. O'Duffy), p.9.
11. M. Coleman, *County Longford and the Irish Revolution 1910–1923* (Dublin: Irish Academic Press, 2003), p.190. For Margaret Ward's critique of this view see M. Ward, 'Gender: Gendering the Irish Revolution', in J. Augusteijn (ed.), *The Irish Revolution, 1913–1923* (Hampshire: Palgrave, 2002), pp.180–1.
12. M. Ward, *Unmanageable Revolutionaries: Women and Irish Nationalism* (Tralee: Brandon, 1983), pp.157–8. WS 1576 (Peg Duggan) and WS 1561 (Mrs Margaret Lucey).
13. For a few examples in the witness statements of women working directly with the flying columns see WS 1690 (Nora Cunningham), WS 699 (Josephine Clarke née Stallard), WS 1336 (Patrick Lennon), p.9, WS 1716 (Seán MacEoin), pp.149–50, WS 1591 (Richard Russell), p.24 and WS 1033 (Patrick Glynn), p.21.
14. WS 1525 James Moloney, pp.18–19. See also ARMAGH – WS 658 John Grant), p.4; CAVAN – WS 365 (Thomas Fox), p.9; CLARE – WS 1462 (Séan Moroney), p.15; CORK – WS 1587 (Daniel O'Keeffe), WS 1591 (Richard Russell), p.24, WS 1428 (Michael O'Connell), WS 443 (Frank Neville); DERRY – WS 803 (Michael Sheerin); DUBLIN – WS 481 (Simon Donnelly), p.7, WS 748 (John J. Doyle), p.16, WS 819 (Liam Archer), p.8; GALWAY – WS 1033 (Patrick Glynn), p.21, WS 1173 (Michael Hynes), WS 1334 (Joseph Standford); KERRY – WS 1118 (James Houlihan), p.11, WS 1319 (David McAlliffe), pp.5–6, WS 1190 (Michael Pierce), pp.19–20; KILDARE – WS 1571 (James Dunne), p.16; LEITRIM – WS 1263 (Charles Pinkman), p.14, WS 1194 (Bernard Sweeney), p.17; LIMERICK LONGFORD – WS 1716 (Seán MacEoin), pp.149–50; MAYO – WS 872 (Thomas Ketterick), WS 896 (Edward Moane), p.9, WS 1735 (P.J. Kelly), p.27; MEATH – WS 1650 (Patrick O'Reilly), p.11, p.15; MONAGHAN – WS 530 (P.V. Hoey), p.22; TIPPERARY – WS 1553 (Liam Hoolan), p.6, WS 1701 (Maurice A. McGrath), p.13, WS 151 (James Ryan), p.9; WATERFORD – WS 1182 (George C. Kiely), WS 1130 (Edward Power), WS 887 (Patrick J. Paul); WESTMEATH – WS 1336 (Patrick Lennon), p.9.
15. McCoole, *No Ordinary Women*, p.73. WS 648 (Catherine Rooney), pp.17–18, WS 1682 (Margaret Broderick-Nicholson), p.5.
16. WS 1336 (Patrick Lennon), p.12. See also WS 1193 (Mrs Bridget Dohery), pp.5–6, WS 385 (Mrs Sean Beaumont), WS (John Grant), p.4, WS 803 (Michael Sheerin), pp.16–17, WS 1194 (Bernard Sweeney), p.17 and WS 1263 (Charles Pinkman), p.14.
17. WS 1029 (Moira Kennedy O'Byrne) and WS 624 (Mary Flannery Woods).
18. WS 648 (Catherine Rooney), pp.2–3.
19. Josephine Browne later married the Intelligence Officer and Adjutant of Cork no. 1 Brigade and later Adjutant of the 1st Southern Division of the IRA, Florence O'Donoghue. For an account of her intelligence activities during the War of Independence while working as typist for the 6th (Munster) Division of the British Army in Victoria Barracks in Cork city see J. Borgonovo (ed.), *Florence and Josephine O'Donoghue's War of Independence* (Dublin: Irish Academic Press, 2006), pp.110–24.
20. For the activities of Lankford (née Creedon) and Barrett see S. Lankford, *The Hope and the Sadness: Personal Recollections of Troubled Times in Ireland* (Cork: Tower Books, 1980), pp.132 and 163, and WS 1133(Annie Barrett).
21. Mernin, a cousin of Piarais Beaslai, was eventually dismissed from Dublin Castle in February 1922 and suffered a nervous breakdown. She was later employed in Oriel House and then the Department of Defence. For Mernin's activities see WS 441 (Lily Mernin) and Department of Defence to Secretary to the President Michael McDunphy, 27 February 1929, National Archives of Ireland, Department of the Taoiseach, S 5778.
22. M. Hopkinson, *The Irish War of Independence* (Dublin: Gill & Macmillan, 2002), pp.69 and 199.
23. WS 1133 (Annie Barrett), p.4.
24. WS 1133 (Annie Barrett), p.6. Seán Moylan was OC North Cork Brigade of the IRA 1920–21; OC 3rd Southern Division in 1921–22, Member of IRA Executive and Army Council during the Civil War and was later a Fianna Fáil TD and Minister for Education.
25. M. Cullen, 'How Radical was Irish Feminism between 1860 and 1920?', in P.J. Corish (ed.), *Radicals, Rebels & Establishments* (Belfast: Apple Tree Press, 1985), p.195.
26. Colm Campbell, *Emergency Law in Ireland, 1918–1925* (Oxford: Clarendon Press, 1994), p.163.

27. McCoole, *No Ordinary Women*, p.93.
28. Ibid., p.15.
29. J. Knirck, *Women of the Dáil: Gender, Republicanism and the Anglo-Irish Treaty* (Dublin and Portland, OR: Irish Academic Press, 2006), pp.74–5.
30. Ryan, L. 'Furies and Die-hards: Women and Irish Republicanism in the Early Twentieth Century' in *Gender & History*, Vol. 11, no.2 (July 1999), p.270.
31. Military Service Pensions Act 1924, Irish Statute Book 1922–1998: Acts of the Oireachtas, http: www.irishstatutebook.ie/1924. Accessed 1 July 2007.
32. Military Service Pensions Act 1934 Irish Statute Book 1922–1998: Acts of the Oireachtas, http: www.irishstatutebook.ie/1934; and Seanad Éireann, Vol.19, 24 August 1934, columns 296–7 and 30 August 1934, column 561. http://www.oireachtas-debates.gov.ie. Staines had been a pro-Treaty TD and the first Garda Commissioner.
33. Ward, 'Gender: Gendering the Irish Revolution', p.180. See also Honorary Secretary of the Association of Old Cumann na mBan Bridget O'Mullane to President de Valera, 18 May 1937, Department of the Taoiseach, NA, S 9800.
34. Letter M. McKeown, Main St, Longford to Mr Ryan 23 March 1939, Seán MacEoin Papers, P151/1141 (1), University College Dublin Archives. For the Treaty stance taken by Cumann na mBan in Longford see Coleman, *County Longford and the Irish Revolution*, pp.188–9.
35. Caitlin Brugha, Mary MacSwiney, Countess Markievicz and Dr Kathleen Lynn all abstained.
36. M.E. Daly, '"Oh, Kathleen Ni Houlihan, Your Way's a Thorny Way": The Condition of Women in Twentieth-Century Ireland', in A. Bradley and M. Gialanella Valiulis (eds), *Gender and Sexuality in Modern Ireland* (Amherst, MA: University of Massachusetts Press, 1997), p.108.
37. K. Offen, *European Feminisms, 1700–1950: A Political History* (Stanford, CA: Stanford University Press, 2000), pp.279–80; S. Kingsley Kent, *Making Peace: The Reconstruction of Gender in Inter-war Britain* (Princeton, NJ: Princeton University Press, 1993), p.113; and Liam O'Dowd, 'Church, State and Women: the Aftermath of Partition', in C. Curtin, P. Jackson and B. O'Connor (eds), *Gender in Irish Society* (Galway: Galway University Press, 1987), p.7.
38. The 1924 and 1927 Juries Acts effectively barred women from sitting on juries. The Public Service bar introduced by Fianna Fáil in 1932 banned married women from the civil service and later the teaching professions. The Conditions of Employment Act, although never enforced, still gave the Minister for Industry and Commerce the right to limit the number of women working in any industry. The 1937 Constitution identified women's primary role in society to be that of wife and mother. C. Beaumont, 'Gender, Citizenship and the State in Ireland, 1922–1990', in S. Brewster, V. Crossman, F. Becket and D. Alderson (eds), *Ireland in Proximity: History, Gender, Space* (London and New York: Routledge, 1999), pp.97–9.
39. K. and C. O'Céirin, *Women of Ireland: A Biographic Dictionary* (Galway: Tír Eolas, 1996), p.133.
40. P. Lynch, 'North Cork – 1920', in *Capuchin Annual* 37 (1970), pp.355–8. See also WS 838 (Seán Moylan), WS 808 (Richard Willis and John Bolster), WS 991 (Owen Harold), WS 451 (George Power), WS 1428 (Michael O'Connell), WS 978 (Leo O'Callaghan), WS 787 (Con Meany) and WS 785 (Daniel Browne).
41. For example see the letter written by Deirdre Little to Sighle Humphries, 1967, P106/1405, UCDA. The papers of Coyle and Humphries are held in the University College, Dublin Archives and contain questionnaires, original documents and material relating to Military Service Pension applications by Cumann na mBan members.
42. From letter to Cumann na mBan ex-members, date as postmarked, Eithne Coyle Papers P61/4, UCDA.
43. J. Doyle and F. Clarke, *An Introduction to the Bureau of Military History 1913–1921*, Military Archives, Dublin (2002), p.2.
44. The Ernie O'Malley notebooks contain seventeen interviews with women: UCDA P17b. There are ten women among Father Louis O'Kane's interviews with Northern activists held in the Archdiocese of Armagh Records Centre, Armagh City. There were eight female interviewees among the testimonies taken over 1965–66 in the Marron papers, Monaghan County Museum.

45. M.E. Daly, 'Women in the Industrial Workforce from pre-Industrial to Modern Times', *Saothar* 7 (1981), p.78.
46. Jane Kissane, who worked for the Bureau from 1949–54, was a sister of Fianna Fáil TD for the Kerry North constituency, Eamon Kissane. During the revolutionary period she had been an organizer of the Belfast Boycott and secretary to the First Dáil's Minister for Labour, Joe McDonagh. Dismissed from government employment in February 1922 'on political grounds' for opposing the Treaty, she was reinstated as High Executive Officer attached to the Department of Agriculture in 1934. See Miss Jane Kissane, reinstatement in the Civil Service, April 1934, NA, S 2891.
47. BMH WSO 2-3-4 (incoming statements ledger), Military Archives.
48. G. O'Brien, *Irish Governments and the Guardianship of Historical Records, 1922–72* (Dublin: Four Courts Press, 2004), p.136.
49. Bridget McGrath, wife of the Adjutant of 3rd Tipperary Brigade Maurice A. McGrath and Bridget Ryan, who was married to the former commandant of 1st Battalion, 2nd Tipperary Brigade Jerry Ryan. S. 3011 Mrs M.A. McGrath, PC 788 Liam Grace collection, Military Archives.
50. For instance, ten out of the thirty-four members of Cumann na mBan's Executive in 1921 were interviewed. WS 1054 Miss Eilis Aughney, WS 1754 Mrs Tom Barry (née Leslie Price), WS 385 Mrs Sean Beaumont (née Maureen McGavock), WS 568 Bean Eilis Ui Chonnaill (née Eilis Ryan), WS 209; 855 (Madge Daly), CD 160 Bean Domhnaill Ui Donnchadha (née Sighle Humphries), WS 399 Mrs Richard Mulcahy (née Min Ryan), WS 1752 Mrs Eileen MacCarvill (née McGrane), WS 450; 485 (Bridget O'Mullane) and WS 541; 587; 732 (Nancy Wyse-Power). Agenda for the Cumann na mBan Annual Convention 22–23 October 1921, Sighle Humphries Papers P106/1130.
51. A few sympathizers or unaligned witnesses of famous events also made contributions.
52. J. Augusteijn, *From Public Defiance to Guerrilla Warfare: The Experience of Ordinary Volunteers in the Irish War of Independence 1916–1921* (London: Irish Academic Press, 1996), p.57.
53. T. Garvin, *Nationalist Revolutionaries in Ireland: 1858–1928* (Dublin: Gill & Macmillan, 1987), p.112.
54. 'Complete Statement of Personal Involvement in the Struggle for Independence', Eithne Coyle Papers, UCDA, P61/2 (2), p.22; and McCoole, *No Ordinary Women*, pp.119–20. WS 214; 418 (Una Stack, née Gordon): Austin Stack was a commander of the Irish Volunteers in Kerry during the Easter Rising. He was elected Sinn Féin TD for Kerry while in prison, was Deputy Chief of Staff of the IRA during the War of Independence and Dáil Minister for Home Affairs from 1919–22. He took the Republican side in the Civil War and died in 1929.
55. Just over 260 statements cover events after 1921 and about 140 testimonies discuss the Civil War.
56. O'Brien, *Irish Governments and the Guardianship of Historical Records*, p.142.
57. WS 432 (Pauline Keating), p.3.
58. McCoole, *No Ordinary Women*, pp.153, 181, 191, 156 and 204.
59. Military Service Pensions 1928–50, Sighle Humphries Papers, P160/1430.
60. O'Céirin, *Women of Ireland*, pp.118 and 133.
61. Hopkinson, *The Irish War of Independence*, p.97. Over 60 per cent of Volunteer contributors were from Dublin or Munster.
62. Sheehan, 'Cumann na mBan: Policies and Activities', p.92.
63. For the activities of Cumann na mBan in Cork and Kerry see Director of Organization Leslie Price's report to its Annual Convention in October 1921, Sighle Humphries Papers P106/1130. Price's witness statement deals only with the 1916 Rising in Dublin. See WS 1754 (Mrs Tom Barry).
64. Coleman, *County Longford and the Irish Revolution,* pp.188–9. Bureau witness WS 259 (Bridget Lyons Thornton), niece of the Sinn Féin TD Joseph McGuinness elected in the May 1917 by-election in Longford, procured arms for the Longford IRA in 1920: pp.10–12.
65. WS 1716 (Seán MacEoin), pp.58–60. For a discussion of Cumann na mBan in Longford see M. Coleman, *County Longford and the Irish Revolution*.
66. Refusals to Co-operate with the Bureau – General File, S1385, Military Archives.
67. Diana Norman, *Terrible Beauty: A Life of Countess Markievicz: 1868–1927* (London: Hodder & Stoughton, 1987), p.13.

68. WS 391 (Helena Molony), Letter to Seán O'Fáolain 6/9/1934 Appendix A, pp.1–2.
69. Seán O'Fáolain, *Constance Markievicz* (London: Century Hutchinson Ltd, 1934, 1987).
70. WS 385 (Mrs Séan Beaumont), p.7. Aherne also made a statement, listed under her married name: WS 303 (Josephine McNeill). She makes no mention of O'Malley.
71. WS 258 (Mrs Maeve McDowell, née Cavanagh), p.3.
72. WS 480 (Eileen Murphy), WS 3198 (Bridget Martin Ni Fhoghludha), WS 419 (Mrs Martin Conlon), WS 355 (Kitty O'Doherty), WS 1655 (Nora Thornton), WS 399 (Mrs Richard Mulcahy), WS 415 (Eily O'Hanrahan O'Reilly), WS 617 (Bridget Malone), WS 416 (Mairin Ryan), WS 322 (Margaret MacEntee) and WS 258 (Maeve McDowell).
73. WS 258 (Maeve McDowell), p.12 and R.M. Fox, *Rebel Irishwomen* (Dublin: Progress House, 1935), p.159. McDowell wrote nationalist poetry published in the *Irish Freedom, The Irish Worker, The Workers' Republic* and W.P. Ryan's *Peasant*. Helena Molony wrote the preface to the second edition of her book of poetry entitled *A Voice of Insurgency* published on Christmas Eve 1916. Ginger O'Connell was the Irish Volunteer's Director of Training before 1916. He supported MacNeill's countermanding orders. In 1920 he succeeded Dick McKee as the IRA's Director of Training and was Assistant Chief of Staff at the Truce. He supported the Treaty in 1922 and his kidnapping in Dublin by Anti-Treaty forces on June 27 1922 was the pretext used by the Provisional Government to initiate the opening salvo of the Civil War, the attack on HQ of the Republican forces in the Four Courts.
74. McKillen, 'Irish Feminism and National Separatism', p.58. Hanna Sheehy Skeffington, Jenny Wyse Power, Cait O'Callaghan, Countess Markievicz, Helena Molony and Dr Kathleen Lynn had all campaigned for women's suffrage.
75. C.H. Fallon, *Soul of Fire: A Biography of Mary MacSwiney* (Cork and Dublin: The Mercier Press, 1986), p.15.
76. C. Murphy, 'A Problematic Relationship: European Women & Nationalism, 1870–1915', in M. Gianella Valiulis and M. O'Dowd (eds), *Women in Irish History: Essays in Honour of Margaret MacCurtain* (Dublin: Wolfhound, 1997), p.157 and McKillen, 'Irish Feminism and National Separatism', p.66.
77. Sheehan, 'Cumann na mBan: Policies and Activities', p.88.
78. E. O'Malley, *The Singing Flame* (Dublin: Anvil Books, 1978, 1992), p.131.
79. WS 391 (Helena Molony), p.20, WS 919 (Ina Heron) and WS 286 (Nora Connolly O'Brien). James Connolly was also a major influence on the feminist beliefs of Hanna Sheehy Skeffington: M. Luddy, *Hanna Sheehy Skeffington* (Dublin: Historical Association of Ireland, 1995), p.22.
80. G.S. Czira (John Brennan), *The Years Flew by: the Recollections of Madame Sidney Gifford Czira*, Alan Hayes (ed.) (Galway: Arlen House, 2000), p.xiv.
81. See also WS 179 (Nell and Elizabeth Corr) and WS 180 (Kathleen O'Kelly), pp.1–2.
82. Covering letter written by Ina Connolly Heron c.1954; WS 934 (Mary McLoughlin). James Connolly was a socialist and labour organizer who founded the Irish Citizen Army in November 1913 and was general secretary of the Irish Transport and General Workers' Union in 1914. He joined forces with those members of the Irish Revolutionary Brotherhood military committee who planned the Rising in January 1916 and was Commander-General of Republican forces in Dublin in Easter week. He was one of the last leaders to be executed by the British on 12 May 1916.
83. WS 290 (Seán McLoughlin). M. Caufield, *The Easter Rebellion* (New York, Chicago and San Francisco: Holt, Rinehart and Winston,1963), pp.201, 328–34. See also Charles Townshend, *Easter 1916: The Irish Rebellion* (Dublin: Allen Lane, 2005), pp.171–2 and 204–5.
84. Interview with Julia Grennan in Donncha O Dúlaing, *Voices of Ireland conversations with Donncha O Dúlaing, biographies by Henry Boylan* (Dublin: O'Brien Press in association with RTÉ, 1984), p.72.
85. WS 1344 (Máire Fitzpatrick), p.6.
86. Ward, *Unmanageable Revolutionaries*, pp.244–5.
87. Bridget O'Mullane to President de Valera, 18 May 1937, Department of the Taoiseach, NA, S 9800.
88. Army Pensions (no.2) Bill, Dáil Éireann, Vol.18, 8 February 1927, column 320 http://www.oireachtas-debates.gov.ie. Accessed 1 July 2007
89. P.S. O'Hegarty, *The Victory of Sinn Féin* (Dublin: University College Dublin Press, 1924, 1998), p.74.

90. WS 939 (Ernest Blythe), pp.5, 64 and 78.
91. Ibid., pp.131–2.
92. Ibid., pp.5, 64, 169–70. William T. Cosgrave was Dáil Minister for Local Government in 1919, first President of the Executive Council of the Irish Free State in 1922 and founded the Cumann na nGaedheal political party in 1923.
93. See Mary Daly's critique of Tom Garvin on this point in Daly, 'Oh, Kathleen Ni Houlihan, Your Way's a Thorny Way', p.108.
94. Ernest Blythe joined the IRB in 1907. In 1914 he became a full-time organizer for the Irish Volunteers until his arrest in 1915. He was arrested in Easter Week and again in 1918 when he was sent to Dundalk and Belfast prisons. He was elected to the First Dáil and served as Minister for Trade and Commerce. He supported the Treaty and held various ministerial posts as a Cumann na nGaedheal TD.
95. Cumann na mBan Annual Convention, 22–23 October 1921, Sighle Humphries Papers P106/1130.
96. WS 802 (Séan Prendergast), pp.84–5.
97. WS 397 (Thomas Pugh), p.3 and WS 285 (Maeve McDowell), p.17. For a discussion of the separation women see B. Novick, *Conceiving Revolution: Irish Nationalist Propaganda during the First World War* (Dublin: Four Courts Press, 2001).
98. O'Céirin, Women of Ireland, pp.213-14.
99. WS 330 (Mrs Batt O'Connor), p.2.
100. WS 205 (Maude Griffith), p.1.
101. B. Maye, Arthur Griffith (Dublin: Griffith College Publications, 1997), pp.23 and 346.
102. M. Ward, *Hanna Sheehy Skeffington: A Life* (Cork: Attic Press, 1997), p.249.
103. Irish World and Industrial Liberator, 8 April 1922; and Laffan, *The Resurrection of Ireland*, p.201.
104. For an account of Maude Griffith's troubled relationship with the Free State see A. Dolan, *Commemorating the Irish Civil War: History and Memory 1923–2000* (Cambridge: Cambridge University Press, 2003), pp.100-19.

CHAPTER SIX

Sexual Crime and Irish Women's Campaign for a Criminal Law Amendment Act, 1912–35

SANDRA McAVOY

> 'Every man is innocent until proved guilty; every girl and woman witness against a man is guilty of perjury until proved innocent.'[1]

In what ways might introducing gender as a category of analysis bring fresh understandings of Irish political history? This chapter examines an aspect of the process that led to the passing of the 1935 Criminal Law Amendment (CLA) Act to suggest one way in which applying a gender lens might broaden our perspective on political and social developments in post-independence Ireland. The parameters within which post-independence debates on sexuality have been considered were established by historians such as John Whyte and Dermot Keogh and sociologist Tom Inglis whose focus was on the influence of the Roman Catholic Church.[2] Arising from their work, a narrative was established within which the Catholic Church 'monopolised' 'the field of sexuality and debate and discussion of sex'[3] and manipulated the State to impose a moral order on Ireland that involved a singularly Roman Catholic construction of sexuality. The 1935 CLA Act, with sections on sexual crime, prostitution, public decency and the imposition of a ban on contraceptives, has been identified as a stage in the imposition of such a moral order. More recently, Mark Finnane has considered the possible influence of *garda* commissioner Eoin O'Duffy on the 1930–31 Carrigan Committee, established to recommend amendments to existing CLA legislation. He also recognized that developments in Ireland after 1922 were in the 'tradition of the campaigns for the protection of women and children which went back to the 1880s and earlier'.[4] An important point regarding the Carrigan Committee is that eighteen of the twenty-nine witnesses who presented oral evidence were women representatives of political and social work organizations. The first historian to access the Carrigan Committee minutes, James M. Smith, has highlighted aspects of the evidence of these women but did not relate it to pre-independence feminist campaigns on sexual crime and prostitution.[5]

In this chapter I will suggest that consciousness of the importance of a CLA Bill to women campaigners opens up a new perspective on the history of the 1935 legislation and raises new questions. Women's political agency and their roles in pre- as well as post-independence debates on sexuality come in to focus, as does a lobbying alliance between women's organizations and Protestant and Catholic moral purity campaigners during the 1920s. I will also suggest that the gender issue at the nucleus of these campaigns was the one encapsulated in the statement of Irish feminist Marion Duggan, from which the subtitle of this chapter is drawn: that existing CLA legislation on age of consent, unlawful carnal knowledge, sexual assault and prostitution reflected double standards of sexual morality, excused male sexual aggression and exposed woman and girl victims to further abuse in the courts. Recognition of this led to limited legislative change in Britain and Northern Ireland in 1922 and 1923. By the late 1920s Irish CLA legislation was overdue and inescapable, so why were steps taken to avoid Oireachtas debate on a 1934 Bill? Might one reason be that a measure perceived to challenge male privilege by expunging the double standard from the sexual crime sections of existing legislation would not have passed had debate been permitted? Though campaigners expressed related concerns regarding the entry of young girls in to prostitution and Louise Jackson has suggested that where the term 'juvenile prostitution' is used it is a euphemism for 'child sexual assault', the focus of the chapter is on issues dealt with in the sexual crime sections of CLA legislation.[6]

Finnane is correct in relating developments in Ireland during the 1930s and Victorian feminist and moral purity crusades. The issue at the heart of those campaigns was the repeal of legislation that reflected sexual double standards. Campaigners perceived the protection of women from male sexual aggression as vital to female emancipation and, with their allies in purity and religious organizations, explicitly challenged the myth underlying acceptance of such standards: that as male sexual urges were uncontrollable, male sexual transgressions were excusable.[7] These feminist campaigns continued in the twentieth century and evidence suggests that the passing of the 1935 CLA Act followed two decades of continuous Irish feminist consciousness raising and lobbying in a phase of campaigning that probably began with the establishment of a British CLA Committee in 1912. The core demands of Irish women campaigners, as stated in feminist journal the *Irish Citizen* in the teens of the century and in evidence to the Carrigan Committee between 1930 and 1931, reflected those of this 1912 committee and of British feminist lobbyists. These included: that the age of consent be raised from 16 to 18, with further protection up to the age of 21 against employers or guardians who might exert pressure to obtain consent; repeal of a proviso in the 1885 CLA Act that permitted a defence in unlawful carnal knowledge cases that the accused had 'reasonable cause to believe' a girl aged between 13 and 15 years old was of age; and the raising of the statutory time limit for initiating unlawful carnal knowledge cases from six to twelve months after the offence occurred.[8]

A feature of British and Irish feminist action on sexual crime was the establishment of 'Women Watching the Courts Committees': groups of activists who attending hearings, analyzed how gendered inequalities in the law impacted on real women and children and published case reports in feminist journals. Their work provided examples, often poignant, of the ways in which existing legislation disadvantaged women and children. Some reports and opinion columns published in the *Irish Citizen* predate the establishment of an Irish Women's Reform League (IWRL) watching the courts committee in May 1914.[9] These and court reports, many by feminist and socialist Marion Duggan LLB, provide insights into both the feminist perspectives of committee members and Irish women's experience of the law.[10] The aim of these middle-class activists was, as Duggan stated, to 'secure for all girls of all classes' a legal protection from the State that was equal to what they perceived as 'the degree of careful supervision exercised over rich and middle-class girls' by the bourgeois family.[11]

Establishing women's right to remain in court during sexual crime hearings involved the negotiation of gender barriers. Those involved in the legal process were male: police, judges, lawyers and jurors. It was customary to ask 'ladies' to leave the public benches lest they heard anything indelicate. Responding to one judge's assertion that sexual matters should be dealt with by 'men of the world', Marion Duggan suggested the advantages accruing from the involvement of women jurors, one of the feminists' demands:

> Does this not imply that men jurors will be better acquainted with the conduct of 'girls of loose character' than will respectable matrons? The man is to be tried by his moral peers. I decline to believe any sensible man or woman could think that men can understand little girls of 15 better than a jury of responsible women would. So the reference must be to experience of immoral conduct. Or are men to be tried by men and not women by women? We want mixed juries in these cases.[12]

IWRL women remained in their seats when the call came to remove themselves and on a couple of occasions the League engaged counsel to demonstrate a preparedness to 'vindicate the right of adult women to be in court during the trial of sexual cases'.[13] The women involved included Hanna Sheehy Skeffington, Marion Duggan, Emily Buchanan, who would give evidence to the Carrigan Committee as a representative of the Protestant Magdalene Home in Leeson Street, Dublin, and Edith Sanderson, who on occasion reported on cases.[14] As further discussed below, their reports in the *Irish Citizen* (Duggan also reported in socialist paper the *Irish Worker*) exposed how the 1880 and 1885 CLA Acts protected male abusers from punishment. They highlighted, with reference to specific cases, many of the issues considered two decades later by committees deliberating on the 1935 criminal law amendments, including that the defence of belief that a girl was of age made it almost impossible to bring a successful unlawful carnal knowledge prosecution.[15] They demonstrated how a six month statutory time limit meant that no criminal charge could be brought if a girl's pregnancy becoming obvious was the first evidence that a crime had occurred. They illustrated the impact on child abuse cases of a rule that no one could be convicted on the uncorroborated evidence of a child, and the effect on cases involving older girls and women of a rule of practice – applied only in sexual crime, treason and perjury cases – that required judges to warn juries that it was dangerous to convict on the evidence of a single witness, the victim. Some reports made clear the vulnerability of young girls in the workplace, particularly in an era when many entered full employment and adult life at the age of 13 or 14. They also focused on low penalties as signalling that, in law, sexual offences were considered petty crimes. Many such crimes *were* legally minor matters. Though 16 was the age of consent, under the 1885 law offences involving girls over 13 were designated misdemeanours rather than felonies, and the age of consent to undefined 'indecent' acts was 13 under the anomalous 1880

CLA Act, not amended when the age of consent was raised from 13 to 16 in 1885.[16] Ideas about adolescence as a period of emotional upheaval, that fuelled contemporary demands for the raising of the age of consent to protect boys as well as girls, informed occasional references in *Irish Citizen* reports to a 'dangerous' age that could continue until a girl reached her twenties.[17]

Before looking at points arising from the court reports, it should be emphasized that, though some feminists claimed the right to speak about sexual matters on the same terms as men, social convention restricted the language either could use in public.[18] In some *Irish Citizen* articles, unlawful carnal knowledge, though it involved penetration and sometimes pregnancy, was referred to as a 'criminal assault', 'filthy assault', 'assault' and less frequently as a 'completed act'. Such constraints must have reduced readers' understandings of the sense of physical invasion, violation and trauma endured by victims of sexual crimes. Attempts to describe the impact of crimes in clearer terms would have been condemned as lewd and obscene. The court reports did, however, convey the hardship endured by girls made pregnant in these circumstances. If contemporary mores meant they could not speak more clearly on other physical aspects of rape and sexual assault, it was possible for feminists and their allies, particularly those involved in social reform work – as were members of the IWRL and most of the women witnesses to the Carrigan Committee – to press home that one result of failure to protect young girls from sexual crime was that they might become unmarried mothers. The way in which the 1927 Irish government publication, the *Report of the Commission on the Relief of the Sick and Destitute Poor* (Poor Law Commissioners' report),[19] and the 1931 Carrigan Report, related unmarried motherhood and reform of sexual crime law in line with campaigners' demands are indicators of the appropriateness of this approach. In a state that respected men's right to rape their wives, arguments about an unmarried and destitute girl's individual trauma were less likely to carry weight than those about the cost of unmarried mothers and their children to the poor law system.

The IWRL Watching the Courts Reports provide qualitative evidence of women's experience of the legal system and insights into feminist ideas on rebalancing both statute and legal practice along more equitable lines. For example, several issues arose in a 1914 seduction case report involving Lizzy C., a 15-year-old shop-worker, allegedly 'assaulted' and made pregnant in 1911 by James F., her employer's cousin. An unlawful carnal knowledge prosecution in

1912 failed, in part because James F. argued that Lizzie looked of age. The test of this was a male magistrate, judge or jury's assessment of a girl's physical appearance during court proceedings, with little account taken of delays, retrials, physical changes related to pregnancy and growth spurts. Marion Duggan reported not only that the judge in the 1914 civil proceedings, Mr Justice Dodd, expressed surprise at the criminal trial judge's decision that Lizzie looked of age but also that he recognized how sexual ignorance had contributed to her plight.[20] That some form of sex education be introduced to provide girls with the knowledge to protect themselves was an explicit feminist demand, one also presented to the Carrigan Committee two decades later.[21]

A seduction case was the final remedy available to Lizzie C.'s parents when a criminal prosecution failed. Based on an assumption that a woman's services were the property of her employer, or, if she lived at home, of her parent or guardian, such cases involved a parent, guardian or employer suing the putative father of her child for loss of these services because of her pregnancy. Unless the putative father was a man of means there was little to gain but a sense of vindication and in awarding Lizzie C.'s father £35, Mr Justice Dodd regretted that there was little chance the money would be paid.[22] Highlighting such cases was important not only in illustrating the need for legislation permitting women to initiate proceedings in their own right to seek maintenance for children born out of wedlock, but also because calls for a CLA Bill were paired with calls for an Affiliation Orders Bill to enable them to do this. The intention was that, taken together, they would create legal consequences for men who made young girls pregnant. A British Affiliation Orders Act was passed in 1914 but not applied to Ireland, presumably because Irish MPs, focused on the national question, were unconscious of, or indifferent to, women's problems. This may have added to feminist frustration in that year at a press that purveyed myths of national purity and was silent on child abuse and rape.[23]

A July 1913 court report highlighted further problems, including the injustice arising from the six month statutory time limit on initiating unlawful carnal knowledge prosecutions and how the character of a juvenile victim could be undermined. A domestic servant, aged 15 years and 8 months when she gave birth to a child, had allegedly become pregnant as a result of frequent sexual 'assaults' by her female employer's brother. It was claimed that he continued to have intercourse with her during her pregnancy. Though pregnancy provided proof of an offence, no legal action was taken until after the birth, possibly because, as *garda* commissioner Eoin O'Duffy explained to the Carrigan Committee, 'innocent or so shrouded with the shame of the act', girls rarely reported rape and assault so that in some cases it was local authorities or the clergy who informed the police after girls entered the union hospital for delivery.[24] The statutory time limit meant that only offences occurring in the previous six months could be considered, not the event that resulted in pregnancy. It was the second time this case had come before the courts and for a second time the jury failed to agree a verdict. Evidence in such a case was a matter of the word of a servant against that of the accused and the report contains a hint of how easily a young girl's evidence might be undermined. The defence counsel insisted that his client was not guilty and that another brother was responsible for the girl's pregnancy, thereby implying that she lied about the father's identity, may have had sexual relations with two men and neither could be trusted nor regarded as an innocent party. There was an implication that women in general could not be trusted – and that any man was seducible – in what may have been a standard appeal to the masculine anxieties or prejudices of all male juries when defence counsel remarked that 'any one of them might any day find himself in a similar position to the young man in the dock'. In other words that any man might be enticed by a determined girl of bad character. In another reference to the women's movement's objectives, Marion Duggan responded that if women were permitted to serve on juries they 'might have reflected that any young girl might any day find herself in the pitiful plight of the ruined girl'.[25]

The rule of practice requiring judges in sexual crime cases to warn juries that it was dangerous to convict on the evidence of a single witness may also have influenced the verdict. British and Irish enquiries acknowledged that jurors took the judge's warning as an instruction to acquit, even in cases in which there was no reason to doubt the testimony of the alleged victim.[26] If this rule made it difficult to secure convictions in cases involving older girls and adult women, the provision in the 1885 Act that in those involving carnal knowledge, or attempted carnal knowledge of girls under the age of 13, no-one could be convicted on the uncorroborated evidence of the child, made it practically impossible to bring a successful child abuse case.

In the summer of 1914 the *Irish Citizen* and *Irish Worker* reported two cases that illustrated this problem. The cases contrasted in that one involved a working-class offender and victim while in the second both were middle class. In the first a separated man, John Madden, an ice-cream vendor and former coal-yard labourer, was charged with an attempted indecent assault on the 6-year-old daughter of a 'workman', in the hall of a house in Lower Gardiner Street, Dublin: an assault interrupted by an inhabitant of the house not called to give evidence and possibly not identified. As a result, the child was infected with gonorrhoea. The IWRL employed counsel in hopes of establishing a watching brief and being permitted to express '"women's point of view" in order that sympathy with the prisoner may not lead to a short sentence'.[27] The trial ended abruptly when the Crown withdrew the charges on the grounds that the 6-year-old was 'too young to answer questions'. In reporting events, Duggan laid out the IWRL view that children must be listened to, that children's courts must be established in which surroundings and procedures were less intimidating, women as well as men would serve and time would be taken to assess children's ability to give evidence.[28]

In the second case Herbert Jones, a 45-year-old married printer, was accused of 'indecent conduct' towards an 8-year-old girl, the daughter of 'an employer', in the garden of his home in a middle-class district in Drumcondra, Dublin. The case was unusual in that this child's evidence was corroborated by a neighbour who witnessed the assault from a window in her home. Found guilty, Jones received only a six-week sentence. Duggan responded: 'How lucky he did not break a window or steal a pair of boots!'[29]

A number of *Irish Citizen* reports questioned the 'curious scale of values' employed in sentencing for sexual crimes. One report highlighted cases in which an indecent assault on a girl under 16 and the theft of bacon were equally punished with six months with hard labour, while in the same court the theft of clothes and £13.10s brought twelve months with hard labour.[30] Another report on a series of cases involving children under 13 years old referred to sentences of one month, and three months, the latter considered 'most unusual'.[31] A further concern was that middle-class men evaded prosecution: 'We should like very definite proof that offenders of influential position are treated with the full severity of the law, and not merely warned or sent out of the country to be the ruin of innocent little girls elsewhere.'[32]

In the event, Herbert Jones served only two weeks. The fact that a Church of Ireland clergyman appealed for leniency and that Jones was released by the Viceroy, Lord Aberdeen, who with his wife was associated with child welfare projects, astonished the IWRL.[33] They recognized that such crimes were treated as petty because of the view that male sexuality could be uncontrollable, that men were subject to 'natural and irresistible urges', and that many judges, lawyers, jurymen – and it seemed some clergy and the Viceroy – understood this as an aspect of healthy masculinity, particularly when dealing with middle-class men like Jones. This was one reason why the IWRL, whose position was that 'perfect moral purity' was desirable for men as well as women,[34] had sought a watching brief in the Madden case, in hopes of making a statement that disputed these assumptions. The *Irish Citizen* recorded comments by judges and counsel that reflected acceptance of such theories, for example, when in a June 1914 seduction case a judge directed the jury to 'take account of the natural, irresistible impulse animating the man'.[35] Interestingly, in a December 1914 case, Mr Justice Hanna was conscious of criticism on this issue and explained that: 'he only entertained sympathy in the case of young boys who often may not realise what their actions may entail upon the girl',[36] while during a 1915 rape case the defence counsel saw fit to distance himself from 'other men [who] thought these cases suitable for mirth and gefaws [sic]'.[37] In a 1919 *Irish Citizen* article, feminist Margaret Connery raised the issue of this 'false teaching aided and abetted by the corrupt double moral standard (which allows unbridled licence to men in matters of sex)' as encouraging sexual crime.[38]

With an all male parliament and with Irish MPs apparently indifferent to the issues, what chance was there of legislative change? In fact the possibility of legislation was on the cards throughout the period 1912 to 1922. In 1914 the Bishop of London introduced a House of Lords Bill providing for 18 as age of consent, 16 as the age in respect of indecent acts, a twelve month statutory time limit, and the repeal of the reasonable cause to believe clause. With the churches, feminists and moral and social welfare associations all pressing for action it was impossible to ignore the issue. This 1914 bill reached committee stage and provided the skeleton for a 1917 Bill, though in the latter 17 was proposed as age of consent. Numerous clauses were added including some making sexual intercourse while infected with venereal disease an offence and providing for the detention of girls until they reached the age of 19 if they were convicted of a range of offences including prostitution. Such clauses reflected ongoing concern in Britain about public morality, prostitution and what was perceived as increasingly immoral behaviour among young people as the war brought social change, but they made for complex legislation and the reinforcement of double standards. The Bill was defeated by one vote at the

Commons Committee stage. In 1920 three Bills dealing with sexual offences, two of them CLA Bills, were referred to a Select Committee. A brief CLA Act passed in 1922 was, however, directly influenced by the feminist Association for Moral and Social Hygiene (AMSH), which produced a simple model for legislation. Introduced in the Lords, when it failed in the lower house the AMSH condemned 'those in the Commons who are determined not to give girls under 16 effective protection against seduction'.[39] Reintroduced as a government measure, the British 1922 CLA Act raised the age of consent to 'indecent' acts to 16 and the statutory time limit to nine months rather than the twelve sought by campaigners. Following debate, the defence of reasonable cause to believe a girl was of age was retained in cases where the accused was under 23-years-old. Opponents of repeal of the reasonable cause clause raised a spectre that also appeared in Irish debates of the late 1920s, the under-aged girl seducer, blackmailer and danger to men.[40]

The final line of the British Act read: 'This Act shall not apply to Ireland.' 1922 was the year of Irish independence. In 1923 the Unionist northern state abolished the reasonable cause to believe clause and adopted the same provisions on indecent acts and the statutory time limit as in the British 1922 Act. In 1924 it passed an Affiliation Orders Act. This move in Northern Ireland and the fact that the likelihood of further legal change remained on the British agenda must have encouraged Irish feminist and moral purity campaigners who, as discussed below, maintained pressure for reform during the 1920s. In July, 1924 a British departmental committee was established to further consider law and practice on sexual crime against 'young persons'. Its recommendations included that the age of consent should be raised to 17; that the reasonable cause to believe defence should be abolished; that the time limit for taking proceedings in unlawful carnal knowledge cases should be twelve months; and that those involved in 'initiating or conducting prosecutions should bear in mind' that lack of corroborating evidence was 'not a bar to the securing of a conviction'. These reflected many feminist demands.[41] When the Carrigan Committee was established in 1930, barrister William Carrigan's letter of appointment assured him that the existence of the report of this committee would simplify his own work.[42]

Irish State files on the 1935 CLA Act contain extensive evidence of women's campaigning, beginning in November 1923 when Louie Bennett, founder of the IWRL and by then secretary of the Irish

Women Workers' Union (IWWU) sent Cumann na nGaedheal Home Affairs Minister, Kevin O'Higgins, a union resolution calling for the age of consent to be raised to 18.[43] In January 1924 representatives of 'a number of women's associations combined in a deputation' lobbied Attorney General Hugh Kennedy. Laid out on the notepaper of feminist organization the Irish Women Citizens' Association (IWCA), their demands were: that for the protection of boys and girls during 'the chaotic stages of adolescence and the period of curiosity' and to prevent girls from 'slipping into prostitution', the age of consent to any sexual act should be 18; that the reasonable cause to believe clause be repealed; and that the time limit for commencement of proceedings under the new legislation be not less than nine months.[44] In the same period Fr Richard Devane, social purity campaigner and ally of the women's movement on some CLA Bill matters, made clear that a core issue was the double standard of morality inherent in the 1885 legislation, a morality he acknowledged was based on a 'false supposition' that male sex drives were uncontrollable and one that had 'fatal consequences' for women.[45]

The lobbyists had some success. By October 1924 heads for Affiliation Orders and CLA Bills had been prepared and the latter proposed removing the reasonable cause clause and making 18 the age of consent to any sexual act.[46] There was a shortage of parliamentary draftsmen, however, and drafting was not proceeded with because, under Kevin O'Higgins, the Department of Justice did not consider the Bills 'of the same public importance or urgency as finance measures, drainage measures, Shannon Scheme, &c.&c. [sic].'[47]

By June 1925 a 'Committee for the Reform of the Laws Relating to the Protection of Women and Girls' was pressing for action on a range of related measures including CLA, Affiliation Orders and Legitimacy Bills.[48] An alliance of feminists, social work and religious associations, many Protestant, they lobbied as individual organizations and as an umbrella group. Membership included the Children's Care Committee of the IWCA; the Dublin Christian Citizenship Council; the Dublin Council of Women; the Infant Aid Society; the Irish Christian Fellowship; The Irish Women Workers Union; the Magdalen Asylum (the Protestant Leeson Street Asylum); the Mothers' Union; the Nursery Rescue and Protestant Aid Society; the Union of Christian Churches; the Irish Women Citizen's Association; the Women Patrols; the Women's National Health Association. Committee members included Marie Johnson representing the

IWCA,[49] Hon. Ethel Macnaghten; Mrs Wigham; Miss Emily Buchanan; Mrs Cosgrave; Mrs McKean; Miss N. Cunningham; Helen Chenevix; Miss O'Connor; Mrs Booth; Miss Draper-Newman; Mrs Barlee; Mrs Howie; Mrs Bewley; the Church of Ireland Dean of Christ Church Cathedral, Dublin, the Rev. Dr Denham Osborne, who represented the Union of Christian Churches, and Fr Devane.[50] Marion Duggan was not a committee member but was involved with this group.[51]

It was 1929 before an opposition Private Member's CLA Bill, on the lines of the British 1922 Act, was introduced by Fianna Fáil Deputy Paddy Little. During debates on this and on a 1929 Affiliation Orders Bill the blackmailing juvenile seductress was conjured up. In the latter case this resulted in a reduction in the proposed time limit for seeking affiliation orders from twelve months after the birth of a child to six months.[52] During the CLA Bill debate, it was Justice Minister, James Fitzgerald-Kenney, who claimed that if the age of consent were raised 'any person might be made the subject of a considerable amount of blackmail'.[53] If the legislature was more concerned with protecting male interests than serving women's, there was a likelihood that a CLA Bill, involving a more complex rebalancing of rights, would not succeed. More than party political differences, might the dichotomy between those who saw sexual crime in terms of the vulnerability of men to hardened temptresses and those taking the feminist and social purity position that women required protection from male sexual aggression, have made it inevitable that, as happened in Britain, the matter would be passed to a committee of inquiry: the 1930–31 Carrigan Committee?

A July 1930 *Daily Express* article made clear both that Irish women campaigners considered CLA issues were 'entirely women's questions' and their indignation that only two of the six member committee would be women[54]: Dublin Union Poor Law Commissioner, Mrs Jane Power and Miss V. O'Carroll, matron of the Coombe maternity hospital. In addition to barrister William Carrigan, other members were Surgeon Francis Morrin, Rev. John Hannon SJ, and Church of Ireland Dean of Christ Church Cathedral, Dublin, Very Rev. H.B. Kennedy, a cleric long involved with moral purity organization the Dublin White Cross Association.[55] Eighteen of the twenty-nine witnesses who gave oral evidence were women. Some, like Emily Buchanan, had worked on the issues for at least two decades. Many, like Delia Moclair Horne, first woman assistant master of Holles Street maternity hospital, and TB specialist Dr Dorothy Stopford

Price, were highly respected in their professions. The points they made reflected feminist discourse on CLA legislation two decades earlier, including that the age of consent to any sexual acts should be no lower than 18, with the Committee of Medical Women suggesting 21 as a minimum age of consent for women in the workplace and referring to domestic servants, clerks and shop assistants as particularly vulnerable.[56] Margaret Gavan Duffy, representing the Lock Hospital, suggested that the age for employees could be as high as 25. She was supported by Dr Ita Brady who referred to a Dublin case in which an employer infected three members of staff with venereal disease. To address problems arising from sexual ignorance, Gavan Duffy suggested that: 'sex education should be imparted by Lady Doctors who would visit girls' schools for the purpose'.[57] Witnesses considered the 'reasonable cause to believe' proviso made the 1885 legislation 'inoperable' and called for its repeal.[58] Kathleen Kirwan of the Legion of Mary Hostel suggested that child abusers exploited the corroborating evidence loophole and that the evidence of the person to whom a distressed child disclosed what happened should be taken as corroborating.[59] Several witnesses asked that soliciting laws should apply equally to men and women and spoke of women's lack of a legal remedy when sexually harassed in the streets.[60] Other issues raised included that the statutory time limit for bringing unlawful carnal knowledge cases should be twelve months,[61] and that women police and jurors were essential to achieving justice.[62]

The Carrigan report reflected most of the women witnesses' suggestions.[63] Interestingly, drafts of a Department of Justice memo criticized the committee for having 'adopted the views of the organisations of social workers' and quibbled with all its recommendations on sexual crime except that the statutory limit on the commencement of unlawful carnal knowledge prosecutions should be raised to twelve months. Against repealing the 'reasonable cause to believe' clause, their anonymous author cited both the blackmail risk and the stock argument used to maintain the double standard, that men were easily 'seduced by a young woman looking years more than her real age'.[64] A decision not to publish the Carrigan report, that a committee of Dáil deputies, the Geoghegan committee, worked in-camera to draft a CLA Bill and that the agreement of party leaders was sought to pass the measure through the Oireachtas with minimal discussion might reflect a desire to conceal information on serious socio-moral problems. The issues involved had, however, been in the public domain for decades. Might a more pressing reason have been a possibility that a CLA Bill would fail, or be rendered ineffectual, had full discussion of the age of consent and 'reasonable cause' provisions been permitted? The strategy of restricting discussion succeeded but there were compromises that meant the measure fell short of women's demands. Under the 1935 CLA Act the statutory time limit on unlawful carnal knowledge cases was raised to twelve months, the age of consent was raised to 17 rather than 18, but a two-tier system was retained in which offences against girls aged 15 and 16 were treated as misdemeanours and 15 rather than 17 was the age of consent to 'indecent acts'.

While in a chapter of this length there are aspects of both women's political activities and the process that led to the passing of the 1935 CLA Act that cannot be fully considered, it does suggest some of the ways in which introducing gender as a category of analysis opens up new perspectives. The origins of the 1935 legislation can be traced to feminist and social purity campaigns to address double standards of sexual morality that pre-date the establishment of the Irish State in 1922. Women's political agency and their role in pre- and post-independence debates on sexuality come in to focus, as does the alliance of feminist and Protestant social morality groups involved in the lobbying committee in the mid-1920s, with which Catholic purity campaigner Fr Richard Devane also co-operated. Resituating them in this broader social context may permit new interpretations of the activities of the Carrigan and Geoghegan committees and raise new questions about the negotiation of the 1934 CLA Bill. It may also facilitate further considerations of the role of the Roman Catholic Church and open up new and more complex understandings of social and political developments of this period.

NOTES

1. Marion Duggan, 'The Madden Case', *Irish Citizen*, 22 August 1914.
2. J.H. Whyte, *Church and State in Modern Ireland, 1923–1979* (Dublin: Gill and Macmillan, 1980); Dermot Keogh, *The Vatican, the Bishops and Irish Politics 1919–39,* (Cambridge: Cambridge University Press, 1986); Tom Inglis, *Irish Lessons in Sexuality* (Dublin: University College Dublin Press, 1998).
3. Inglis, *Irish Lessons in Sexuality*, p.30.
4. Mark Finnane, 'The Carrigan Committee of 1930–31 and the "moral condition of the Saorstát"', *Irish Historical Studies*, xxxii, 128 (November 2001), pp.519–36 (p.523).
5. James M. Smith, 'The Politics of Sexual Knowledge: the Origins of Ireland's Containment Culture and the Carrigan Report (1931)', *Journal of the History of Sexuality*, 13, 2 (2004), pp.208–33.
6. Louise Jackson, *Child Sexual Abuse in Victorian England* (London: Routledge, 2000), pp.15–16. Though witness statements from women's organizations were not available to me at the time, I examined the process that led to the passing of the 1935 CLA Act in a

1998 PhD thesis in which I focused on the issues of sexual crime, prostitution, public decency, contraception, abortion and infanticide: Sandra Larmour (McAvoy), 'Aspects of the State and Female Sexuality in the Irish Free State 1922–1949' (Unpublished PhD thesis, History Department, University College Cork, 1998).

7. Margaret Jackson, *The Real Facts of Life* (London: Taylor and Francis, 1994), Ch. 2, pp.34–59.
8. Sheila Jeffreys, *The Spinster and Her Enemies* (London: Pandora, 1985), pp.79–85.
9. See 'The Protected Sex', *Irish Citizen*, 23 January 1915, and 'Women Watching the Courts Committee', *Irish Citizen*, 9 October 1915. On the founding and role of the IWRL and its involvement with the National Vigilance Association in Dublin, see Rosemary Cullen Owens, *Louie Bennett* (Cork: Cork University Press, 2001), pp.14–17.
10. Duggan studied Ethics and Logic at Trinity College Dublin, graduating in 1908 and was awarded an LLB in 1910: Susan M. Parkes, *A Danger to the Men? A History of Women in Trinity College Dublin 1904–2004* (Dublin: Lilliput Press, 2004), pp.65 and 239. Until the 1919 Sex Disqualification Removal Act was passed women were not permitted to train for the Bar, to become solicitors, or serve as jurors. Marion Duggan was finally called to the Irish Bar in 1925: 'New Barristers', *Irish Times*, 11 June 1925.
11. See M.E. Duggan, 'In the Courts', *Irish Citizen*, 5 December 1914.
12. M.E. Duggan LLB, 'In the Courts', *Irish Citizen*, 27 June 1914.
13. See 'Current Comment: Women in Court', *Irish Citizen*, 30 January 1915, and 'Ladies and Children to Leave the Court!', 14 August 1915.
14. 'Women Watching the Courts Committee', *Irish Citizen*, 9 October 1915.
15. Under Sections 4 and 5 of the 1885 Criminal Law Amendment Act the terms 'unlawful carnal knowledge' and 'defilement' described the offence of having sexual intercourse with a girl under the age of consent, a criminal offence whether she consented or not.
16. Act to Amend the Criminal Law as to Indecent Assaults on Young Persons, 1880 section 2. Age of consent rose from 12 in 1861, to 13 in 1875, to 16 in 1885 in line with shifting ideas about childhood.
17. 'Sex Education', *Irish Citizen*, 30 March 1914, and M.E. Duggan, 'In the Courts', *Irish Citizen*, 5 December 1914.
18. 'Free Speech on Sex', *Irish Citizen*, 18 October 1913.
19. 'Unmarried Mothers and their Children', in *Report of the Commission on the Relief of the Sick and Destitute Poor Including the Insane Poor* (Dublin: The Stationery Office, 1927), pp.68–74.
20. M.E. Duggan, 'In the Courts', *Irish Citizen*, 27 June 1914.
21. 'Sex Education', *Irish Citizen*, 30 March 1914, and M.E. Duggan, 'In the Courts', *Irish Citizen*, 5 December 1914.
22. M.E. Duggan, 'In the Courts', *Irish Citizen*, 27 June 1914.
23. Editorial, 'Conspiracy of Silence', *Irish Citizen*, 25 July 1914.
24. O'Duffy's written submission to the Carrigan Committee, NAI, D/J file H247/41A pp.6–7.
25. 'The Ruin of Young Girls in Ireland', *Irish Citizen*, 19 July 1913.
26. *Report of the Departmental Committee on Sexual Offences against Young Persons* (London: HMSO, 1925), Cmd. 2561, pp.47–50, para. 69 and Carrigan Report, NAI, Department of the Taoiseach (D/T) file S5998, pp.23–4 and 27–8.
27. M.E. Duggan, 'In the Courts', *Irish Citizen*, 11 July 1914.
28. M.E. Duggan, 'Have you a little daughter?', *Irish Citizen*, 18 July 1914, and M.E. Duggan, 'A Study in Protection', *Irish Citizen*, 23 January 1915.
29. On the Jones case see: *Irish Worker*, 4 and 18 July 1914 and *Irish Citizen*, 11, 18 and 25 July 1914 and 22 and 29 August 1914.
30. 'Property and Persons', *Irish Citizen*, 10 April 1915.
31. 'How Children are "Protected"', *Irish Citizen*, June-July 1919. (By 1919 the journal was produced bimonthly rather than weekly and the method of dating had changed.)
32. 'Current Comment', *Irish Citizen*, 8 November 1913, and M.E. Duggan, 'In the Courts', *Irish Citizen*, 11 July 1914.
33. 'M.E. Duggan, LLB writes:', *Irish Citizen*, 29 August 1914.
34. M.E. Duggan, 'Outrages', *Irish Citizen*, 26 September 1914.
35. M.E. Duggan, 'In the Courts', *Irish Citizen*, 27 June 1914.
36. M.E. Duggan, 'In the Courts', *Irish Citizen*, 5 December 1914. See counsel's remarks in M.E. Duggan, 'Watching the Courts', *Irish Citizen*, 26 June 1915.

37. M.E. Duggan, 'Watching the Courts', 'Ashamed of his Sex', *Irish Citizen*, 14 August 1915.
38. Margaret Connery, 'A Light Calendar', *Irish Citizen*, June-July 1919.
39. Jeffreys, *The Spinster and Her Enemies*, pp.79–85, and Cheryl Law, *Suffrage and Power. The Women's Movement, 1918–1928* (London: I.B. Taurus & Co., 1997), pp.100–101.
40. Alyson Brown and David Barrett, *Knowledge of Evil. Child Prostitution and Child Sexual Abuse in Twentieth-Century England* (Devon: Willan Publishing, 2002), p.78.
41. *Report of the Departmental Committee on Sexual Offences against Young People* (London: The Stationery Office, 1925), Cmd. 2561, summary of recommendations pp.83–8.
42. Letter to William Carrigan from E. O'Frighil, 30 May 1930, NAI, D/J file, H171/39.
43. Letter from Louie Bennett to the Minister for Home Affairs (Kevin O'Higgins) and resolution (untitled), 2 November 1924, NAI, D/J file, H171/39.
44. Hugh Kennedy letter and IWCA statement,14 January 1924, NAI, D/J file, H171/39.
45. December 1923 'Memorandum on Law and Proposed Legislation Dealing with Social Moral Problems. By Rev. R.S. Devane, S.J., Rathfarnham Castle', NAI, D/J file, H266/40.
46. Copies in: Department of Justice file H266/40.
47. Letter signed E. O'Frighil, Department Secretary, 23 June 1925, NAI, D/J file H171/11.
48. The latter provided for the legitimizing of children born out of wedlock when their parents married.
49. Presumably the trades unionist wife of Parliamentary Labour Party leader Thomas Johnson.
50. Details in 18 June 1925 letter in NAI, D/J file H266/40. For letters from individual organizations see also D/J file H171/39. Materials from organizations involved appear in a range of state files on the CLA Bill between 1925 and 1935 and after legislation passed.
51. Letter from Ethel Macnaghten to Kevin O'Higgins names Duggan, 26 February 1926, NAI, D/J file 9/19/1.
52. Dáil Debates, vol.32, 30 October 1929, col. 524 and vol.33, 12 February 1930, col. 124–31.
53. Dáil Debates, vol.34, 27 March 1930, col. 261.
54. 'Women on Dáil Committee', *Daily Express*, 17 July 1930.
55. See Very Rev. H.B. Kennedy B.D., 'Social Service', in Rev. William Bell and Rev. N.D. Emerson (eds), *The Church of Ireland A.D. 432-1932* (Dublin: Church of Ireland Publishing Co., 1932), pp.186–90 and 'Youth and Sex' report, *Irish Times*, 2 March 1931, possibly reflecting the Dean's experience on the Committee.
56. Carrigan minutes, NAI, D/J file 90/4/2: 20 November 1930, Drs Delia Moclair Horne and Dorothy Stopford Price.
57. Carrigan minutes: 15 January 1931, Margaret Gavan Duffy and Dr Ita Brady.
58. Carrigan minutes: 17 October 1920, Mrs T. Kettle; 18 July 1930, Miss Dodd, IWCA; and 17 October 1930, Emily Buchanan for the Protestant Magdalen Asylum.
59. Carrigan minutes: 15 January 1931, Kathleen Kirwan.
60. Carrigan minutes: 18 July 1930 IWCA delegates, 17 October 1930, Emily Buchanan; 20 November 1930, Women Doctors; and 27 November 1930, Mrs C.P. Curran and Mrs Hobson, Saor an Leanbh.
61. Carrigan minutes: 5 February 1931, Hannah Clarke, NSPCC inspector.
62. Carrigan minutes: for example, 18 July 1930, IWCA delegates; 27 November 1930, Saor an Leanbh delegates; and 20 November 1930, Women Doctors.
63. Report of the Committee on the Criminal Law Amendment Acts (1880–85) and Juvenile Prostitution, unpublished, NAI, D/T file S5998.
64. Draft (1) memo dated '9/11/1931' in NAI, D/J file 8/20 and draft (2) more measured October 1932 memo in D/T file S5998.

CHAPTER SEVEN

Virtuous Mothers and Dutiful Wives: The Politics of Sexuality in the Irish Free State[1]

MARYANN GIALANELLA VALIULIS

Following in the wake of the war of independence and subsequent civil war, in 1922 the leaders of the Irish Free State set about the task of establishing and consolidating an independent state. Their ideal was to create a Catholic and Gaelic state – one that would justify their claim to independence. It was not, however, an auspicious moment to try to close one's borders to the 'permissiveness' of the period. The 1920s were, after all, in varying degrees throughout Western Europe and the United States, the age of the 'flapper', the age of jazz, the age of *carpe diem*.

In the Irish Free State, however, the period of the 1920s and 1930s was a time when the new state was defining itself and articulating its identity. In a sense, Irish political and ecclesiastical leaders were conscious that this was their 'historic moment' – the time when they could prove their worth, their ability to govern themselves and disprove all the stereotypes and slurs which had been affixed to them during their long period of colonialism.

Central to the Irish claim for independence was their difference from England. England was described as pagan, Anglo-Saxon, urban and materialistic while the Free State was Celtic, Irish-speaking, rural and Roman Catholic. Above all, it was virtuous. The Irish, according to Free State leaders, were a moral people who would construct a state which embodied and reflected their 'Irishness' – their language, their Gaelic traditions and their superior Catholic morality. With independence – however limited – the Free State could cast off the 'alien standards of public morality' which had been foisted on them by the English and establish their 'own legal standard of public morality', to 'set an example to other nations'.[2] This was a critical part of the ideological justification for independence. Their moral superiority was central; it was key to their identity. The Irish government was determined to create a Catholic, conservative, Gaelic state which would justify its claim to independence.

Women were critical to the Free State's definition of itself as a pure and virtuous nation. The important question was, what role would women play in the new State? In the struggle for independence, women played a vital role in organizations such as Inghinidhe na hÉireann and Cumann na mBan. They ran guns, sheltered IRA men on the run, churned out propaganda, served as judges in the newly established Dáil courts, and in general, did what needed to be done.

However, with the establishment of peace – at least in the twenty-six counties – in the eyes of both Irish political and ecclesiastical leaders, Irish women needed to be returned to the home. The need was to re-establish a traditional gender ideology which sees the hearth and home as women's rightful sphere. Their citizenship, their participation in the State, would be directly related to the home. As the 1937 Constitution would so aptly state years later: 'In particular, the State recognises that by her life within the home, woman gives to the State a support without which the common good cannot be achieved.'[3]

To this end, the Free State enacted gender legislation which tried to remove women from participating in the economic and political life of the State. Throughout the 1920s and 1930s, women were, in effect, barred from serving on juries, were forbidden to sit for the highest examinations in the Civil Service, were subject to the marriage bar, and were restricted from working in certain factories.[4] Their sphere of activity was the home, the private sphere and therein, it was claimed, lay their responsibility, their duty and their contribution to the State.

The dominant religious discourse of the period supported this gender legislation and urged women to shun the changes which saw women in the offices, in the factories, speaking at public meetings and participating in political activities in an active role. Women were urged to stay in the home, in a heterosexual nuclear family, reproducing for the good of the nation in accordance with Catholic doctrine.[5] Women, according to this view, were to be firmly entrenched in the home as mothers, wives and carers. Thus the equality promised in the Constitution was breached and remained, according to the Women's Citizens and Local Government Association in 1928, an 'ideal' not a reality.[6]

These legislative restrictions and ecclesiastical prohibitions reinforced the idea that women's citizenship was rooted in their role in the family as wives and mothers. It was through motherhood especially that women performed their service to the State. Motherhood thus became a 'central mechanism through which women ... [were] incorporated into the modern political order'.[7] Motherhood was given a political status.

The elevation of motherhood in particular and the family in general occurred throughout the years of the Free State. In the gender legislation of the 1920s and 1930s, culminating in the 1937 Constitution, women were defined in an essentialist manner as wives and mothers, as part of a family, situated in the private sphere. In the juries debates of 1924 and 1927, women's role in raising children and keeping the home – in particular, cooking the family dinner – was singled out as one, if not the primary, reason that women should not serve on juries. Who, Kevin O'Higgins asked, would cook the family dinner? And, in the debates on the Civil Service (Amendment) Act of 1925, the critical issue was marriage. Women should not qualify for the highest offices in the Civil Service because, according to the Minister for Finance, Ernest Blythe, they will get married, leave the Civil Service and their entire class will be skewed.

The family itself was privileged in Irish political thought as the source of order and stability. This was stated explicitly in the 1937 Constitution which vested inalienable rights in the family and which describes the family as 'the necessary basis of social order and as indispensable to the welfare of the Nation and the State'.[8] Women were subordinate to their husbands, queen of the house to his king, a helpmate. In a telling example of this hierarchy, the *Irish Press* spoke of the glory of the Irish family during the Eucharistic Congress of 1932: 'Last week showed many things – and one was the steel strength of our home life. Every happening had behind it its father, mother, child. The decorations – father on top of the ladder, mother handing him things – mainly fashioned by herself – and advising, children looking on.'[9] Thus stood the family - the building block of Irish, Catholic society. This view of the family encapsulated both Catholic teaching and Catholic aspiration. The family was the building block of the nation. Strong families meant a strong nation. Catholic conservative families were integral to the political structure of the State. Central to the strong family, strong nation argument were women; women as wives; women as mothers; women as guardians of the hearth and home.

Women's citizenship – the way in which they participated in, and contributed to, the State – was rooted in the private sphere, in the domestic arena, in the family and directly related to motherhood within marriage. Because it was related to motherhood, it was tied to heterosexuality and it was the heterosexual, nuclear family that was privileged and glorified in the gender ideology of the period. The ideal of the virtuous and pure woman was critical in providing ideological justification for independence and thus had to be ensured through law. However, this emphasis on the virtues of the idealized woman meant that the State's attitude towards motherhood and women's sexuality was sometimes contradictory, often problematic. Only virtuous women were wanted as mothers and to ensure this, women's sexuality had to be regulated and controlled. In fact, given the double standard of the day, women had to be controlled.

It was not an easy task. Despite the gender legislation of the period, despite ecclesiastical warnings and threats of damnation, the state of the country definitely seemed to fall short of the ideal. For example, an editorial in the *Irish Times* in 1927 declared:

> Throughout the centuries, Ireland has enjoyed a high reputation for the cardinal virtues of social life. She was famous for her men's chivalry and for her women's modesty. To-day every honest Irishman [*sic*] must admit that this reputation is in danger ... Our first need is full recognition of the fact that today the nation's proudest and most precious heritage is slipping from its grasp.[10]

And a 1932 report of the Committee on the Criminal Law Amendment Act and the question of Juvenile Prostitution – the Carrigan Report – asserted that:

> the moral condition of the country has been gravely menaced by modern abuses ... The testimony of all the witnesses, clerical, lay, official is striking in its unanimity that degeneration in the standard of social conduct has taken place in recent years. It is attributed primarily to the loss of parental control and responsibility during a period of general upheaval, which has not been recovered since the revival of settled conditions. This is due largely to the introduction of new phases of popular amusement ... being carried on in the Saorstát in the absence of supervision ... the cause of ruin of hundreds of young girls, of whom many are found in the streets of London, Liverpool and other cities and towns in England.
>
> The commercialized Dance halls, picture houses of sorts, and the opportunities afforded by the misuse of motor cars for luring

> girls, are the chief causes alleged for the present looseness of morale.[11]

These same sentiments were echoed endless times from the pulpit where priests moved from public denouncements of immorality to threats of religious injunctions if the immoral behaviour was not stopped. The 1925 statement of the Irish Bishops meeting in Maynooth stated the importance of this issue:

> There is a danger of losing the name which the chivalrous honour of Irish boys and the Christian reserve of Irish maidens have won for Ireland. If our people part with the character that gave rise to the name, we lose with it much of our national strength … Purity is strength and purity and faith go together. Both virtues are in danger these times, but purity is more directly assailed than faith.[12]

If there were any doubt about who had to bear responsibility for this state of affairs, societies like the Catholic Truth Society made it abundantly clear who was to blame:

> The women of Ireland, heretofore renowned for their virtue and honour, go about furnished with the paint-pot, the lip-stick … and many of them have acquired the habit of intemperance, perhaps one of the sequels to their lately adopted vogue of smoking. A so-called dress performance or dance today showed some of our Irish girls in such scanty drapery as could only be exceeded in the slave markets of pagan countries.[13]

Or as one bishop more moderately noted: 'They could not have a clean and noble race till woman was restored to her former dignity.'[14]

The perception was that far from being morally pure and virtuous, the country was sliding down the road to perdition. In particular, it seemed as if the Free State was brimming with all sorts of sexual activity – much of which was classified as 'immoral and decadent' according to the dominant discourse of the day. These charges of immorality went beyond a violation of religious moral teaching. Immorality struck at the heart of Irish identity. It was a political matter. That is what made it such a potent concern.

Certainly the Free State government was concerned. It pondered the truth of the popular perception of an abundance of immoral sexual activity and it wondered what should be its response, its policy in this area. In October 1932, a Department of Justice memorandum on the Carrigan Report concluded that:

> Apart from the question as to whether the Report should be adopted, is the question whether is should be published. The view of the Department of Justice is that it should not be published. It contains numerous sweeping charges against the state of morality of the Saorstát and even if these statements are true, there would be little point in giving them currency.[15]

This was one possible response – to ignore the allegations and not to give publicity to the various charges of immorality. Other possibilities, however, presented themselves. The State could deny the extent of the problem – claiming that, as one Senator said, the 'over-exaggerated' talk about immorality defamed the people of Ireland.[16] It could also blame the problem on 'foreign imports' – foreign newspapers (England), foreign music and dances (the US), foreign fashions (France).

All these tactics were employed but most significantly, the Government also blamed Irish women. It believed that Irish women were failing to observe traditional Irish morality, especially Irish mothers, who were seemingly swept up in the latest fads, exhibiting a lack of modesty, purity and deference. What was particularly appalling to ecclesiastical leaders was that in Catholic Ireland which they believed had a history of noble and virtuous mothers, there were now to be found mothers 'who shirked or neglected their duty to their children ... There were mothers who preferred the fashionable and crowded thoroughfare to their own quiet home; there were mothers who preferred talking on a platform or in a council chamber to chatting with their children in a nursery.'[17] If, as one of the bishops said, Irish women spent more time rocking the cradle and less time in public, they would be better mothers.[18]

In the end, the State decided that these issues – traditionally seen as domestic concerns or private sphere issues, were so critical as to warrant public redefinition and intervention. The Government used its powers to legislate for what it believed would be a more moral society. In effect, the State sought to control women's sexuality which it deemed to be the nub of the problem. It was too important an issue simply to trust women to take up their proper roles.

Throughout the 1920s and 1930s, there were numerous studies, committees and ultimately legislation dealing with aspects of morality. Sources of the period seem to indicate that, in fact, there did seem to be a great deal of sexual activity going on throughout the Free State – in urban and rural areas, among the working class, middle class and upper class. It seemed, as the Carrigan Report noted, sexual activity, especially the use of contraception, was widespread: 'The practices so advocated have become extremely prevalent, not only in the cities and larger towns, but also in villages and remote parts of the South and West of the country.' Moreover, the purchasing of contraceptive devices was blatantly obvious:

> We hear evidence ... that so common in some places were such articles in use that there was no attempt to conceal the sale of them, and places were mentioned to which the supply of such articles comes regularly by post to recognised vendors. At the same time quantities of contraceptive advertisements are in circulation, and price lists are extensively distributed throughout the country by cross-Channel agencies.[19]

On the one hand, what this implies is that women were, to some degree, active agents. They were engaging in sexual activity and, to a limited extent, were controlling their reproduction by means of birth control, abortion and even infanticide. This point was made in the Dáil and Seanad debates as Senators spoke of the consequences of outlawing contraception as being an 'increase in crimes such as criminal abortion and criminal infanticide'.[20] The idea, therefore, that somehow women were passive recipients of government and ecclesiastical dictates does not correspond with the reality of women's lives. On the other hand, such reported sexual activity strengthened the desire of the government to control women's sexuality.

While the government wished to control women's sexuality, what the politicians did not want to do was to talk publicly about sexuality, especially women's sexuality. They established commissions and committees so as to lessen the need for public discussion. For example, in a discussion of the Criminal Law Amendment Act, Senators agreed that 'because of the delicate nature of the discussions that may arise, it would be better ... that these discussions should take place in private, and that the result of the special Committee's deliberations, should afterwards be brought to the House'.[21] The sense was that sexuality was unseemly, embarrassing and while it had to be regulated, it did not have to be publicly discussed. Sexuality, when it came to political discourse, was defined as being a private matter, better left in the domestic realm. Sexuality, however, when it came to issues of political identity, had to be controlled, had to be legislated for, to ensure that the State was properly perceived as virtuous.

By defining women's primary responsibilities in the domestic sphere and defining women's role within the family as the basis for citizenship, political leaders were, in fact, emphasizing women's difference. The question of sexuality highlighted the issue of difference. Women were sexual beings, were wives and mothers, were 'embodied' – that is, linked to nature, to reproduction, to everything the ideal male citizen traditionally was not. It was their bodies that made them different – it was an embodied difference. It was their bodies that relegated them to marginal citizenship. It was their bodies that caused members of the Dáil and Seanad such embarrassment as it seemed clear that these discussions were not proper topics for political debate. However, it was their bodies that the State decided it must control.

Perhaps one of the clearest examples of this desire to control sexuality was the specific issue of birth control. Political and ecclesiastical leaders were clearly concerned about the influx of imported literature on birth control into Ireland and the growing number of women who were practising birth control. This posed a particular threat because it was believed that the literature on birth control was being imported into the State by the English tabloids and by cheap English novels and thus directly threatening the purity of the people, and, in some eyes, their very existence as a race.

The Censorship Act of 1928, among its other provisions, forbade the importation into the State of any books, newspapers or advertisements which advocated contraception.[22] This was followed by the Criminal Law Amendment Act of 1935 which outlawed the contraceptive devices themselves.[23] It spoke to the overall intention of political leaders that at the same time that the government was outlawing contraceptive devices, it was also piloting a bill through the Dàil and Seanad which gave the Minister for Industry and Commerce the right to limit the number of women employed in any given industry. Taken together these two bills were powerful directives to restrict women to the home and to construct women only as wives and mothers.

The Catholic Church and, by extension, its followers in the Irish Free State government, abhorred birth control. In terms of Catholic morality, it was quite straightforward. Birth control was outlawed by the Catholic Church and hence was to be seen as a matter of faith and morals. Or as the Archbishop of Cashel more colourfully stated: 'there should be no compromise with the purveyors of filthy, impure literature, and no compromise with the promoters of the empty cradle'.[24] For some Irish Protestants, the issue was more complex. Some felt that there were women – moral and respectable women – who because of the circumstances of their lives, might need to use contraception. But all agreed that contraception among younger single people who used it to avoid the consequences of sexual activity was to be condemned. Freeing vice, i.e. freeing unmarried sexual activity, from one of its most powerful restraints – pregnancy – was condemned by all. But, interestingly enough, these were not the main arguments in the debate.

In the main, the debates about birth control centred on what was called 'race suicide'. Throughout the debates, this was the way birth control was referred to. From a historical perspective, this might have referred to the Great Famine of the nineteenth century and the tremendous loss of population Ireland experienced. Perhaps the Famine was lingering in this discussion and the desire to achieve a higher population was to enable the Free State 'to bury the ghost of the Great Famine'.[25]

Within the European context, the discussion about birth control/race suicide can be viewed as part of the pro-natalist discourse of the period.[26] It appears that the term race suicide was used to mean the demise of the Irish race. As the Minister for Justice, Mr Fitzgerald Kenney, said:

> The nation which does not progress goes backwards, and the nation that falls off in population falls off in everything, and it is undoubtedly a safe thing to say that great nations do commit race suicide. This is not a new problem. You have only to look at the decay of one of the greatest nations of the world. France cannot keep up its population ... the greatest nation in the world ... is steadily dying out with loss to mankind. That is an evil we are not going to have in this country.[27]

Equating birth control with race suicide was important for two reasons: 1) it indicated a change in nationalist thinking; and 2) it shifted the attention away from the morality issue to one which could be construed as the attempt by the forces of the former colonial power to exert a negative influence on a virtuous Irish population.

During the debate on birth control, much was made of the attempt of the English press to export literature on birth control in particular and what was seen as 'immoral literature' in general to a pure and virtuous people. It was about reputation, about appearing to the world as a moral people. Thus, the debate, for the most part, was not about the numbers of Irish people who were embracing birth control – that would not fit with the picture the Free State political leaders had painted of their new State – rather it was about the attempt by the English to impose these evil devices on a population that should grow and send its people all over the world. Morality was side stepped and race suicide was inserted. It is worth noting, that one of the most galling things about this entire debate to certain members of the Dáil was that opponents of both censorship and birth control made their case to the greater public and embarrassed members of the Dáil.

Moreover, equating birth control with race suicide indicated a change in nationalist thinking. Emigration – the evil which earlier nationalist movements had blamed on Ireland's colonial status and which it was predicted would cease under a free and indigenous government – continued with the establishment of the Free State.[28] It was a dilemma for the government. However, during this debate, which was in reality so much about image, emigration was portrayed as a good thing – the opportunity for the Irish people to populate other sections of the world, bringing with them their culture, their values, their beliefs and giving the Free State itself influence beyond its shores. As one Senator noted:

> In our own country, on the contrary, the general absence of contraceptive measures in our family life produced a surplus population which made the Irish people an immense factor in the lives of the new and sparsely populated countries like America and Australia, and I think that is an important point of view outside the moral one.[29]

The desirability of populating other sections of the world shifts the debate away from the morality issue in the Free State to one of a people bringing their values and beliefs to the rest of the world. It had, among other things, direct implications for women and their role in the new State.

Obviously women are the reproducers of the nation. According to the view expressed in the Dáil, their duty was not to try to control their fertility, but to have numerous children and send at least some of their children to populate 'new' lands and extend the influence of the Free State. The ideal was to have large families – fewer marriages and large families. Reproduction thus becomes a political act and family size a political concern.

Yet, according to the dominant discourse of the period, women did not have a public identity, nor did they belong in the public sphere. This was the basis of much of the gender legislation of the period which restricted their political and economic rights. The issue of birth control and the larger issue of reproduction revealed a contradiction in the heart of the government's attitude toward women. The debate on birth control revealed the emptiness, the hollowness of the claim that women could not be 'full' citizens because they were rooted in the family, because their activities were not political, but domestic. Birth control and family size were quite clearly a political, public issue which had ramifications for the image of the nation abroad.

It is also interesting to note that the debate on birth control reveals quite clearly the fact that legislation was often generated on the basis of prescriptive literature – articles, reports and sermons – and that this legislation had a great deal to do with image and the justification of identity. Based on a relatively affluent middle-class heterosexual model, this ideal did not resonate with the world of many women who had to work outside the home, for example, or who would have chosen to limit the size of their families had they had the opportunity, or who were forced to emigrate because their job prospects were limited by the government's policies. The reality of women's lives did not seem to impinge on the Irish political and ecclesiastical elite. They based their abstracted view of women on the prescriptive ideal of women as wives, mothers and carers. They needed women to be virtuous mothers and dutiful wives. It was vital to Irish identity. Real women were not part of this debate.

The abstract ideal of the virtuous mother and dutiful wife had serious consequences for all Irish women but its dominance was destabilized and challenged by various groups of women. As noted, virtuous motherhood was seen to be the means by which women served the State and were incorporated into the State. The emphasis was on virtuous. This meant, of course, that not any female body could be a mother: 'not just (any) body can be a citizen anymore, for some bodies have been marked by the State as non-productive of babies and no economic gain'.[30] Significant groups of Irish women were left out of this ideal. As the feminist theorist Diane Richardson has noted:

> In so far as the nation-state is constructed as heterosexual, this does not mean that all forms of heterosexuality are necessarily regarded equally. It is heterosexuality as marriage and the traditional, middle-class nuclear family that is commonly held up as a model of good citizenship, necessary for ensuring national security and a stable social order. By implication, other forms of heterosexuality, for instance, young women who are single mothers, imperil the nation.[31]

This clearly resonated with the Irish experience. Single heterosexual women, unmarried mothers and lesbians challenged the dominant ideal. Single women were clearly less valued than married women. In the gender hierarchy of the day, they were the most expendable. Legislation such as the Civil Service (Amendment) Act restricted their employment prospects and emigration records demonstrate the fact that single women left the country in significantly high numbers.

Lesbian women were not directly acknowledged or seen as part of the collectivity of Irish women who were pure and virtuous. During the various debates on sexuality, lesbianism is rarely directly mentioned. Homosexuality, for example, was condemned outright in the Carrigan Report but not lesbianism. It was, however, a subtext in the debate. For example, it is interesting to note that among the books specifically mentioned as suitable for banning during the censorship debate were books by Margaret Sanger, Maria Stopes and Radclyffe Hall's *The Well of Loneliness* – a clear indication of the link between motherhood, heterosexuality and citizenship.

Of all the women discussed in the Dáil and Seanad, the most important group of women in this particular discussion are those who stand in marked contrast to the virtuous 'Madonna' image of motherhood – those women who became mothers outside of marriage, especially those who had more than one child and were not in a State-sanctioned union. These women are marked as 'Eve', and were, in the words of the Minister for Justice, Mr Fitzgerald Kenney, 'a danger to the community'.[32] The contrast vividly demonstrates the construction of women's sexuality in the rigid Madonna/Eve dichotomy.

Debates in the Dáil and Seanad are useful in illuminating this division. During the debates on the Illegitimate Children (Affiliation Order) Bill of 1930, most of the views expressed by Senators and TDs about the nature of women tended to be within this stereotypical context. They reveal yet again one of the contradictions at the heart of government policy – while women were exhorted to be mothers, not all mothers were equally valued or accepted.

The Illegitimate Children (Affiliation Order) Bill was aimed at identifying putative fathers in order to force them to pay maintenance for their alleged child. On the one hand, women's groups, social workers and some priests who were involved in the moral purity crusade took up the defence of the unmarried mother who gave birth to her first child. The first child was an important qualifier because sympathy waned appreciably for women who had two or three children outside of State-sanctioned unions. In the main, this group saw first-time mothers as 'innocent victims' or 'ignorant girls' who were lured into sexual activity by 'male prowlers'.[33] Fr Devane, a leading light in the moral purity crusade, wrote that 'young blackguards ... roam the streets and frequent dance-halls for the purpose of seducing girls'.[34] Nor would he accept the charge of blackmail currently being hurled at these girls as being accurate. Devane cites the Sisters of the Good Shepherd convents in Ireland in 'denying the imputation' of blackmail. He also says that he 'consulted some of the most experienced Dublin priests and heads of the Dublin Rescue societies ... They were in unqualified agreement with the Sisters' views.' Moreover, they maintained that far from alleging blackmail the 'difficulty was often times experienced in inducing girls to give any information about their seducers, no matter how they had been wronged'.[35] These women were described as overcome by the shame of what they had done and the disgrace which they had brought upon their families. Their advocates wished to see legal reforms – such as legal proceedings held in camera and the naming of the putative father – which would protect these girls from unwanted publicity and afford them some financial recompense.

Those who opposed giving such protection or advantages to the unmarried mother repeatedly spoke of her as a 'seductress' and very frequently mentioned the opportunity for blackmail which would present itself, for example, if a putative father were named before the truth of the allegation could be verified. Examples were given of unscrupulous female servants who tried to take advantage of their employers or who named the most prosperous of their acquaintances as the alleged father. As the Minister for Justice noted:

> some Senators seem to be of the opinion that all girls are virtuous girls, and that men are always responsible when girls fall. That, of course, is not the fact at all. It has to be recognised that there are a considerable number of immoral women in the world. It is quite possible that a woman through her own fault, may apply for a fourth, fifth or even sixth affiliation order.[36]

Not only were not all girls virtuous, but the Minister was at pains to point out that not all mothers were virtuous:

> Senators should remember also that all mothers are not completely virtuous women. If a girl is in the family way, and there is the possibility of the real father of the child being a pauper, and if there is somebody of substantial means against whom the charge could be made, though he is innocent ... there will be a tremendous temptation in the case of a great number of mothers to urge their daughters to make a charge against that innocent person.[37]

And, in a remarkably revealing statement of class bias, the Minister went on to say:

> I do not say that would happen in the case of a respectable woman whose daughter fell by accident. There are, however, certain classes of people and illegitimacy seems to be almost hereditary with them. The mothers are illegitimate. In my opinion an illegitimate mother who has got an illegitimate daughter, would be just the type of person who would urge that daughter to bring a charge of that kind.[38]

The Minister's sentiments encapsulated much of the thinking of Irish political leaders at the time concerning women, their virtues, their purity or the lack thereof. Above all, it demonstrated both the complexity and ambiguity surrounding motherhood as an institution.

Motherhood was women's service to the State. Located in the family, it was the basis for their participation in the State and central to a definition of Irish identity. But what the morality legislation of the period seemed to indicate was the underlying belief that, in the very important question of identity, of purity and morality, women were failing to be the paragons of virtue they were alleged to be in sermon and song. Hence women could not be trusted to act in what was perceived to be the best interests of the nation. Legislation was, therefore, necessary to ensure that they would act in a correct manner. In fact, women seemed to be more Eve than Madonna, not up to the task of being the markers of Irish moral superiority. Thus, it was necessary for the political sphere, the realm of men, to intrude upon the domestic sphere, the realm of women, and generate legislation.

The Free State had a particular type of motherhood in mind for its self-definition. Not just (any) body could be a mother – issues of sexual orientation, of class, of status, of respectability came into play. As a number of theorists have noted, citizenship is closely associated with ideas about moral behaviour: what is and is not considered fit and proper conduct.[39] Clearly it was not simply about reproducing the nation. It was about reproducing the nation with virtue which demanded nothing less than virtuous mothers and dutiful wives. The control of Irish women's sexuality was too important to be left simply to women.

NOTES

1. This chapter was developed from a paper presented at the Women's History Association, Ireland at University College Cork, 2006.
2. Rev. R.S. Devane, SJ, 'The Unmarried Mother – Some Legal Aspects of the Problem', *Irish Ecclesiastical Record*, XXIII (January 1924), pp.55–68.
3. Article 41.2, 1937 Constitution cited in J.M. Kelly, *The Irish Constitution* (Dublin: Jurist Publishing Co., University College Dublin, 1984, 2nd Edition).
4. These acts were the Juries Acts of 1924 and 1927, the Civil Service Amendment Act of

1925, the Marriage Bar of 1931 which first applied to married women teachers and was later extended to the entire civil service, and the Conditions of Employment Act of 1935.
5. Catholic doctrine asserting that women's place was in the home was articulated in papal encyclicals, Lenten pastorals and articles in the Catholic press.
6. Letter to the Editor, *Irish Independent*, 6 October 1928, p.8 from Mary Cosgrave, Chairwoman, Women's Citizens and Local Government Association.
7. Carole Pateman, 'Equality, Difference, Subordination: The Politics of Motherhood and Women's Citizenship', in Gisela Bock and Susan James (eds), *Beyond Equality and Difference* (London: Routledge, 1992), pp.18–19.
8. Article 41.1, 1937 Constitution cited in Kelly, *The Irish Constitution.*
9. *Irish Press*, 27 June 1932.
10. Editorial, *Irish Times*, 9 March 1927, p.6.
11. *Report*, Committee on the Criminal Law amendment Act and the Question of Juvenile Prostitution [Carrigan Report]. Department of the Taoiseach files, National Archives, S5998, 1930.
12. *Cork Examiner*, 30 November 1925.
13. *Irish Independent*, 13 October 1926.
14. *Irish Independent*, 28 February 1927.
15. *Memorandum* on the Report of the Committee on the Criminal Law Amendment Act and the Question of Juvenile Prostitution [Carrigan Report], Department of Justice, 27 October 1932, p.13.
16. *Seanad Debates*, Vol.12, 11 April 1929, Censorship of Publications Bill, 1928, col. 114.
17. *Irish Independent*, 25 October 1924.
18. Ibid.
19. *Report*, Committee on the Criminal Law Amendment and the Question of Juvenile Prostitution [Carrigan Report].
20. Dáil Debates, Vol. 53, 1 August 1934, Criminal Law Amendment Bill, col.2020. For a discussion of infanticide, see Clíona Rattigan's chapter in this volume.
21. *Seanad Debates*, Vol.19, 12 December 1934, Criminal Law Amendment Bill, col.794–795.
22. The Censorship Bill was primarily concerned with 'immoral literature' and much of the debate centred on establishing the mechanism whereby literature so deemed could be censored. Under this provision, literature advocating birth control was to be prohibited.
23. The Criminal Law Amendment Act was primarily concerned with issues of juvenile prostitution and the age of consent. As part of this discussion, contraceptive devices were outlawed.
24. *Irish Independent*, 18 October 1928, p.7.
25. Mary E. Daly, 'The Irish Family Since the Famine: Continuity and Change', *Irish Journal of Feminist Studies*, 3, 2 (Autumn, 1999), p.14.
26. France, for example, despite its anti-clerical government, was firmly against practices of birth control.
27. *Seanad Debates*, Vol.12, 11 April 1929, Censorship of Publications Bill, 1928, cols. 128–129.
28. For a discussion of emigration in the Free State, please see Jennifer Redmond's chapter in this volume.
29. *Seanad Debates*, Vol.12, 11 April 1929, Censorship of Publications Bill, 1928, cols. 72–73.
30. Alexander M. Jacqui, 'Not Just (Any) Body Can be a Citizen: The Politics of Law, Sexuality and Postcoloniality in Trinidad and Tobago and the Bahamas', *Feminist Review*, 48 (Autumn 1994), p.6.
31. Diane Richardson, *Re-Thinking Sexuality* (London: Sage Publications, 2000), p.80.
32. *Dáil Eireann Debates*, Vol. 33, 12 February 1930, Illegitimate Children (Affiliation Order) Bill, col.131.
33. *Report*, Committee on the Criminal Law Amendment Act and the Question of Juvenile Prostitution [Carrigan Report], p.20.
34. Rev. R.S. Devane, SJ, 'The Legal Protection of Girls'. Irish Ecclesiastical Record, Fifth Series, 37 (February 1931), pp.20-40.
35. Ibid.
36. Seanad Debates, Vol.13, 19 March 1930, Illegitimate Children (Affiliation Order) Bill, cols. 708–709.
37. Ibid.
38. Ibid.
39. Richardson, *Re-thinking Sexuality*, p.88.

CHAPTER EIGHT

'Crimes of passion of the worst character':[1] *Abortion Cases and Gender in Ireland, 1925–50*

CLÍONA RATTIGAN

In his address to the jury in an abortion case that was tried in the circuit criminal court in Dublin in June 1945, Judge McCarthy stated that:

> The woman who takes part in a matter of this kind is regarded by the law, by public opinion, by justice, with a very serious eye. In the woman it is bad. In the man it must be infinitely worse. He takes no risk. He submits to no operation. His life is not put in jeopardy at the hands of the Mrs Moloneys of this world with their needles; he merely supplies the money to hire the professional abortionist so that he can get rid of the responsibility he has brought upon himself and upon the girl as a result of his own shameful conduct.[2]

The judge clearly regarded men who covered the cost of their girlfriends' abortions with contempt and considered that their conduct was far more reprehensible than that of women who submitted to such illegal operations. How accurate was his assessment of the gender dynamics at play in these cases? Did the women who 'submitted' to such operations do so against their will? Were men who were anxious to get rid of the responsibility of a pregnancy outside marriage the driving force behind these criminal transactions?

SINGLE WOMEN AND ABORTION

This chapter focuses on unmarried Irish women who had abortions or attempted to abort between 1925 and 1950. Some women were assisted by their male partners, while others consulted female friends or made arrangements with abortionists on their own. 'Abortion for the purpose of fertility control', as McAvoy has noted, 'was a criminal act' during the period under review and under Section 58 of the 1861 Offences Against the Person Act 'all parties to abortion, including the woman seeking the operation, faced penalties up to life imprisonment'.[3] My research is based on the records of twelve cases tried in Northern Ireland and twenty cases that came before the courts in the South between 1925 and 1950. The sample for this chapter includes cases of criminal abortion involving unmarried women that were tried in the Circuit Court and Central Criminal Court as well as cases that went before the Court of Criminal Appeal, and catalogued abortion cases involving single women that are held in the Public Record Office of Northern Ireland. A further two cases quoted in this chapter were sourced in police files in the National Archives, Kew and involved Irish women who died as the result of abortions in London. As McAvoy has observed, 'given the scale of emigration of women from Ireland to Britain ... it is likely that there was a high level of awareness of the possibility of obtaining "back-street" abortions in England. For those with that knowledge and sufficient funds, or contacts they could visit in Britain, it was an option.'[4] The full names of individuals in cases quoted in this chapter are available in the original material. Individuals who feature in cases held in the National Archives of Ireland and the National Archives, Kew are referred to by their first names and the initial of their surnames, except where the individuals are well known and have been named in other studies, such as William Coleman. As infanticide cases in the Public Record Office of Northern Ireland are subject to a one hundred year rule I am unable to identify defendants by name.

Some Irish women who had emigrated to Britain during the period under consideration were certainly aware of the abortion networks in existence there. At least one Irish woman died as the result of a back-street abortion obtained in England during the period under review and another Irish woman died following an attempt to self-abort. In September 1929 Margaret R. was found dead on the pavement outside 16 King's Place in London.[5] Margaret was originally from Co. Wexford and had been living in London for five years when she died as the result of an abortion. In June 1938 Moira S. died in Manchester as the result of self-abortion.[6] She may have been Irish. The police had very little information on her but one woman who read a report about police attempts to trace the woman's relatives contacted them to say that she had employed an Irish girl of that name and description as a maid a number of months before her death. In another instance, Rita N. died as the result of peritonitis in London in October 1925. She did not have an abortion in London but left Dublin for London following an attempt to self-abort.

Abortion was undoubtedly a dangerous procedure at the time. Some single Irish women became seriously ill following attempts to control their fertility by resorting to abortion. In his deposition Dr. Alex Spain, master of the National Maternity Hospital, stated that Ellen T. was 'gravely ill' when she was first admitted to hospital.[7] She was suffering from peritonitis following a 'backstreet' abortion, which was allegedly performed by Mary Anne Cadden in October 1944. A total of seven single women in this sample died as a result of attempts to self-abort or as the result of abortions performed by others. Two cases came before the courts in Northern Ireland during the period under review where investigations were begun shortly before the women died. E.B. made a short statement to police 'having the fear of death before [her] and being without hope of recovery'.[8] A special court was held at A.B.'s bedside before her death.[9]

Unmarried, pregnant women who aborted during the period under review were usually desperate to avoid the stigma associated with single motherhood. According to a report in the *Irish Times* in June 1944, Karmel M. had 'begged' medical student John S. 'to remove the dead foetus because she was unmarried and did not want to go to hospital'.[10] John S. said that he 'had urged her to go to hospital, but she refused, as she was not married'.[11] Karmel's reluctance to seek medical attention in a maternity hospital is perhaps understandable in light of the attitudes towards unmarried mothers held by members of hospital committees, hospital staff and patients in many parts of Ireland at the time. Indeed there is plenty of evidence to suggest that members of some hospital committees and county health boards were hostile towards single expectant women who sought admittance to maternity wards during the period.[12] The women in this sample belonged to a society that condemned unmarried motherhood without qualification and offered little support for single mothers and their children.

As Arnot and Usborne noted in their study on gender and crime, the records of criminal trials often 'give precious insights into private relations usually hidden from history because they are deemed too intimate to be openly discussed'.[13] This is certainly true of abortion cases that were tried in Ireland between 1925 and 1950. The records of abortion cases that came before the courts during the period under review contain detailed information about the private lives of unmarried couples.

Little is known about how couples dealt with the prospect of an unplanned pregnancy outside marriage in Ireland between 1925 and 1950 and studies on abortion have often overlooked the role played by men in cases that went to trial. This chapter will explore the role played by men and women in abortion cases that came before the courts in Ireland, both North and South, between 1925 and 1950 and through a micro-level analysis of a small number of abortion cases, will examine the gender dynamics that led to a couple's decision to terminate an unplanned pregnancy. The records of a further two cases involving the deaths of two single Irish women in London, as the result of a backstreet abortion or through attempted self-abortion, will also be discussed.

The records of criminal trials are undoubtedly a rich historical source. However, the evidence in some of the cases quoted in this chapter is quite complex. In a small number of cases, moreover, a woman's and a man's versions of events were completely at odds with each other. For instance, while Sheila D. alleged that her employer, Harold M., had sexual intercourse with her on a regular basis, advised her to take abortifacients and sent her to England to seek an abortion, Harold denied all involvement in the affair and claimed that Sheila had told 'a pack of lies' in court.[14] In October 1949, Margaret A. alleged that brothers Robert and John T. had given her abortifacient drugs in order to cause her to miscarry. A Garda investigation followed. However, it later emerged that there was no substance to the allegations and Margaret admitted that she had been motivated to bring charges against the brothers in order to gain revenge as she had been insulted and rejected by Robert T., the man she claimed was responsible for her pregnancy. Both men were found not guilty by direction in the Central Criminal Court in February 1950. Therefore, a considerable degree of caution must be exercised when dealing with these records.

The records of abortion trials afford the researcher access to intimate aspects of the personal lives of both men and women and often shed light on 'the dramas enacted between women and men as sexual partners'.[15] However, the voices that emerge from the statements taken by the police and in the transcripts of trials are voices that were shaped and controlled to varying degrees by the investigator and the prosecutor. Yet, even allowing for the coercive environment of disclosure, the records of criminal trials undoubtedly remain an invaluable source.

'IN A STATE OF GREAT MENTAL DISTURBANCE'

Testifying in an abortion trial in Dublin in 1931, Dr. Paul Carton said that single women 'go mad when they are pregnant' and are inclined to 'do anything'.[16] Dr. O'Donnell Browne asserted that practically every single girl who becomes pregnant 'is in a state of great mental disturbance'.[17] The prospect of lone motherhood would undoubtedly have been extremely stressful and worrying for single Irish women who found themselves pregnant during the period under review. This would be particularly true for women whose partners were not supportive or understanding of them in their predicament. It is certainly clear from the cases in this sample that single women became extremely anxious when faced with an unplanned pregnancy and were often willing to take considerable risks in order to seek an abortion. Three examples will suffice. Judith M. told the court that she consulted two doctors in order to determine if she was pregnant. She said that she made an appointment with a second doctor because she felt that she would not get the result from the first doctor quickly enough. She did this, she said, 'because [she] was very nervous about it and [she] was rather frightened and [she] wanted to know quickly'.[18] Dennis B. recalled how Karmel M. 'seemed to be in a semi-hysterical condition wanting something done about it' shortly after she realised that she was pregnant.[19] As Mr McGilligan pointed out in court, Karmel M. was 'undoubtedly in distress' when she realized that she was pregnant and began taking ergot which made her ill.[20] She was also in danger of losing her job. If she carried her pregnancy to term she would have had to leave her job 'without being in a position to earn anything.'[21] In March 1947, Josephine M. asked Kathleen Gilbourne 'to do something for her to get rid of her pregnancy'.[22] She allegedly said that she would drown herself if Mrs Gilbourne refused to assist her.

Most women in this sample would have found it extremely difficult to raise an infant on their own limited means and many single women who tried to terminate their pregnancies between 1925 and 1950 would have been anxious to avoid the shame associated with single motherhood. Some women may have feared that they would lose their jobs if their employers learned that they were pregnant. As Cooper Graves noted in relation to women who deliberately chose to commit infanticide in Victorian England, such a course of action 'could not only save women from economic ruin, it could release her from being held a lifelong hostage to the constraints imposed by motherhood'.[23] This is also true of single pregnant women who contacted abortionists or attempted to self-abort during the period under review. Women like Bridie K. and Margaret B. who had already given birth would have known from experience how difficult it was to raise an infant on their own limited means. Moreover, women who had already given birth outside wedlock may have been reluctant to tell their relatives and friends that they were pregnant for a second or third time. While some families may have been willing to accept one child born outside wedlock they may not have been prepared to accept a second transgression. This may have motivated single pregnant women to seek an abortion.

'THIS GIRL IS GETTING VERY EMBARRASSED'[24]

Single women who had sought abortions were often the main witnesses for the State when the cases went to trial. As Mr Moore pointed out in an abortion case that came before the courts in 1944, 'it was not customary to prosecute a woman on whom an abortion had been performed'.[25] McAvoy has noted that 'women traced by police, whose depositions are in State Files, and who appear to have given evidence for the prosecution, were presumably advised that they might avoid prosecution by co-operating'.[26] In most cases women who had undergone illegal abortions were subject to lengthy and detailed cross-examination in court. Bridie K.'s cross-examination was 'of a most comprehensive and testing character and extended over many hours'.[27] When Carrie D. was asked to describe how the abortionist carried out the procedure she turned to the judge to enquire if she was obliged to answer the question. Carrie was clearly uncomfortable as 'there [were] men on the balcony' of the courtroom listening to her evidence.[28] Judith M. said that it was 'very disagreeable' for her to have to give evidence in court.[29] It is perhaps understandable that Judith M. would have found it disagreeable to give evidence in court given that she was questioned about private aspects of her personal life. During the course of her cross-examination Judith was asked when she first began having sexual intercourse with Alphonsus M., whether they used contraceptives, and if they ever had sexual intercourse 'in the precincts of Trinity College'.[30] She was also asked whether she practised her faith. The barristers who defended those charged with procuring abortion clearly attempted to discredit single women who had had illegal abortions and who were called on to give evidence against their clients in court.

MEN AND ABORTION

Many abortions in Ireland were carried out by women and in some cases the trial records contain no references to the man who was responsible for a single woman's pregnancy. However, men were at the centre of a number of abortion trials that came before the courts during the period under review. Charges were brought against the male partners of twelve unmarried women in this sample. Although the boyfriends or fiancés of three more women in this sample provided their pregnant girlfriends with financial assistance and helped them establish contact with abortionists, they were not charged. Male involvement clearly varied from case to case and their input ranged from advising their girlfriends to jump off tables, to making arrangements with an abortionist.

Margaret A. said that when she informed her boyfriend that '[her] periods were stopped' he allegedly advised her 'to get up on a table and jump off it and [she] would be all right'.[31] Sheila D. said that Harold M., her employer and the man allegedly responsible for her pregnancy, told her to take some quinine-sulphate tablets when she told him that she 'feared that [she] might be pregnant'.[32] He later told her to 'try a few really high jumps'.[33] John D. said that when he realised that Bridie K. was two months pregnant he made arrangements with a nurse 'to fix her up'.[34]

In her study of infanticide in Chicago between 1870 and 1930, Oberman noted that while 'a determined and resourceful pregnant woman could have identified an abortionist and borrowed the money needed to secure an illegal abortion', 'a more passive or socially isolated woman might have desired an abortion but have been unable to locate or afford one'.[35] Poor, single women living in rural areas of Ireland without the knowledge or financial means to seek an abortion and without partners to provide them with money or to make contact with abortionists on their behalf were perhaps more inclined to commit infanticide. Rose has noted that while Ireland had a relatively low rate of illegal abortion in comparison with Northern Ireland, Scotland, Wales and England 'they have also had during the same period the highest rates of infanticide, concealment of childbirth and abandonment of children under two years of age, than has had any of the areas investigated in the British Isles'.[36]

Many unmarried women who were charged with the murder or concealment of birth of their illegitimate infants between 1925 and 1950 seem to have been poorly informed about pregnancy and childbirth.

Few, if any, single women charged with the murder or concealment of birth of their illegitimate infants seem to have used any form of contraception.[37] At least two women in this sample who terminated their pregnancies had used contraception on a regular basis and some women had had more than one abortion. Judith M.'s fiancé said that he 'always used contraceptives except in the safe periods, immediately before and immediately after menstruations'.[38] Alphonsus M. usually purchased the contraceptives in Northern Ireland but he had also bought them from Northern students in Trinity College 'a couple of times'.[39] Margaret R.'s fiancé told police that 'every time [he] had intercourse with Miss R. [he] took precaution not to put her in the family way'.[40] He went on to explain that these precautions 'consisted of withdrawing and sometimes [he] used a French letter'.[41] In his statement he also mentioned the fact that Margaret used a whirling spray after intercourse. Some couples relied on *coitus interruptus*. When he was questioned in court Dennis B. referred to the fact that *coitus interruptus* was 'the usual practice' with Karmel M.[42] However, other couples did not use any form of fertility control. As McLaren noted, 'for some abortion was a primary, rather than a back-up, method of birth control'.[43] This is evident in a small number of cases in this sample. When asked if he adopted 'practices against conception' Marks R. admitted that he had adopted 'none whatsoever' even though he had sex frequently with Bridie K.[44]

Some of the single women in this sample may have been better educated and more confident and resourceful than most of the unmarried women who were charged with the murder or concealment of birth of their newborn infants in Ireland between 1925 and 1950. Harold M., who was charged with procuring the miscarriage of Sheila D. in January 1950, told the court that Sheila 'has considerable intelligence and verve ... she is definitely lively and intelligent and has talent in the things she does'.[45] According to Judge Davitt, 19-year-old Trinity student, Judith M., who was the main witness for the State in the case against William Coleman in July 1944 was 'perhaps, not the ordinary or quite ordinary type. She is not very conventional.'[46] Judith M. was well educated, self-assured and admitted to being a lapsed Catholic who made up her own mind about questions of morality. A second-year student of English and Spanish, she had considered sitting the scholarship examinations in Trinity College before she became pregnant.

In some cases the attitudes and actions of the men they had been involved with seemed to have impacted on a woman's decision to seek an abortion. According to Brookes, between 1900 and 1967

English men frequently assisted their wives' efforts to abort. Brookes referred to the cases of Edith Daynes and Frances Smedley, who were both aided by men in their attempt to procure an abortion and argued that it was because of the men in their lives that both women had 'the knowledge and resources necessary to seek a 'backstreet' abortion'.[47] Brookes has asserted that 'in each of these cases ... the woman's decision was influenced by the attitude of the man responsible for the pregnancy'.[48] It is surely significant that four single women who sought abortions in Dublin and Cork between 1939 and 1950 were having affairs with older, married businessmen who were in a position to provide them with money and contacts.

'IT COULDN'T TAKE PLACE WITHOUT THAT MONEY'

Access to financial assistance was essential for single women who wished to terminate an unplanned pregnancy. Although the evidence in a 1948 Co. Laois case and in several cases that came before the courts in Northern Ireland demonstrated that some abortionists catered for poorer women, the fees charged by Dublin-based abortionists such as William Coleman, Christopher Williams and Mary Moloney meant that abortions were out of reach for most single, working-class women who were faced with an unwanted pregnancy during the period under review.

Thirteen men in this sample provided their pregnant girlfriends with financial assistance.[49] Such financial assistance was vital, particularly considering that most of the women who were implicated in these cases were not well-paid. Most of the women in this sample worked as shop assistants or domestic servants and would not, therefore, have been able to pay for an abortion or for abortifacient drugs on their own. Convicted abortionists Moloney and Williams generally charged between £25 and £35, while Alphonsus M. allegedly paid William Coleman £60 to terminate his fiancée's pregnancy in March 1944.

Some women were clearly dependent on their partners for financial assistance. Karmel M. was unable to cover the cost of an abortion herself and was reliant on Dennis B., a man she had slept with on a number of occasions, to provide her with the necessary money. Karmel M. wrote to Dennis shortly after she realized that she was pregnant to ask him if he could provide her with the money she needed to pay for a backstreet abortion more quickly: 'perhaps you will think the matter over in the meantime and let me know if there is any possibility of speeding things up', she wrote.[50] The couple had already discussed the matter but Karmel appeared anxious to have her pregnancy terminated as soon as possible as it was affecting her ability to work. 'As I have been feeling desperately ill all week, I have been wondering whether it would be possible to get the operation done next Sunday afternoon', Karmel wrote.[51] She was clearly afraid that she might lose her job. 'I have had to knock off work three times this week and of course there are questions being asked. I have been taking very strong doses of ergot and this has left me very weak – as I was warned it would do – and standing for eight hours a day doesn't improve matters ... frankly I'm in dread of losing this job'. Karmel's final remark in her letter to Dennis B. underscored her sense of dependency on him. 'Needless to say, I'll fall in with any suggestion you make', she remarked before signing off. Karmel was clearly grateful to Dennis for the financial assistance he provided. Following a successful termination she wrote to him and thanked him for his help. She told him that he had 'faced up to it decently' and wished him good luck.[52] However, it is also clear that if unmarried pregnant women whose boyfriends did not provide financial assistance were determined to terminate their pregnancies and had access to financial resources or useful contacts, then they would seek an illegal abortion.

When addressing the jury during Dennis B.'s trial, Judge Davitt noted that the man allegedly responsible for Karmel M.'s pregnancy 'provided the means which were the only means of enabling the operation to take place. It couldn't take place without that money.'[53] This was true, not only in the Dennis B. case, but in a number of other cases. When questioned in court during George J.'s trial in June 1945, Carrie D. said that she would have been unable to pay the fee that Mrs Maloney charged. Although Carrie worked in a furrier's at the time, she said she 'had no money and ... would not have been able to pay'.[54] Under cross-examination George J. admitted that 'no such job would enable her to pay for this operation out of her own earnings'.[55] It seemed more than likely that he had paid for the cost of the procedure. The situation was similar in the Netherlands. In his study on cultures of abortion in The Hague in the early twentieth century de Blécourt argued that 'on the whole ... it was mainly lovers who felt responsible and found other men to perform the operation. They made the appointment, paid 50 or 100 or even 200 guilders for it.'[56]

Some men were undoubtedly glad to be relieved of the burden of having to pay for the maintenance of an illegitimate child and were content to pay towards the cost of backstreet abortions or abortifacient drugs. Before sentencing Dennis B. in June 1944, Judge Davitt said that the defendant was not 'very young suddenly submitted to temptation' but a 'man who had taken his fun where he found it and was glad to pay his proportion of the cost' towards Karmel M.'s abortion.[57] In her study of women and reproduction in Britain between 1860 and 1939 Brookes referred to a case where the man responsible for a single woman's pregnancy 'was happy to pay her father for his part in her pregnancy rather than marry her'.[58] Part of the sum of money paid to her father, according to Brookes, seems to have gone towards the cost of an abortion. De Blécourt has argued that in The Hague in the early twentieth century 'an unwritten rule on the abortion market appears to have been that the responsibility of boyfriends or lovers for pre- or extra-marital pregnancies entailed a large sum of money, in contrast to the small sum women usually paid. It was expected on both sides as proper restitution of the woman's honour, at least as long as marriage was not considered.'[59]

'I GOT THE PILLS AND SENT THEM TO HER TO TAKE TO HELP HER OUT'

Seven men in this sample bought abortifacient drugs for their girlfriends or gave them the money to purchase the drugs. Abortifacient drugs were often a first option for couples who wished to terminate a pregnancy. If the drugs failed to take effect then couples often considered seeking an abortion. When Bridie K. told Marks R. that the pills she had taken 'were not doing any good and were awful to take', he allegedly told her 'that there would be an illegal operation done'.[60] In January 1939 G.H. was charged with unlawfully supplying 'a noxious thing called Dr. Raspail's Female Pills, containing steel, pennyroyal and bitterapple, knowing that the same was intended to be unlawfully used with intent to procure the miscarriage of a woman named A.G.', the woman with whom he was involved.[61] When he was arrested G.H. told police that he knew that 'the girl A.G. was in trouble and in the family way'. He also admitted sending her pills 'to help her out'. He said he sent her 'a couple of bottles of them' in November or December 1938. In her statement A.G. said that when she realized that she was pregnant she wrote to G.H. and

> asked him if he could do anything for me. He replied stating that he would procure some pills which I should take to bring it away. About the end of that month I received from him by post about two dozen pills in a packet and he told me that he had purchased them in Mr P.'s Chemist shop, A. They were known as Dr.

> Raspail's Female Pills and bore that name in print on the outside of the packet. H. instructed me to take one of the pills three times daily after meals. I did as he directed and took all the pills but they had no effect on my condition.[62]

G.H. wrote several letters to his pregnant girlfriend in November and December 1938. The letters were later used as evidence against him in his trial. It is clear from G.H.'s letters that both he and A.G. hoped that the abortifacient drugs he had sent her by mail would cause her to miscarry. The level of anxiety the couple experienced seemed to intensify in each letter, as it became increasingly unlikely that the pills would have the desired effect. In mid-December 1938, about a fortnight after A. had first started taking Dr. Raspail's pills, G. began to discuss the possibility of A. undergoing 'a slight operation'. G. told A. that he hoped that the tablets would be effective as 'the next remedy does not seem very pleasant'.[63]

'HE SAID HE HAD FOUND A DOCTOR WHO WOULD PUT THINGS RIGHT WITH ME'

A number of men implicated in abortion cases between 1925 and 1950 established contact with abortionists on behalf of their girlfriends or made inquiries about men or women who would be willing to terminate a pregnancy and put their girlfriends in touch with such people. The man Elizabeth H. had been keeping company with approached Kathleen Gilbourne in February 1947 when Elizabeth was two months pregnant. He said '[he] asked Mrs Gilbourne if she could do anything for a girl that was pregnant and she said she would if [he] would bring the girl up to her house'.[64] In the case of Judith M., while her fiancé Alphonsus M. did not pay for her pregnancy to be terminated – Judith M. approached a friend and told him that she was in 'a frightful jam' and needed seventy pounds – he supported her decision and he arranged an appointment for her with William Coleman.[65]

In the letters he sent to his pregnant girlfriend, G.H. made it clear that he had made a number of enquiries about abortionists. He told his girlfriend that he had spoken to a chemist. In another Northern case G.C. told police that he had discussed his girlfriend's pregnancy with 'a good few people' before he brought her to see a chemist in Belfast in September 1945.[66] He said that 'contact was made for [him]' with the chemist who performed the abortion. G. said that his girlfriend, who subsequently died, 'did most of the talking' to the chemist when they got to Belfast.[67] However, it is clear that he had helped to organize the abortion.

Sheila D. told *gardaí* that when the abortifacients she had taken failed to work, Harold M. arranged for her to visit a doctor in London. Sheila said that Harold gave her the address of a doctor to go to, as well as £120 to cover her travelling expenses, hotel expenses and the doctor's fees. He also gave her a gold ring to wear. 'He said he had found a doctor who would put things right with me. When I said I didn't like the thoughts of this, – when I said that, he said it would be nothing at all, – just D.N.C. The D.N. I don't remember but the C. is for curette.'[68] Sheila travelled to London by air on the 21st January 1950 and took a taxi to the address Harold M. had given her.

Men also provided what could be termed moral support by accompanying a woman to the abortionist and bringing her home afterwards. Six men in this sample accompanied their girlfriend to abortionists. Although none of the men were present when the abortion was being carried out, they waited until the abortionist had completed the procedure and in most cases they then accompanied their girlfriend home. Alphonsus M. said that after his fiancée[69] had had an abortion 'she appeared to be very shaken indeed when she came out of the dressing room. She was very pale and she was alarmingly weak. She could not walk. She just hopped over to where I was. She sat down at the desk when she came out of the dressing room, for four or five minutes, and when we went away I had to help her along the street.'[70] Charles W. brought Elizabeth H. to Mrs Gilbourne's house and waited outside while Mrs Gilbourne attempted to cause her to miscarry. Margaret R.'s fiancé Frederick J. accompanied her to the abortionist's house and waited outside for her. Usborne uncovered evidence of similar forms of support and co-operation in the records of German abortion cases. Having studied the records of 200 cases of criminal abortion in the Weimar Republic Usborne noted that in most cases, men accompanied their pregnant partners to the abortionist and some even provided assistance during the procedure. 'Most men accompanied women to the operation and at least 18 husbands and 7 lovers were also present during the operation, giving moral support and even practical help like holding the lamp.'[71]

There are other examples of the ways in which men assisted their girlfriends after an abortion. Two men in this sample seem to have disposed of the foetus once their girlfriends had miscarried. L.C. told police that A.B., the woman he had been keeping company with, informed him when she miscarried and gave him a parcel and asked him to burn it. He said that '[he] took the parcel, brought it to Belfast with [him] and dropped it in the Lagan'.[72] Bridie K. claimed that after she had miscarried Marks R., the man who was responsible for her pregnancy, took the foetus away and burnt it. 'I told R. I had been in pain all night and that the baby had come away – that he would have to do something with it as I would not have anything to do with it. I showed it to him and he rolled it up in paper, and he put it in his pocket. I saw him the next day and asked him what he did with it and he told me that he burned it.'[73]

After she had had a successful abortion Karmel M. wrote to the man who was responsible for her pregnancy and who had provided her with the money she needed in order to pay for an abortion, to inform him that she had 'ended up as an emergency case in Holles Street Hospital' but that she was no longer pregnant.[74] In one of the letters Karmel wrote to Denis B. she remarked, 'you will be relieved I'm sure to know that everything is successfully over with'. Karmel told Denis that the 'last four months have been like a horrible nightmare'. 'I cannot tell you how relieved and happy I am to know that the worry and sickness is at an end', she wrote.[75] The ordeal of an unplanned pregnancy and an illegal abortion clearly put a strain on heterosexual relationships and could, as Usborne has observed, exacerbate 'existing tensions between partners'.[76]

'FIGGIS WAS VERY UPSET AT THE DEATH OF THE YOUNG WOMAN WHO WAS THE SUBJECT OF THE HENDON INQUEST'

Some men were deeply affected by the deaths of partners who died after attempting to terminate an unplanned pregnancy. When Rita N., a 21-year-old Irish woman died in London in October 1925 as the result of peritonitis, following an abortion, the body of the man who was responsible for her condition was found in a gas filled hotel room just over a week after her death. One newspaper noted that Darrell Figgis, a writer, Sinn Féin activist and politician, who had been responsible for Rita N.'s condition 'was very upset at the death of the young woman'.[77] He was apparently unaware that she had injected glycerine into her womb until after her death. When one of the doctors who had treated Rita informed Figgis that his deceased girlfriend had used a syringe and glycerine in order to cause a miscarriage he apparently 'looked very astonished, but said nothing and went away very excited'.[78] Rita joined Darrell in London after her attempt to self-abort in September 1925. She had informed him that she was pregnant and that she had experienced violent pains, which she said she could not understand but she never informed him that she had tried to self-abort. She had begun to miscarry by the time she reached London and was later hospitalised. Rita eventually told the doctor who treated her that she 'used a syringe with a long narrow nozzle which [she] got from a chemist's'. She said that 'there was glycerine in it and [she] disinfected the syringe before using it'.[79] The knowledge that Rita had tried to abort and her subsequent death is likely to have been a major factor in Figgis' suicide.

'MISS M. WAS AN ACTIVE AGENT'[80]

Some women did not refer to the men responsible for their pregnancies in their statements. Margaret B. did not name the man who was responsible for her pregnancy. She seems to have made arrangements to terminate her pregnancy on her own. She said that she went to see William Coleman in December 1936, 'told him [she] was pregnant and asked him if he could do something for [her]'.[81] Neither S.B. nor H.R., who had had abortions in Belfast in 1930 and 1937 respectively, mentioned the men who were responsible for their pregnancies. Their boyfriends were not suspected of having been involved in the cases. In fact, both women seem to have approached other women for information about abortionists.

In her study of abortion in England from 1900 to 1967 Brookes uncovered evidence of a female subculture where 'working-class women shared information and helped each other procure abortion when necessary'.[82] According to Brookes 'the reputations of amateurs and doctors who "helped" women spread quickly'.[83] She argued that there seemed to have been a 'freemasonry amongst women'[84] as workmates, friends or neighbours often knew a 'woman who knows another woman' with whom they could get in touch.[85]

From the records of abortion cases tried in Belfast between 1930 and 1945 it is evident that such a female subculture also existed in Northern Ireland. McAvoy has noted how a 1948 Co. Laois abortion case offered 'insight into a rarely documented rural, working-class women's culture in which women assisted each other in pregnancy and childbirth without reference to the medical profession and in which the knowledge that it was possible to terminate pregnancies passed by word of mouth'.[86] Karmel M.'s friend, Mabel, may have helped put her in touch with John S., a Nigerian medical student who was charged with terminating her pregnancy. Maureen F.'s workmate put her in touch with a man who introduced her to an abortionist. Maureen was employed as a waitress in the Savoy restaurant on Dublin's O'Connell Street. When she confided in her fellow employee, Elizabeth T., about her unwanted pregnancy, Elizabeth put her in contact with George Ian McCabe who in turn introduced her to abortionist Christopher Williams. Usborne found that in Weimar Germany 'an unwanted pregnancy constituted a crisis that activated single-sex networks' and that 'if women desired an artificial miscarriage they turned to a female network of information and support and they preferred a female to a male abortionist.'[87] Although some single, pregnant women in this sample turned to female acquaintances for advice, most single women who had abortions in Dublin during the period under review did not turn to a female network of information and support. Nor do they appear to have preferred female abortionists.

In just under half of the cases in this sample, unmarried pregnant women clearly took the decision into their own hands. Five women in this sample bought abortifacient drugs themselves. During the course of the investigation into an illegal abortion that was allegedly carried out by William Coleman in Dublin in December 1936, it emerged that Margaret B. had taken steps to attempt to bring about a miscarriage before she went to see Coleman. A search of Margaret's room revealed that she had taken glauber salts, two boxes of ergot powder and had purchased quinine tablets. A glass syringe was also found in her bedroom. Karmel M. told John S., a Nigerian medical student who was convicted of using an instrument to procure an abortion in June 1944, that she had been taking ergot. Karmel approached John S. herself and asked him to operate on her. John claimed that he merely removed the dead foetus from her womb but he was convicted and sentenced to three years' imprisonment.

In another example, Judith M. seems to have been determined to terminate her pregnancy. Although her fiancé supported her, the decision to visit William Coleman and to seek an abortion seems to have been hers. When he was called on to give evidence in court, Alphonsus M. said that it 'was entirely up to [Judith]'.[88] He maintained that she suggested the possibility of terminating the pregnancy to him and said that if he had not approved of her decision to seek an abortion 'she would have gone just the same'.[89] He told the court that she had secured financial assistance from a friend and she could have phoned Coleman and made the arrangements herself if he had refused to assist her. It is possible, however, that both Judith and Alphonsus may have deliberately downplayed his role in the case because they were concerned that he could be charged as an accessory. Alphonsus and Judith married the day after Coleman was arrested and it was suggested during the course of the trial that the couple 'had married with the object of defeating the ends of justice'.[90]

In a similar case, although Margaret R.'s fiancé Frederick J. was aware that Margaret wished to terminate her pregnancy and accompanied her to the residence of an abortionist on at least one occasion, Margaret seems to have made most of the arrangements herself. She had had a successful abortion previously. Frances Duncan, a chambermaid in the Russell Hotel where Margaret had been employed, introduced Margaret to the woman suspected of having performed the abortion. The judge who tried the case said that while the evidence against Anne C.P. was 'very suspicious', it was not 'definite'.[91] Abortifacient pills were found in Margaret's bedroom. According to her fiancé, Margaret began taking pills and powders several days before she died. During the trial it was also suggested that Margaret may have given herself a soapy injection before she went to Anne C.P.'s house on 10 September 1929.

Twelve women in this sample managed to pay for abortions themselves or to secure loans from friends, and one woman's mother paid for her abortion. Four of the five unmarried women whose pregnancies were terminated by Kathleen Gilbourne paid the fee she charged themselves. Some women were unable to pay the fee all at once. In her statement Josephine M. said that she paid Mrs Gilbourne's two pound fee in weekly instalments at a rate of seven and six pence. There were at least two cases where women who did not obtain financial assistance from the man who was responsible for the pregnancy approached friends instead and managed to persuade them to lend them money. Twelve women organized an appointment with an abortionist themselves. De Blécourt has noted that while the verdicts in abortion cases tried in The Hague in the early twentieth century 'do not disclose much about who took the initiative', he suggested that 'it presumably came from the women'.[92] He cited one case where a lover insisted that his pregnant girlfriend have an abortion but noted that there was no further sign of lovers enforcing abortions and concluded that 'women's own agency is more apparent'.[93] While women's own agency is also apparent in Irish abortion cases, the actions and attitudes of the male partners of single women who sought abortions during the period under review was clearly an important factor in many cases.

'I TOLD G., WHO WANTED TO MARRY ME, BUT I REFUSED BECAUSE WE ARE OF DIFFERENT RELIGIONS'[94]

It was often assumed that single women who became pregnant would want to marry the man who was responsible for the pregnancy, if he was willing to do so. A closer analysis of these cases reveals that this was not necessarily so. A woman like Judith M., who was attending university, may have had ambitions that extended beyond becoming a wife and mother and an unplanned pregnancy would have ended such ambitions. Moreover, Judith apparently 'felt that if she married [Alphonsus] in these circumstances she would always feel there was an element of compulsion, that he was forced to marry her'.[95] Alphonsus M. told the court that 'quite a number of times I wished her to marry and I was quite emphatic about it'.[96] S.M. said that when she told the man she had been keeping company with for the past three years that she was pregnant he said he wanted to marry her. However, S. refused his offer because they were of different religions.

Some of the women in this sample may never have intended to marry the men with whom they were intimately involved. As Brookes has noted in relation to abortion cases in England, 'some women preferred the risk of an abortion to that involved in a shotgun wedding'.[97] Other women may have preferred to have an abortion than to marry while pregnant. Some were clearly concerned about the shame associated with pre-marital pregnancy and were anxious to avoid upsetting their families. In October 1925 Darrell Figgis said that he told Rita N. that he thought the right thing to do would be 'to marry at once'.[98] He suggested wiring for Rita's family in order to explain the situation to them but Rita made him promise that he would do nothing of the kind. According to Darrell 'the suggestion terrified her'.[99] She did not want her family to know that she had been pregnant. Extramarital conception was clearly considered shameful in Ireland, even when marriage followed.

'HE SWORE AT ME AND TOLD ME THAT IF I DID NOT DRINK IT HE WOULD THROW IT ROUND ME'

Nevertheless, while it is evident that for some women the decision to have an abortion was theirs, other women in this sample may have been pressured by their partners into undergoing an abortion or consuming abortifacient drugs. When 17-year-old M.C. told her boyfriend that she was pregnant in July 1930, C.W. assured her that 'he would get her something to make her all right'.[100] He later produced a bottle containing tincture of iron. Although M. was reluctant to take the liquid she said that she eventually drank it because C. frightened her. She told police that 'he swore at [her] and told [her] that if [she] did not drink it he would throw it round [her]'.[101] Soon afterwards M. became ill and her mother took her to see a doctor. C.W. was later charged with causing M.C. to take 'a certain noxious thing to wit Tincture of Iron with intent by means thereof to procure miscarriage'.[102]

In another case, in September 1931, Marks R. told an acquaintance that he had trouble with a girl named Bridie K. Bridie was pregnant again and while Marks 'wanted a second operation performed', she would not consent to this.[103] Bridie K. claimed that Marks R. put her under pressure to have an abortion the second time she became pregnant but she refused to consent. Marks R. was a married man and he was clearly anxious to prevent his family from learning about his affair with Bridie.

This pattern of behaviour is also evident in other European countries. In her study of abortion in the Weimar Republic, Usborne noted that 'coercive abortion by men on their own mistresses was ... not uncommon'.[104] She also pointed to the fact that while the decision to seek an abortion could have an adverse affect on heterosexual relationships and led, in some instances, 'to manifestations of tension and even violent behaviour between men and women, both between husbands/lovers and their wives/mistresses or male abortionists and their women clients', there were as many if not more incidents where men and women co-operated.[105] This is also evident in the records of abortion cases that came before the courts in Ireland during the first half of the twentieth century. While an unplanned pregnancy caused tension and bad feeling within some relationships and even led, in some cases, to the breakdown of relations between couples, there were many instances where men and women co-operated and supported each other in seeking to abort.

While there are few cases in which there is evidence to suggest that women were pressured by their partners into undergoing an abortion or consuming abortifacient drugs, it could be argued that in most cases unmarried pregnant women were subject to other forms of pressure and were motivated to seek abortions because of the stigma associated with single motherhood, lack of financial resources and the lack of support from the man responsible for the pregnancy.

Single pregnant women did not only come under pressure from

their boyfriends or fiancés to terminate their pregnancies. The compulsion to protect a family's sense of honour and reputation in the community was particularly strong in Ireland during the first half of the twentieth century. In some instances the relatives of single, pregnant women collaborated in order to arrange an abortion so that the shame and disgrace of a birth outside marriage could be avoided. The evidence in one Belfast case suggests that one woman's mother put her under considerable pressure to consent to an abortion. Indeed, E.F.'s mother made all the arrangements for the abortion. When she discovered that her daughter was four months pregnant E.'s mother first invited the man responsible for her daughter's condition to her house to discuss the matter. However, when T.B. refused to marry her, saying that 'I cannot keep a wife', M.F. approached a woman she knew and asked her 'if she would give her [daughter] a soap injection to relieve her of her pregnancy or if she knew of any other person who could do so'.[106] Mrs F. was clearly anxious for her daughter to avoid the shame associated with single motherhood. E.M. told the police that she heard her say that she was 'not going to have [her] daughter disgraced she has got to be cleared'. In his statement E.F.'s boyfriend said that she was very upset the last time he saw her and told him that 'all those people downstairs except my grandmother want me to go to a woman and have threatened to bring her here to me'. Although Mrs F. said she would never 'do anything to my wee girl', her actions led to her daughter's death.[107]

'THIS IS A COURT OF LAW: IT IS NOT A COURT OF MORALS'[108]

In their addresses to the juries in four of the cases in this sample, judges reminded the members of the juries that the courts in which various abortion cases were tried were not courts of morals. They impressed upon them the fact that they were required as jurors to separate legal fact from morality. Yet, Judge McCarthy's comment in the Jackson case is particularly revealing. He declared that this is not a court of morals before adding, 'perhaps one often wishes that it were'.[109] According to Brookes, juries in England were 'usually sympathetic to the abortionist and appreciative of the heavy sentences' and as a result were often reluctant to convict.[110] Brookes has also noted that 'the anomaly of a law that inflicted severe penalties for an act to which everyone involved consented raised comment from the bench'.[111] There was little popular sympathy with abortionists in southern Ireland during the period under review. Despite the fact that several women involved in the abortion cases in this sample had instigated the crime, they were not prosecuted, whereas a number of men who had provided them with the means of paying the abortionist's fee were convicted and sentenced to terms of imprisonment. Women like Karmel M., as Judge Davitt observed, were 'fully consenting [parties] in all that was done to [them]'.[112] Yet Irish juries seem to have been unmoved by the fact that Karmel M. appeared as a State witness even though she 'had been aborted on a previous occasion and who on her own admission, had taken ergot, and had permitted the use of an instrument on her'.[113] During the trial of three Nigerian medical students who were charged with using an instrument to procure Karmel M.'s abortion in June 1944, Mr Fahy referred to this as 'a strange justice'.[114] McAvoy has argued that during the 1940s the State seemed determined 'to use existing law to the full to destroy the abortion trade'; Sections 58 and 59 of the 1861 Offences Against the Person Act were more strictly applied in the Irish Free State during the 1940s than in previous decades.[115] The State pursued both abortionists and accessories to abortions during this period and heavy sentences were imposed on those convicted. However, men in Northern Ireland were perhaps less likely to be charged with procuring abortion in cases where they provided their girlfriends or fiancées with financial assistance. For instance, even though G.C. arranged for his girlfriend to meet with an abortionist in Belfast, drove her there and may have paid for the cost of the procedure, he was not charged.

There was a tendency among some judges to gender stereotype and to regard single women who had had abortions as hapless victims who had been heavily influenced by their male partners into terminating their pregnancies. During George J.'s trial the judge told the jury that 'the whole purpose [of abortion] is to get rid of the result of the unbridled passion of some man who has wronged the girl'.[116] He referred to women who sought abortions as 'unfortunate girls' and praised their 'splendid courage' in coming to court to give evidence 'when they realise the full enormity of their offence and expose themselves to the shame and disgrace of being associated with this event and make an attempt to undo the result of their misconduct and to point out to others who may be tempted to do likewise the evil of their own ways'.[117]

A closer reading of abortion trials in Ireland between 1925 and 1950 reveals that the reality was somewhat more complex. It is clear from the records of abortion cases that came before the courts in Ireland, both north and south, during the period under review that single women who sought to terminate their pregnancies were not, for the most part, unfortunate victims. Many of the women who gave evidence in these cases appear to have been willing sexual partners. A number of women had had abortions before or had previously given birth. Several had had more than one sexual partner, yet it was often assumed in Irish courtrooms that the decision to have a sexual relationship and to seek an abortion in the event of an unplanned pregnancy rested with the man. It seems highly unlikely that any woman gave evidence in court in order to attempt to undo the 'evil' of her misconduct or to act as warning for others. In fact, Carrie D. appears to have been reluctant to make a statement against her former boyfriend George J. However, she had little choice but to give evidence against him as the Gardaí took her identification card and residence permit which she required in order to return to her home in Belfast.

The records of abortion trials in Ireland reveal much about gender dynamics in Ireland between 1925 and 1950. An analysis of the roles played by both men and women in abortion cases that came before the courts reveals both what contemporaries refused to acknowledge – that the decision to seek an abortion was often the result of joint decision-making on the part of the couples involved or a woman's own choice – and what contemporaries were more willing to accept – that some women had been pressurized or threatened by their male partners into taking abortifacient drugs or terminating an unplanned pregnancy.

The judicial records of abortion cases in this sample suggest that women often took the initiative to terminate an unwanted pregnancy themselves, but the records also point to the fact that in many instances the attitude and actions of their male partner was often a key factor in a woman's decision to seek an abortion. Single women who aborted and single women suspected of killing their illegitimate infants or concealing the birth of their newborns were motivated to break the law for similar reasons. Whether they terminated their pregnancy at an early stage or carried the pregnancy to term and took their infant's life shortly after self-delivery seems to have depended on the knowledge available to them and whether they had access to money and useful contacts, as well as the outlook of their male partners.

ACKNOWLEDGEMENTS

I would like to thank the Irish Research Council for the Humanities and Social Sciences for funding the research on which this chapter is based.

NOTES

1. National Archives of Ireland (NAI), Court of Criminal Appeal (CCA), 60/1945.
2. Cited in National Archives of Ireland (NAI), Court of Criminal Appeal (CCA), 60/1945.
3. Sandra Larmour (McAvoy), 'Aspects of the State and Female Sexuality in the Irish Free State, 1922–1949' (Unpublished PhD Thesis, History Department, University College Cork, 1998), pp.233–4.
4. Sandra McAvoy, 'Before Cadden: Abortion in Mid Twentieth-Century Ireland', in Dermot Keogh, Finbarr O'Shea and Carmel Quinlan (eds), *Ireland in the 1950s: The Lost Decade* (Cork: Mercier, 2004), pp.153–4.
5. National Archives (NA), Kew, MEPO 3/412.
6. NA, Kew, MEPO 3/1028.
7. NAI, Dublin Circuit Court, 1945, ID 27 11.
8. Public Record Office of Northern Ireland (PRONI), BELF/1/1/2/141/28.
9. PRONI, BELF/1/1/2/126/5.
10. *Irish Times*, 10 June 1944.
11. *Irish Times*, 9 June 1944.
12. See *The People* (Wexford), 25 May 1929 and 22 June 1929 and the *Irish Times*, 20 June 1927. In May and June 1929 the Wexford county health board discussed the admission of single expectant mothers to the county home. Some members objected to the fact that 'respectable married women would be put into the same ward as the unmarried mother' (*Wexford People*, 22 June 1929). One member of the Wexford county health board referred to unmarried mothers as 'people who don't deserve respect' (*Wexford People*, 25 May 1929). In June 1927 at the monthly meeting of the Galway hospital and dispensaries' committee, the members of the committee learned that five unmarried mothers had recently been admitted to the hospital. They were clearly dissatisfied and unanimously passed a resolution calling on members of the Catholic hierarchy to appeal to the people of Ireland to 'return to the old Gaelic customs under which such scandals were practically unknown' (*Irish Times*, 20 June 1927).
13. Margaret L. Arnot and Cornelie Usborne, 'Why Gender and Crime? Aspects of an Institutional Debate', in Margaret L. Arnot and Cornelie Usborne (eds), *Gender and Crime in Modern Europe* (London: UCL Press, 1999), p.22.
14. NAI, CCA 50/1950.
15. Arnot and Usborne, 'Why Gender and Crime?', p.22.
16. NAI, CCA, 23/1931.
17. NAI, CCA, 8/1937.
18. NAI, CCA, 83/1944.
19. NAI, CCA, 72/1944.
20. Ibid.
21. Ibid.
22. NAI, Central Criminal Court (CCC), ID 29 7, 1948, Co. Laois.
23. Donna Cooper Graves, '"...in a frenzy while raving mad": Physicians and Parliamentarians Define Infanticide in Victorian England', in B. Bechtold and D. Cooper Graves (eds), *Killing Infants: Studies in the Worldwide Practice of Infanticide* (Lampeter: Edwin Mellen, 2006), p.134.
24. NAI, CCA, 60/1945. During George J.'s trial the judge suggested that 'all decent young men who have no business here should leave the court. This girl is getting very embarrassed. And I am sure it is no pleasure to anybody to listen to her story.'
25. NAI, CCA, 18/1945.
26. Larmour (McAvoy), 'Aspects of the State and Female Sexuality in the Irish Free State, 1922–1949', p.244.
27. 'The Attorney General v. Hyman L.', *The Irish Reports*, 1932, p.166.
28. NAI, CCA, 60/1945.

29. NAI, CCA, 18/1945.
30. NAI, CCA, 83/1944.
31. NAI, CCC, ID 29 4, Dublin, 1950.
32. NAI, CCC, ID 29 5, Dublin, 1950.
33. Ibid.
34. NAI, CCC, ID 11 95, Cork, 1939.
35. Michelle Oberman, 'Understanding Infanticide in Context: Mothers who Kill, 1870–1930 and Today', *Journal of Criminal Law and Criminology*, 92, 3 and 4 (2002), p.721.
36. R.S. Rose, 'An Outline of Fertility Control, Focusing on the Element of Abortion, in the Republic of Ireland to 1976' (Unpublished PhD Thesis, Institute of Sociology, The University of Stockholm, 1976), p.173.
37. These findings are based on a sample of almost 200 infanticide cases involving single women that were tried in the Central Criminal Court, Dublin between 1922 and 1950. My PhD thesis examines cases where unmarried women were charged with the murder or concealment of birth of their illegitimate infants in Ireland during the first half of the twentieth century. Clíona Rattigan, '"Dark Spots" in Irish Society: Unmarried Motherhood, Crime and Prosecution in Ireland, 1900–1950' (PhD thesis, Trinity College Dublin, 2008).
38. NAI, CCA, 83/1944.
39. Ibid.
40. NA, Kew, MEPO 3/412.
41. Ibid.
42. NAI, CCA, 72/1944.
43. Angus McLaren, *Twentieth-century Sexuality: A History* (Oxford: Blackwell, 1999), pp.76–7.
44. NAI, CCA, 23/1931.
45. NAI, CCA, 50/1950.
46. NAI, CCA, 83/1944.
47. Barbara Brookes, *Abortion in England 1900–1967* (Beckenham: Croom Helm, 1988), p.30.
48. Ibid.
49. Margaret R.'s fiancé, Frederick J., may also have contributed to the cost of her visits to an abortionist in London in September 1929. However, Margaret died before the police investigation began and as Frederick J. did not refer to financial matters in the statements he made it is not possible to know whether he contributed towards the cost of the procedure.
50. NAI, CCC, ID 24 139, Dublin, 1944.
51. Ibid.
52. Ibid.
53. NAI, CCA, 72/1944.
54. NAI, CCA, 60/1945.
55. Ibid.
56. Willem de Blécourt, 'Cultures of Abortion in The Hague in the Early Twentieth Century', in Franz X. Eder, Lesley A. Hall and Gert Hekma (eds), *Sexual Cultures in Europe: Themes in Sexuality* (Manchester: Manchester University Press, 1999), p.207.
57. NAI, CCA, 72/1944.
58. Barbara Brookes, 'Women and Reproduction c.1860–1919', in Jane Lewis (ed.), *Labour and Love: Women's Experience of Home and Family 1850–1940* (Oxford: Basil Blackwell, 1986), p.161.
59. De Blécourt, 'Cultures of Abortion in The Hague in the Early Twentieth Century', p.209.
60. NAI, CCA, 23/1931.
61. PRONI, BELF/1/1/2/119/7.
62. Ibid.
63. Ibid.
64. NAI, CCC, ID 29 7, 1948, Co. Laois.
65. NAI, CCA, 83/1944.
66. PRONI, BELF/1/1/2/141/28.
67. Ibid.
68. NAI, CCA, 50/1950.
69. Alphonsus and Judith M. were not officially engaged when Judith became pregnant but the couple claimed that they had been unofficially engaged for some time before Judith realized that she was pregnant.

70. NAI, CCA, 83/1944.
71. Cornelie Usborne, 'Wise Women, Wise Men and Abortion in the Weimar Republic: Gender, Class and Medicine', in Lynn Abrams and Elizabeth Harvey (eds), *Gender Relations in German History: Power, Agency and Experience from the Sixteenth to the Twentieth Century* (London: UCL Press, 1996), p.157.
72. PRONI, BELF/1/1/2/126/5.
73. NAI, CCA, 23/1931.
74. NAI, CCC, ID 24 139, Dublin, 1944.
75. Ibid.
76. Usborne, 'Wise Women, Wise Men and Abortion in the Weimar Republic', p.157.
77. *The Times*, 30 October 1925.
78. NA, Kew, MEPO 3/2578.
79. Ibid.
80. NAI, CCA, 72/1944.
81. NAI, CCA, 8/1937.
82. Brookes, *Abortion in England 1900–1967*, p.3.
83. Ibid., p.34.
84. Ibid.
85. Ibid., p.35.
86. McAvoy, 'Before Cadden: Abortion in Mid-Twentieth-Century Ireland', p.158.
87. Usborne, 'Wise Women, Wise Men and Abortion in the Weimar Republic', p.168.
88. NAI, CCA, 83/1944.
89. Ibid.
90. 'The People (at the suit of the Attorney General) v. William H. Coleman', *The Irish Reports*, 1945, p.237.
91. NA, Kew, MEPO 3/412.
92. de Blécourt, 'Cultures of Abortion in The Hague in the Early Twentieth-Century', p.207.
93. Ibid.
94. PRONI, BELF/1/1/2/118/6.
95. NAI, CCA, 83/1944.
96. Ibid.
97. Brookes, *Abortion in England, 1900–1967*, p.33.
98. NA, Kew, MEPO 3/2578.
99. Ibid.
100. PRONI, BELF/1/1/2/93/61.
101. Ibid.
102. Ibid.
103. NAI, CCA, 23/1931.
104. Usborne, 'Wise Women, Wise Men and Abortion in the Weimar Republic', p.155.
105. Ibid., p.156.
106. PRONI, BELF/1/1/2/123/5.
107. Ibid.
108. NAI, CCA, 83/1944.
109. NAI, CCA, 60/1945.
110. Brookes, *Abortion in England, 1900–1967*, p.28.
111. Ibid., p.37.
112. NAI, CCA, 72/1944.
113. Ibid.
114. *Irish Times*, 10 June 1944.
115. Larmour, 'Aspects of the State and Female Sexuality in the Irish Free State, 1922-1949', p.244.
116. NAI, CCA, 60/1945.
117. Ibid.

CHAPTER NINE

Gender, Emigration and Diverging Discourses: Irish Female Emigration, 1922–48[1]

JENNIFER REDMOND

INTRODUCTION

Two dominant aspects of the discourses on Irish women's emigration centred on the questions: what they were *supposed* and *feared* to be doing, and what were they *actually* doing when they emigrated to England? As I have argued elsewhere, marital status played a key part in moral and welfare concerns over Irish women: their singleness was interpreted as a factor that made them simultaneously vulnerable to and capable of sinful behaviour.[2]

This chapter considers the different yet converging discourses surrounding Irish women's emigration experiences in the period 1922 to 1948.[3] These discourses will be juxtaposed with published oral history testimonies of Irish female emigrants to show the various disjunctions between articulations of the lived experiences of female emigrants and the rhetoric surrounding them. It is necessary to highlight the fact that the experiences considered do not explicitly refer to those of female migrants who travelled to the UK because of an illegitimate pregnancy, but reference will be made to this cohort in the course of the chapter.[4]

METHODOLOGICAL CONSIDERATIONS

The inherent difference in the answer to the question posed here is explored through a variety of sources. Official documents such as government memos and reports, as well as newspaper articles, reports of sermons and other Catholic literature are used to sketch the dimensions of the public discourses on female emigrants. This is contrasted with private discourses emanating from female emigrants themselves, captured through a variety of oral history collections published from the 1980s onwards. As might be expected, these sources differ tremendously in tone, viewpoint and agenda.

It is important to note the methodological considerations that must be attended to in such an approach. An obvious point is that public documents, be they commissioned reports, statements, newspaper or journal articles, are written with a specific audience in mind. Recognizing the 'subjectivity' inherent in such documents negates claims to objectivity as has been the norm in historical writings. Thus, as McKenna has reminded us, it is important to remember that every document has an author, and 'no form of record is "pure", capable of offering a truth untouched by author, intended audience or context'.[5] Thus even 'objective' documents held in State archives were written by *someone* with a particular reader in mind.

Media articles in particular are written with attention to capturing the interest of the reader through eye-catching or dramatic headlines. The present study on which research for this chapter is based examined a range of Catholic and national daily newspapers for evidence relating to this topic.[6] Newspapers were, according to Louise Ryan, the dominant mode of communication in Ireland during this time, rendered particularly effective by the high rates of literacy.[7] A discernible change is noticeable in the layout and design of such newspaper pages in the period under consideration, with the use of larger and varied fonts, greater collation of similarly themed articles and a less condensed use of space contributing to more effective transmission of information. There was clearly an attempt made to make newspapers more 'readable' in order to more effectively convey messages. They are thus important to analyze in terms of their message and tone in relation to the topic of female emigration.

It seems that women's emigration was a topic particularly used to draw the reader's attention, and there are instances of references to women's emigration being used in the headline of articles which have little to do with women at all.[8] Clearly, references to the 'girl emigrant problem' were used intentionally to draw notice to the issue or to other stories peripherally related to the topic. Thus newspapers can be seen not only to propagate a certain agenda/stance towards the topic, but also to ensure that it stayed in the news despite the failure of successive governments to seriously address the issue through policy measures, funding or legislation. This reflects the fact that emigration was not seen solely as a demographic or economic problem, but was viewed by many as a moral problem.

Evidence from oral history collections must also be assessed with their particular limitations or subjectivities in mind. Thus practitioners of oral histories warn us of the specific dynamics of the interview process, which can determine what is remembered and what is chosen to be told. Narratives can also be shaped, rehearsed, falsified, contracted or expanded at will. However, their strength lies in the fact that oral history testimonies offer what Ken Howarth has termed 'a voice to the unheard and the unseen'.[9] There are also interactive possibilities not generally available in the research of documentary evidence: 'at least you can ask your informant questions: typefaces do not tend to answer back'.[10] Similarly, memoirs and autobiographies written by women (and men) must be analyzed with attention to their unique subjectivity. These are crucial forms of evidence, particularly in relation to women who are often less likely to record their lives in this medium. The historian, Diarmaid Ferriter, asserts that memoirs are 'an important and legitimate source material if treated with the same care and sometimes scepticism that we should treat all documentary evidence'.[11]

THE NATION AND EMIGRATION

The connection between the formation of the nation state in Ireland and emigration is key because of the emphasis at this time of political change on definitions of national identity, both legal and ideological, which focused on ideal forms of citizenship. The type of citizenship espoused by the State was highly gendered, as can be seen in the legislative measures that sought to define and restrict women's role in public life.[12] It is clear that the issues of women's identity and citizenship were conceptualized in tandem when enacted legislation is analyzed: in 1935 the Irish Nationality and Citizenship Act, the Aliens Act, and the Criminal Law Amendment Act were all passed by the Oireachtas, while the 1936 Conditions of Employment Act was also being discussed.[13] Thus, who was considered to be inside and conversely, outside, the national collective was legislatively defined at the same time as moralistic measures were adopted to legislate the sexual lives and choices of Irish citizens. When viewed in tandem, it seems obvious that who Irish people *were* was formulated at the same time as measures to frame *what* they could do.

The Irish Free State was born at a time of upheaval and dissolution, and the first government, formed by Cumann na nGaedheal,[14] relied on support from the Catholic Church to foster peace and reconciliation in order to establish civil society. Thus, from its inception, Church and State were closely allied, and the 'imagined community'[15] of the nation had a Roman Catholic ethos that was to maintain its hegemony for many decades. This influenced notions of what it meant to be Irish – i.e. to be Roman Catholic – and what it meant to be a citizen of the newly independent nation. It also somewhat explains the concern over Irish female emigrants to Britain. The idealized image of Irish virtue was embodied by women and must be maintained, especially when Irish women were 'representatives' of the nation in other countries. As Yuval-Davis argues, women are often symbolically projected as the embodied representatives of a nation, and 'they are constructed as the symbolic bearers of the collectivity's identity and honour, both personally and collectively'.[16] The concern of the Catholic Church over Irish female emigrants' welfare is viewed by Louise Ryan as a fear of losing control over them: 'The moral constraints that had controlled these young women in Ireland would not be able to protect them in England.'[17] Thus female citizens were constructed as in need of guidance, more so than Irish males, particularly when they left Irish shores, despite the fact that both males and females would have had little experience of living away from home, and might both have benefitted from help and support. Clearly, issues of control rather than guidance were paramount in the minds of those who objected to female emigration.

Emigration was also an important issue because of the sheer numbers of emigrants leaving the newly formed State. Emigration rates were high throughout the period, a fact that was both startling and embarrassing to the new leaders. It had been naively assumed that emigration was a 'problem' that would be solved by throwing off the colonial yoke – but this did not turn out to be the case. As many, including Tom Garvin, have argued, emigration was 'almost proverbially, a way of life' that seemed to be an indication that 'the entire independence project was a failure'.[18]

To briefly contextualize the issue of emigration during this time period, it is known that by the mid-1920s, 43 per cent of Irish born men and women were living overseas, in comparison with a European average of approximately 5 per cent of their population living outside their native country.[19] The high rates of female emigration were commented upon from the early years of the new Free State, with the *Freeman's Journal* remarking on the latest statistics in 1923 that 'the excessive emigration of women emigrants from Ireland is, next to the ages of the emigrants – two out of every three emigrants being between 20 and 30 years old – the most deplorable feature of the emigration returns'.[20] By the 1946–51 period, eight out of ten Irish emigrants were going to England, Wales and Scotland,[21] and between 1926 and 1931 alone, 161,021 people emigrated to the UK.[22] The alarm at this rate of emigration is evident from the fact that the above statistic on numbers emigrating to the UK featured as front-page news in *The Irish Press.* By the time of the 1951 Census, there were only 964 females for every 1,000 males in the country, compared to a high of 1,049 females per 1,000 males in 1851.[23]

Irish female migrants, in general terms, fitted a particular profile: they tended to be very young, with one third between the ages of 15 and 19 years, and a further third between 20 and 24 years;[24] they were usually from a rural area,[25] and generally destined for domestic service jobs, although there is also much evidence to suggest that they worked in the large factories that surrounded London and elsewhere at that time, as well as the large shops, and in pubs and restaurants.[26] Rates of emigration increased with the onset of the Second World War, and women were recruited as teachers, nurses, midwives, domestics in hospitals and hotels, as well as workers in the munitions factories, the cotton mills and the transportation system, particularly bus conducting.[27]

'LURED BY THE GARISH DISTRACTIONS OF THE GREAT WORLD'

The conjectured arguments on Irish female migrants' motivations for going to England are exemplified in Church, State and media commentary on such women, and in fact at times it seems as if there was a competition to be the *most* outraged by the situation. The debate on female migrants focused more on the *idea* of them leaving and their reasons for emigrating rather than the reality of their lives once they got there. Thus a sensationalist depiction of the *emigrant* was sustained at the expense of a reasoned analysis of the *immigrant*. Dr. McNamee, Bishop of Ardagh and Clonmacnoise, for example, claimed in 1931 that girls were emigrating due to their uncontrollable 'fascination [with] ... the garish distractions, and the hectic life of the great world as displayed before their wondering eyes in the glamorous unreality of the films'.[28] This says nothing of the economic necessities, lack of life opportunities or the family obligations which many emigrants had. Women were, therefore, excluded from being considered as rational economic migrants, and pigeonholed instead as being capricious and shallow.

The commentary on female migrants typically ranged from condemnation of their reasons for migrating, the morality of their employment choices, their rejection of their home life and culture and their social activities once there. This commentary was rarely paralleled to the same extent on their male counterparts, although recent evidence on impoverished, isolated and homeless Irish male immigrants in England suggests that perhaps it should have been.[29] The main thrust of the interest in female migrants seems to be from a desire to prohibit potential immoral behaviour, and to preserve the ideal of a Gaelicised, pure and moral Irish womanhood, which was now also the formula for female citizenship, as expressed most particularly in the 1937 Constitution.[30]

Women were simultaneously constructed on an ideological level as 'the essence of traditional Irish virtue and morality as well as [embodying] the threat of immorality and sexual impurity'.[31] For example, Dr. McNamee again can be quoted when, in 1937, he perceived a crisis in female emigration to England, and cautioned that 'Emigrants may find themselves in jobs where modesty and virtue may be exposed to great dangers' and that girls 'will have a better chance of happiness in the country homesteads of Ireland than anywhere else on earth'.[32] Thus the connection is explicitly made between migration and immorality, and conversely, settlement in Ireland and virtue.

This tone of censure was also evinced by de Valera once in office, although prior to this he had stressed the duty of the State to provide employment. For example, in a speech made in 1926 at the inaugural meeting of Fianna Fáil, de Valera argued that:

> I have said it before, and I repeat it here, and I believe most right-thinking men will agree with me, that it is a primary duty for any government in any civilised country to see that men and women will not starve and that little children will not starve through opportunity for useful work being denied to the breadwinner.[33]

This reveals two interesting facts: employment was understood solely as employment for men and emigration is implicitly posited as an issue for the government to remedy by providing more employment. Emigrants themselves were not accused of rejecting jobs at home as in his later statements, such as in 1947 when he insisted that there were plenty of jobs in Ireland and that people were often leaving for other reasons, again alluding to non-economic causes as predominant, and therefore out of the control of the government: 'A good deal of psychological matter – it is not solely economic matters – is responsible.'[34] This is different from his earlier statements on the matter, shifting the emphasis from the economic duty of the State to selfish desires and opportunism by its citizens. This is despite the fact that the economic climate had not significantly improved. Indeed, the only major societal alteration that had occurred between the two statements was that Fianna Fáil was now in government and not in opposition.

This argument was part of the nationalist critique of emigration to Britain, which was viewed as an insidious form of population degeneration. As McLaughlin has argued: 'Nationalists condemned the haemorrhaging of Mother Ireland through emigration, arguing that England condoned Irish emigration because it was depriving Mother Ireland of her sons, and more especially, her daughters.'[35] The reality, however, was that in order to sustain even a basic standard of living, emigration was necessary, and as J.J. Lee comments: 'In no other European country was emigration so essential a prerequisite for the preservation of the society.'[36] The need for emigration did not fit with Irish nationalist principles, and thus it was denied its rational framework. Women in particular, as indicated by McLaughlin, were 'lost' to Ireland, referencing a fear of 'race suicide' that emerged in certain newspaper articles.

Due to the difficulties of a depressed economy, de Valera's optimistic economic outlook was simply not true for many. Numerous people, males and females alike, had very limited opportunities available to them in Ireland, either socially or economically. When questioned why they left Ireland, many female emigrants simply stated there was no other option: 'I really felt I had no choice but to leave. That's one of the biggest regrets I have about going to England. I really didn't have a choice.'[37] An Irish priest, Fr Séamus Fullam interviewed by Catherine Dunne as part of the *Unconsidered People* collection, worked with the Irish community in London for decades. Fr Fullam verifies the view of Irish emigration as forced or necessary, as he stated: 'Those Irish I met were people who had to leave home because there was nothing for them. They came on a boat with nothing.'[38] The evidence of oral history testimonies suggests that emigration was primarily motivated by economic imperatives, and for many was not a choice based on personal preferences. This is particularly true for female migrants whose opportunities for employment in Ireland were limited, and further reduced by the State through the Conditions of Employment Act (1936)[39] and the marriage bar for female public servants.[40] This is one of the key gender differences between migrants who left Ireland: women's opportunities for paid employment were curtailed on the basis of what was thought to be 'gender appropriate', whereas men's opportunities were not limited in that way. This is not to say that men did not have their own economic disadvantages, with high rates of temporary working and low wages, but they were not restricted in the same ways as women either by law or custom in taking up work.

The low wages for women's work must also be viewed as a motivating factor for female emigration from Ireland. Although gendered wage differentials existed in most countries at the time for which data is available, they were more extreme in Ireland:[41] female rates of pay throughout the 1940s up to the 1960s were just over half those of men.[42] Such were the differences in pay for female domestic servants, for example, that some Irish women left factory jobs to go into service in England. In a very small survey of six women emigrating from Tralee to Great Britain, the Commission on Emigration and Other Population Problems found two cases of women leaving Denny's bacon factory to go into service which the women described as 'bettering themselves'.[43] This was found to be the case in other areas, and in 1948 the Irish Housewives Association (IHA) pointed out to the Commission that resident maids with some experience received £1.17.6d. per week in Britain in comparison to just 25/- in Ireland.[44] However, monetary incentives must be viewed in conjunction with the improvement in status that many Irish women perceived upon entering domestic service jobs in Britain as opposed to Ireland. As Enda Delaney has commented: 'Domestic servants ... were viewed as an inferior form of life by both employers and the community at large' in Ireland, and this perception seems to have been acutely felt by many women, who preferred to engage in this form of employment abroad.[45]

The incentives of such monetary reward and improvements in conditions of work were viewed by some as strictly bad for Irish emigrants. Speaking specifically about female emigrants, government officials stated that economic independence for girls was one of the key factors that led to their moral downfall in Great Britain:

> Boredom in surroundings often remote and friendless, the lack of restraints of home environment and the possession of more money than experience would enable them to apply to their own advantage are some of the other factors which usually operate to the moral detriment of immature girls who emigrate to Britain.[46]

This type of discourse is prevalent throughout the 1920s, 1930s and 1940s, demonstrating the gendered attitudes to financial independence as well as emigration. Such a viewpoint was expressed by *St.*

Mary's Magazine, an English publication, in which it was argued that Irish newspapers should exercise caution in advertising jobs in England for Irish women and that they should try to institute a system whereby applicants were tracked for an initial period.[47] The Editor of the *Irish Catholic* commented on the infeasibility of this proposal, but suggested that 'Admonitions published from time to time, addressed to both maids and mistresses, would, in our opinion, be more effective and more feasible'.[48] The necessity of regular admonitions to girls about their employment choices is thus presented as merely common sense, ignoring the fact that economic constraints and obligations often dictated female emigration, rendering such admonitions irrelevant.[49]

Many women represented in oral history accounts left Ireland due to economic imperatives that impacted on their lives in a number of ways. Their families often needed them to work in order to contribute to the home economy, and working abroad and sending remittances could often most successfully achieve this. It seems that many emigrants retained money for the necessities only, sending much of their wage packet back home in order to maintain family ties: 'The minute I'd get my wage packet I'd put the money into an envelope and send it to my mother. And then I felt better ... And I felt I was actually with my mother when I sent the money.'[50] In addition to providing remittances, by leaving the country, female emigrants were no longer a financial burden on the family, and could thus contribute without costing anything in terms of food, accommodation and other necessities.

Apart from the financial benefits for women's emigration, a motivating factor can be seen in the opportunity for women to pursue a career for personal fulfilment not possible in Ireland due to the legislative and socio-cultural constraints on women's employment. This is attested to by one female migrant who stated that:

> There were no opportunities for women in my day. If a woman got married and then started to work in the 1930s, she'd be criticised all over the place. 'God, she didn't make much of a match, he can't even keep her.' It never dawned on anybody that a person might like to go out to work.[51]

'PATHOLOGISING' FEMALE EMIGRANTS

Whilst all emigrants were condemned by certain modes of nationalist and cultural rhetoric, as Gray argues, women were particularly negatively cast as deficient or immoral due to their 'choice' in leaving Ireland:

> Women emigrants were pathologised for leaving, for being attracted or lured away from the country where they rightly belonged. While pathologising Irish women, these discourses also acknowledged, at an implicit level at least, the potential of Irish women to undermine a patriarchal and family-oriented Irish national identity.[52]

Viewing women's emigration as their rejection of patriarchal constraints may be a modern construction of their actions, but Irish women were certainly reacting to (and against) their limited economic opportunities and their decreasing ability to fulfil desired roles in Ireland. There was a distinct focus on the idea of rejection in discourses on female emigration, with arguments being made for viewing female emigration as a rejection of morally appropriate standards of behaviour.

The secular press often focussed on the most negative experiences of Irish female emigrants and posited them as the norm. This created a discourse of panic, shame and alarm over the welfare and behaviour of Irish female emigrants that tainted their motives and character. Gertrude Gaffney of the *Irish Independent* highlighted the issue of female emigration to Britain in a series of articles in December 1936, later followed by a pamphlet. Her articles have been quoted widely as they were the most extensive review of the issue from a journalistic point of view at this time. They represent a clear case of generalizing from the specific circumstances *some* female emigrants found themselves in to the wider female population. The articles addressed different perspectives on the emigrant experience, from the emigrants themselves as well as religious and charity workers.

While Gaffney did state at the beginning of the series of articles that girls generally did well for themselves in England, she also stressed the misfortunes of those who 'fell by the wayside', stating that they could be found in 'every shelter for the destitute, in every maternity hospital, in every home for unmarried mothers, or worse still, in the common lodginghouses in certain parts of the great cities'.[53] This commentary sets up a dichotomy between successful and unsuccessful emigrants, the pivotal factor being the exercise of female sexuality. Those women who fail to control their sexuality and purity are thus twice exiled – from the community in their homeland, and from their community in their new land. As Ryan comments: 'Women's sexual behaviour marks the boundaries between inclusion and exclusion from national collectivities.'[54]

The issue of women's sexuality was thus a theme that ran throughout many of the discourses on emigration. In the view of Dr.

Gilmartin, Archbishop of Tuam, the behaviour of 'modern young girls' was primarily to blame for the low marriage rates in Ireland:

> It was abominable to see young girls doing what they liked then fleeing to England to hide their shame. Laxity of parental control was too apparent, and in this respect mothers were worse than fathers ... Those girls who lend themselves for amusement are keeping boys from getting married. Respectable men tell me that is the reason for the great numbers of bachelors, and say they don't want to marry these modern girls, who go about gallivanting at late hours with painted faces. If the girls are good so will the boys.[55]

Thus the morality or immorality of young women was supposed to set – and maintain – the moral tone for the community. Women and girls were the bearers of decency, and any deviation from expected standards would lead to a crisis in the morality of the community, particularly in relation to men. Dr. Gilmartin's statements also seem to imply that if the girls did have to go to England 'to hide their shame' it was their fault, or else it was their mother's fault for improper guidance. The conspicuously absent factor of male responsibility in this rhetoric, as either a mate or a father, is telling of the bias against women's sexual behaviour at this time.

What is necessary to point out in relation to the discourses on female emigrant behaviour is the distinction between the women in the maternity and unmarried mother's homes and other emigrant women. While some women undoubtedly 'fell' after emigration, it is estimated that many more emigrated from Ireland *because* of illegitimate pregnancy. Paul Michael Garrett refers to the fact that by the 1950s 'PFI' or 'Pregnant from Ireland' had become 'part of the everyday vocabulary of the social workers who dealt with unmarried mothers arriving from Ireland'.[56] Migration due to pregnancy has been outlined elsewhere as part of the 'hidden history' of Irish migration. For example, Lyndsey Earner-Byrne and Garrett have both written on the repatriation scheme that operated between Ireland and England from the 1930s.[57] As argued by both, the government was eager not to involve itself in this matter too deeply, seeing it as more of a pastoral matter and thus official control of the repatriation scheme was handed over to the Catholic Church under the auspices of Archbishop John Charles McQuaid at the end of the 1930s. Both Earner Byrne and Garrett have revealed the large network of organizations that were involved in the scheme through the Catholic Church, and the extent of the flow of pregnant women coming from Ireland. By focusing on such women, however, Gertrude Gaffney in the *Irish Independent* presented this cohort as illustrative of a significant trend in Irish female emigration, and this ignored the fact that the many who did not 'get into trouble' simply went unnoticed by such welfare organizations.

An examination of these discourses highlights the disparity between the speculation and the actual experience of most Irish female emigrants – what they were really doing was generally less salacious than what they were imagined to be doing. The fact is that numerous Irish female emigrants *did not* get pregnant outside of marriage as a result of migrating to the UK. One female migrant, speaking of the very young Irish girls she worked with in domestic service in the 1940s in England commented: 'It's a miracle more of them didn't get into trouble. Still, we had the best contraception of all – fear!'[58] Many Irish female migrants were also active in the church community throughout the UK, and many were involved in Catholic societies such as the Legion of Mary. One such woman, interviewed by Catherine Dunne, helped unmarried mothers as part of her Legion work, meeting them off the trains at Euston Station and organizing places for them to stay.[59]

IRISH FEMALE EMIGRANTS AND IRISH CULTURAL TIES: BREAK AWAY OR NEGOTIATION?

Throughout the period under review here, there were frequent media stories about a loss of faith and connection with the Catholic Church upon emigration. An example of this trend appeared in *The Irish Catholic* in an article entitled 'Keep your Daughters at Home' on female emigrants to England, wherein it was stated as a matter of fact:

> With very few exceptions these girls have never previously been separated from their Catholic home environment, but being naturally very impressionable – much more so than English girls – they rapidly adapted themselves to their new pagan environment, usually with disastrous results.[60]

This comment reveals two accepted 'truths': that Irish women were naive and lacking in judgement, and that England was a 'pagan' country. While there was a 'leakage' problem to some extent, some migrants were actively involved in maintaining both religious and cultural ties to Ireland. The maintenance of such ties was buttressed by the familial support networks that often arranged their emigration and provided them with places to stay and employment. What comes across clearly in oral history testimonies by Irish female migrants is that a sense of cultural continuity was important throughout their lives, and many maintained traditions and links with their homeland and their local Irish community. Sharon Lambert comments that: 'Irish emigrant women were maintaining their Irish identities within their families and, by their extensive links with their family homes in Ireland, they were transmitting an Irish cultural identity to their children.'[61] Lambert's interviews with Irish women who emigrated to Lancashire revealed only two cases (out of forty) of women specifically leaving Ireland due to perceived excessive parental control, and one of these women continued to send remittances, thus not breaking familial or cultural ties, but 'managing' them from a distance.

This continuity of ties may also have been maintained because for many, emigration was supposed to be a temporary working arrangement, and 'I never meant to stay' is a common phrase in their accounts. Thus, while it is obvious that all emigrants faced a negotiation of their identity when they became immigrants, it is more common to find accounts of emigrants whose behaviour maintained traditional values of Irish morals than those who radically altered their behaviour on arrival in England. To give an example of female emigrant experience, Phyllis Izzard, an emigrant who settled in London at the age of 17, commented on the importance of religion to her when she arrived. She also noticed some differences between the practice of faith in her native home in Kilkenny and her new home: 'I felt that here people went to Mass of their own accord, whereas at home, in those days, people went to Mass because they would have been talked about if they didn't.'[62] This contradicts fears that migrants would lose their faith once they left Ireland, or worse, would be converted to Protestantism. It also exposes the potentially shallow nature of demonstrations of religiosity in Ireland, a reaction referred to as 'excessive enforced piety'[63] by Ferriter.

The evidence also suggests that much of Irish immigrants' social lives revolved around parish clubs, where many met future husbands and wives. Indeed, social networks often constituted siblings and other relatives, as well as fellow migrants from the same areas in Ireland – all of which suggests a transplantation and negotiation of cultural life, not abandonment. The evidence thus suggests a widening of kin networks, rather than a linear process of moving from one community to the next. Original letters given to the author emanating from an exchange between a future husband and wife in the 1940s also shows this trend.[64] Josephine Nestor asks Paddy Corless to 'remember her to Jimmy Kelly' in one of the letters, referring to the fact that Paddy was socializing with people from the local community.

It shows emigrants' ability to keep close ties with their native town/village whilst in England. Further evidence is given as to the desire for cultural continuation by Noreen Hill, a Cork woman who left for England during the Second World War:

> When I was bringing up my children it was very important to me to try and pass on a sense of Irishness to them. I told them about Irish history, read Irish story books to them, tried to teach them a little bit of the Irish language, tried to teach them their prayers in Irish.[65]

Hill's experience and feelings are likely to be shared by many Irish men and women anxious to maintain their cultural identity in a land where difference based on skin colour was increasingly becoming prominent.[66] However, it must be remembered that the ability – and indeed desire – to maintain a distinct Irish identity is only likely to exist where a critical mass of Irish people were living. Similarly, Rossiter emphasizes the relationship between women and the Catholic Church in the UK, particularly in relation to their parish-based activities:

> Through fund-raising for vast church building programmes, parish devotional associations, sodalities, guilds, confraternities, welfare organisations and not least, Catholic schools, the Church established strong links with the immigrants. While men dominated virtually all the secular organisations, women formed the backbone of church-based activities and ... the magnitude of their work is, as yet, hidden from history.[67]

The gender division in terms of religious participation is neatly articulated by a Galway emigrant, Kathleen Morrissey, one of Catherine Dunne's interviewees: 'Women tended to join the Church; men went to the pub.'[68]

Irish women's participation in such activities, while not a universal experience, is likely to have been one shared by many women, either as a way to make new contacts, or as a means of maintaining existing networks of friends and relatives. Indeed, it was the steadfastness of Irish religious belief, particularly in the nineteenth century, that led to such distrust and fear of the Irish community in Britain.[69] However, as Herson has argued in his analysis of Irish identity in the town of Stafford (which experienced low rates of Irish immigration), 'there was little incentive to maintain an Irish identity in the face of the need to survive and prosper in a new environment'.[70] This is confirmed by evidence collated by Stanley Lyon on behalf of the Commission on

Emigration and Other Population Problems, whereby a priest in Southampton – also having a small Irish community – thought it was harder for workers (particularly men) to maintain their religion there than it would have been for those in Manchester or London where a bigger Irish community existed.[71] Thus the maintenance of family networks and the transmission of cultural identity is mitigated by geographical location and the presence of an ethnic Irish community. The evidence therefore suggests a significant maintenance of family ties, particularly through religious practice by women, contradicting fears of women losing their faith and morals through the process of emigration.

CONCLUSION

It is obvious from an examination of the discourses that there are significant disjunctions between what the State, the media and the Church said Irish female emigrants were doing, and what they report they were actually doing. While such subjective articulations of memory and the complexity of interactions within the interview setting must be taken into account, the frequency with which certain statements appear in different collections of oral histories about this period cast doubt on the broad assertions within the press at this time about female emigrant behaviour. This is particularly evident in statements made about economic need and the importance of maintaining family ties and religious practice as a form of support. It is also reported that many female emigrants are reluctant to participate in oral history collections, believing their stories are too uninteresting and non-eventful to warrant historical recording.[72] This is in stark contrast to hyperbolic assertions on their profligate lifestyles that appeared regularly at this time in national newspapers.

All aspects of their migration – from their reasons for leaving the State to their actions whilst in Britain – were framed within the context of immorality, or else negatively constituted as being due to disloyalty, wilfulness or abandonment of tradition. By combining the different types of discourses available to us in the study of women's emigration, evidence presented can be compared and contrasted. In the documents available to us at present, inconsistencies and gender ideologies emerge which highlight the different ways men and women were discursively constructed. The discrepancies between what women were reported to be doing and what they reported themselves to be doing can also clearly be seen.

Sensationalism is obviously an influencing factor in the style of the reporting that characterized the newspaper articles on Irish women emigrants. However, that does not explain the gender disparities between the reporting on men and women in the context of emigration. While both men and women were targeted within reports that raised alarm over loss of faith, other topics saw a distinct difference in attitudes towards male and female emigration. This was particularly the case in terms of employment. Men were warned not to migrate when there were fears of unemployment in Britain, and a sympathetic tone is evident in reports of cases where young men found themselves unable to obtain work or found themselves unemployed shortly after arrival. For young women, the tone was less sympathetic and more condemnatory of them for not being satisfied to accept their lot in Ireland. Being unemployed in England was also equated with being in moral danger for women. This is to deny, however, the networks of contacts, and thus resources, that both male and female emigrants had to draw upon.

It seems that the pattern of focusing on the 'worst case scenario' or the minority of emigrants who had 'failed' to make a successful life in their new land became the norm in reports and conceptions of female emigrants. However, emigration was a major event in the lives of Irish women, and was not a decision undertaken lightly due to the influence of films or the lure of glamorous city life. Many experienced hardship and hard work in the UK in order to sustain their families at home. These women were also interested in maintaining their sense of Irishness, hence their engagement in Irish 'ex-pat' community life and with the Catholic Church. What they were really doing was surviving, but this may have made a much less interesting topic to write, politicize, berate, read, and sermonize about.

NOTES

1. This chapter was developed from a paper presented at the New Research in Irish Feminism Conference, Trinity College, 2005.
2. J. Redmond, 'Sinful Singleness? Exploring the Discourses on Irish Single Women's Emigration to England, 1922–1948', *Women's History Review*, 17 (July 2008), pp.455–76.
3. This is the era in which Ireland gained independence from Britain in the form of dominion status, and progressed politically to a twenty-six county republic, thus it was the first major stage of nation building. The term 'Ireland', therefore, throughout this chapter refers to the twenty-six counties only.
4. This topic has been covered excellently by historians such as L. Earner-Byrne and P.M. Garrett, thus it is not explored in-depth here. Female emigration as a whole is considered here, and reference is made to morality and sexuality rather than illegitimate pregnancy *per se*. See Lindsey Earner-Byrne, '"Moral Repatriation": The Response to Irish Unmarried Mothers in Britain, 1920s–1960s', in Patrick J. Duffy (ed.), *To and from Ireland: Planned Migration Schemes c.1600–2000* (Dublin: Geography Publications, 2004), pp.155–74; Paul Michael Garrett, 'The Abnormal Flight: The Migration and Repatriation of Irish Unmarried Mothers', *Social History*, XXV, 3 (2000), pp.330–43; Paul Michael Garrett, 'The Hidden History of the PFIs: The Repatriation of Unmarried Mothers and Their Children from England to Ireland in the

1950s and 1960s', *Immigrants and Minorities*, 19, 3 (2000), pp.25–44.
5. Y. McKenna, *Made Holy: Irish Women Religious at Home and Abroad* (Dublin: Irish Academic Press, 2006). Further discussion of sources is contained in the methodology section below.
6. The present chapter was drawn from research conducted in completion of a PhD from the Centre for Gender and Women's Studies (CGWS), Trinity College Dublin and supervised by Dr. Maryann Gialanella Valiulis. Catholic and secular newspapers were researched for the period 1922–48. These include such titles as *The Irish Catholic*, *The Standard*, *The Irish Independent*, *The Irish Times* among others.
7. L. Ryan, *Gender, Identity and the Irish Press, 1922–1937: Embodying the Nation*, (Lewiston: Edwin Mellen Press, 2002), p.6.
8. An example of this is the leader story of the *Irish Catholic*, 31 January 1925 appearing with the headline 'Irish Emigrant Girls, Measures for their Protection' which was about the work of the Mission of Our Lady of the Rosary. However, the article deals mainly with the travel restrictions imposed due to the quota system in America, and the work the Mission does in helping emigrant girls. One interesting aspect of the report, however, is the statement that 'the claims and fitness of the relatives or friends who call the immigrants discharged to the home' on arrival in the US is undertaken by the Mission, indicating a level of monitoring, even of a girl's relatives.
9. Ken Howarth, *Oral History: A Handbook* (Phoenix Mill: Sutton Publishing Ltd, 1998), p.v.
10. Ibid., p.viii.
11. Diarmaid Ferriter, *The Transformation of Ireland, 1900–2000* (London: Profile Books, 2005), p.6.
12. For more on this point, see particularly the work of Maryann Gialanella Valiulis, Louise Ryan and Rosemary Rowley: Maryann Gialanella Valiulis, 'Engendering Citizenship: Women's Relationship to the State in Ireland and the United States in the Post Suffrage Period', in Mary O'Dowd and Maryann Gialanella Valiulis (eds), *Women and Irish History* (Dublin: Wolfhound Press, 1997), pp.159–72; Valiulis, '"Free Women in a Free Nation": Nationalist Feminist Expectations for Independence', in B. Farrell (ed.), *The Creation of the Dáil* (Dublin: Blackwater Press, 1994), pp.75–90; Valiulis, 'Defining Their Role in the New State: Irishwomen's Protest Against the Juries Act of 1927', *The Canadian Journal of Irish Studies*, 18, 1 (July 1992), pp.43–60. Louise Ryan, 'Constructing "Irishwoman": Modern Girls and Comely Maidens', *Irish Studies Review*, 6, 3 (1998), pp.263–72; Ryan, 'Irish Female Emigration in the 1930s: Transgressing Space and Culture', *Gender, Place and Culture*, 8, 3 (2001), pp.271–82; Ryan, 'Sexualising Emigration: Discourses of Irish Female Emigration in the 1930s', *Women's Studies International Forum*, 25, 1 (2002), pp.51–65; Ryan, *Gender, Identity and the Irish Press*. Rosemary Rowley, 'Women and the Constitution', *Administration*, 31, 1 (1989), pp.42–62.
13. The Criminal Law Amendment Act officially was 'An Act to make further and better provision for the protection of young girls and the suppression of brothels and prostitution, and for those and other purposes to amend the law relating to sexual offences'. It also prohibited the sale and importation of contraceptives, and thus did not apply only to young girls but to all women in Ireland. The Aliens Act defined aliens as all those who were not citizens of Saorstát Éireann, and, as might be expected, obliged them to obey all rules of the country. It also allowed for the State to regulate an alien's movements, and to determine their nationality when this was 'unknown or uncertain'. Irish nationality was guaranteed by birth in the country and by descent, and the 1935 Irish Nationality and Citizenship Act sought to define more clearly an Irish identity distinct from a British or Commonwealth identity. See note 39 for further details of the Conditions of Employment Act.
14. Cumann na nGaedheal became Fine Gael in 1934.
15. For further discussion of this phrase, see Nira Yuval-Davis, *Gender and Nation* (London: Sage Publications, 1997) and Benedict Anderson, *Imagined Communities* (London: Verso, 1991 revised edition).
16. Yuval-Davis, *Gender and Nation*, p.45.
17. Ryan, 'Sexualising Emigration', p.59.
18. T. Garvin, *Preventing the Future: Why was Ireland so Poor for so Long?* (Dublin: Gill and Macmillan, 2004), p.xiv.
19. Ryan, *Gender, Identity and the Irish Press*, p.109.
20. Editorial article, 'Irish Emigration', *Freeman's Journal*, 4 April 1923, p.4.
21. R.E. Kennedy, *The Irish: Emigration, Marriage and Fertility* (Berkeley, CA: University of

California Press, 1973), p.75.
22. 'Irish Emigration Statistics', *The Irish Press*, quoting the Department of Industry and Commerce statistical abstract, 10 December 1931, p.1.
23. Central Statistics Office, *Census of Population 1951: Preliminary Report*, Table E, p.12. The lowest proportion of women in comparison to men was in the province of Connacht, with the highest in Leinster in 1951.
24. P. Travers, '"There was nothing for me there": Irish Female Emigration, 1922–71', in P. O'Sullivan (ed.), *Irish Women and Irish Migration* (London: Leicester University Press, 1995), pp.148–67 (p.148).
25. Females, for example, constituted 55 per cent of emigrations from Munster and Connacht between 1946 and 1956, with emigration from these counties being higher than from Leinster or Ulster. *Census of Population 1951: Preliminary Report*, p.18.
26. See C. Dunne, *An Unconsidered People* (Dublin: New Island, 2003). Many may also not have been in paid employment before emigrating and may have put their intended employment down at times when this was recorded. See J. Meenan, *The Irish Economy Since 1922* (Liverpool: Liverpool University Press, 1970), p.211.
27. A. Rossiter, 'Bringing the Margins in to the Centre: A Review of Aspects of Irish Women's Emigration from a British Perspective', in A. Smyth (ed.), *Irish Women's Studies Reader* (Dublin: Attic Press, 1993), pp.177–202 (p.191); and M. Muldowney, 'The Impact of the Second World War on Women in Belfast and Dublin: An Oral History' (Unpublished PhD Thesis, Trinity College Dublin, 2005), and her subsequent book, *The Second World War and Irish Women: An Oral History* (Dublin: Irish Academic Press, 2007).
28. Taken from the reports in *Irish Independent* of the Lenten Pastoral given by Dr. McNamee, 8 February 1937, p.7.
29. For example, the work of the Aisling Project shows the extent of homelessness, social isolation and substance abuse among many Irish male long-term migrants to Britain. See http://www.aisling.org.uk/html/new_intro.php for further details of the project.
30. I am referring most particularly to Article 41 which states that: 'In particular the State recognises that by her life within the home, woman gives to the State a support without which the common good cannot be achieved. The State shall, therefore, endeavour to ensure that mothers shall not be obliged by economic necessity to engage in labour to the neglect of their duties in the home.'
31. Ryan, *Gender, Identity and the Irish Press*, p.2.
32. 'Matrimony and Emigration', article on the Lenten Pastoral of Dr. Gilmartin, *Irish Independent*, 8 February 1937.
33. Speech made on 16 May 1926 at La Scala theatre in Dublin.
34. De Valera, *Dáil Debates*, Volume 108, Col. 2133, 20 November 1947.
35. J. McLaughlin, 'The Historical Background to "New Wave" Irish Emigration', in J. McLaughlin (ed.), *Location and Dislocation in Contemporary Irish Society: Emigration and Irish Identities* (Cork: Cork University Press, 1997), pp.5–35 (p.22).
36. J.J. Lee, *Ireland, 1912–1985*, as quoted in Dunne, *An Unconsidered People*, p.1.
37. Dunne, *An Unconsidered People*, p.30.
38. Ibid., p.140.
39. Under this Act the Minister for Industry and Commerce had the power to prohibit female industrial employment, or else fix the proportion of female workers permitted to be employed in any organization. See section 16 (1) of the Act for further particulars.
40. The marriage bar came into effect through a regulation instituted by the Minister for Finance, Ernest Blythe to Section 9 of the Civil Service Regulation Act (1924) on 26 April 1924 whereby it was decreed that 'Female Civil Servants holding established posts will be required on marriage to resign from the Civil Service' (Unnumbered Statutory Rules and Orders).
41. M.E. Daly, *Women and Work in Ireland* (Dublin: Irish Economic and Social History Society, 1997), p.53.
42. R. King and H. O'Connor, 'Migration and Gender: Irish Women in Leicester', *Geography*, 81, 4 (1996), p.313.
43. Rural Survey, Tralee, conducted by Mr Honohan, Arnold Marsh Papers 8306/S6, Trinity College Dublin.
44. Evidence taken from a memo submitted by the Irish Housewives Association relating to 1948, Arnold Marsh Papers 8305/9, Trinity College Dublin.
45. E. Delaney, 'Irish Migration to Britain, 1921–1971: Patterns, Trends and Contingent Factors'

(Unpublished PhD thesis, Queen's University Belfast, 1997), p.302.
46. Unsigned Memorandum for Government, 'Emigration of Irish Girls for Employment in Great Britain', Arnold Marsh Papers 8300/12/2, Trinity College Dublin.
47. 'A "Domestic" Problem: Irish Girls and Employment in England', *The Irish Catholic*, 29 May 1926, p.2.
48. Ibid.
49. Sharon Lambert found evidence in her research of women being compelled to emigrate by their families in order to support younger siblings. See S. Lambert, 'Irish Women's Emigration to England: 1922–60: The Lengthening of Family Ties', in A. Hayes and D. Urquhart (eds), *Irish Women's History* (Dublin: Irish Academic Press, 2004), pp.152–67.
50. M. Lennon, M. McAdam and J. O'Brien, *Across the Water: Irish Women's Lives in Britain* (London: Virago Press, 1988), p.94.
51. Ibid., p.33.
52. B. Gray, 'Unmasking Irishness', in J. McLaughlin (ed.), *Location and Dislocation in Contemporary Irish Society: Emigration and Irish Identities* (Cork: Cork University Press, 1997), pp.209–35 (p.209).
53. Gertrude Gaffney, 'Irish Girl Emigrants: The Dangers they Encounter', *Irish Independent*, 7 December 1936, p.5.
54. Ryan, 'Sexualising Emigration', p.61.
55. 'Painted Girls of the Dance Halls: Achbishop's Denunciation', *The Irish Catholic*, 16 May 1931, p.5. It is interesting to note that this rather explicit sermon was given after a children's confirmation ceremony in Claremorris.
56. Garrett, 'The Hidden History of the PFIs', p.26.
57. Ibid. and his other article on the subject: Garrett, 'The Abnormal Flight'; and L. Earner-Byrne '"Moral Repatriation"', and her earlier article, 'The Boat to England: An Analysis of the Official Reactions to the Emigration of Single Expectant Irishwomen to Britain, 1922–1972', *Irish Economic and Social History*, XXX (2003), pp.52–70. This subject has also been dealt with by Maria Luddy and Cliona Murphy (eds), *Women Surviving: Studies in Irish Women's History in the 19th and 20th Centuries* (Dublin: Poolbeg Press, 1990), although space does not permit a detailed examination of the history of unmarried mothers and welfare policies in Ireland.
58. Dunne, *An Unconsidered People*, p.104.
59. Reference is made to Sheila Dillon (a pseudonym) in Dunne, an *Unconsidered People*, p.155.
60. 'Keep your Daughters at Home', *The Irish Catholic*, 8 August 1936, p.8.
61. Lambert, 'Irish Women's Emigration to England: 1922-60', p.152. Lambert's analysis is based on interviews with forty Irish women who emigrated to Lancashire between 1922 and 1960.
62. Dunne, *An Unconsidered People*, p.48.
63. Ferriter, *Transformation of Ireland*, p.334.
64. This collection of letters, which I have termed the Nestor–Corless Letters were shown to me after a public appeal for original source material. The letters were written by Josephine Corless née Nestor, who was in Dunmore in Galway, to Paddy Corless who travelled around England in pursuit of work during the war era. The letters referred to here are from 1944. A selection of the letters, as well as Paddy Corless' official travel documentation, have been given to Trinity College Manuscripts Department.
65. Lennon, McAdam and O'Brien, *Across the Water*, p.99.
66. For more on Irish people in England and ethnicity, see B. Walter, *Outsiders Inside*: *Whiteness, Place, and Irish Women* (London: Routledge, 2001).
67. Rossiter, 'Bringing the Margins into the Centre', p.193.
68. Dunne, *An Unconsidered People*, p.83.
69. J. Walvin, *Passage to Britain: Immigration in British History and Politics* (Middlesex: Penguin Books, 1984).
70. J. Herson, 'Family History and Memory in Irish Immigrant Families', in K. Burrell and P. Panayi (eds), *Histories and Memories: Migrants and their History in Britain* (London: Tauris Academic Studies, 2006), pp.210–33 (p.220).
71. 'Employment and Living Conditions of Irish Workers in Great Britain'. Prepared by Mr. S. Lyon, Arnold Marsh Papers 8306/S24, Manuscripts Department, Trinity College Dublin.
72. See, for example, S. Lambert, *Irish Women in Lancashire 1922–1960: Their Story* (Lancaster: University of Lancaster Press, 2001).

CHAPTER TEN

Doing Gender History Visually

ÚNA NÍ BHROIMÉIL AND
DÓNAL O DONOGHUE

INTRODUCTION

This chapter critically engages with ways in which visual methodologies can be used in gender history research. We propose a radical reconceptualization of the place and purpose of the visual in this field. As Fintan Cullen observes, historians do not tend to analyze the visual in terms of its own discipline but rather misuse it as 'a silent resource ... the uncommented use of art as illustration'.[1] Taking up Cullen's call to historians to 'confront the visual in a more considerate fashion and accept that it is as much part of the cultural mix of a period as contemporary diaries and other text-based sources',[2] we propose and model ways of engaging the visual in gender history research. Our aim here is to map out and articulate methodological approaches located in contemporary art practice and visual narrative that, we believe, provide powerful ways of making visible gender constructs in historical moments. We do this from two very different disciplinary and methodological backgrounds, with different understandings of the role, and indeed potential, of the visual in gender history. Following Ball, collectively we show how engaging in, with and through the visual requires a shift in emphasis, a new way of doing and engaging with scholarship, and how it extends the sites of dissemination already available for work undertaken in this field. As Ball claims, 'To be committed to the development of different ways of knowing through the development of different methodologies, and alternative writing strategies, necessitates the development of different research/scholarly practices.'[3]

In conceptualizing how we might engage the visual in gender history research we draw on our respective studies of the masculinizing practices and feminizing practices of two single-sex primary teacher training colleges in Ireland in the early twentieth century. For both our respective inquiries we sourced visual and textual data, individual, group and college photographs, college prospectuses, a college rule book and teaching practice reports. We sourced data that extended over a period between 1900 and 1938. For the purposes of clarity, we deal with each study on its own. This allows us to articulate and make visible the types of data and methods of analysis and representation that we undertook in our respective research studies.

UNCOVERING MASCULINIZING PRACTICES AND THE SOCIAL CONSTRUCTION AND REGULATION OF MASCULINITIES IN A SINGLE-SEX MALE TEACHER TRAINING COLLEGE

This inquiry focused on the masculinizing practices in a male single-sex residential teacher training college in Ireland during the opening decades of the twentieth century. For the purpose of this study, masculinizing practices are conceptualized as all those social, discursive, material and institutional practices and performances that confront, challenge, form, shape and influence male subjectivities and masculine identities. In the study, particular attention was devoted to what happened in Practicing Schools,[4] when student-teachers practised teaching. During this period which occurred for a total of six weeks each year (in two three-week blocks) student-teachers taught large classes of boys in front of their college professors, namely the Professor of Method and his Assistant. Their performances were observed, written about and graded. The written accounts (which speak of how students taught, what they taught, and how in the process they projected, performed and negotiated their identities in this space) appear in handwritten and leather bound report books. When closely read, these reports provide significant insights into how male identities and masculine subjectivities were played out, performed, monitored and surveyed and recorded. As John Beynon claims 'recent critical studies address masculinity directly as a socio-historical cultural concept, [but] older texts deal with it indirectly, even obliquely, and can be profitably reread against the grain'.[5] Similarly, David Morgan discusses what a deconstructive reading of such texts, a reading which involves 'reading between the lines', a searching for themes that are not always clearly stated, a reading of 'absences as well as presences, to decode the text or to discover hidden or suppressed meaning',[6] might offer in coming to understand how identities are constructed, performed, negotiated and played-out. Following Beynon and Morgan, in this study the teaching practice reports were closely read, themes were identified and patterns mapped out which demonstrated the ways in which masculinities were constructed and regulated in, with and through narratives of teaching and teacher practice.

The outcomes of this analysis were first disseminated in academic publications.[7] These publications demonstrate how the management of the body during Teaching Practice was central to the acquisition of status and distinction as a man, and as a male teacher. Certain bodily forms and bodily performances were recognized as possessing value; some were valued more than others, and certain bodily forms and performances carried a greater exchange value when it came to the awarding of grades. Legitimate and deviant ways of managing and experiencing bodies were identified and articulated. They were further categorized as manly or unmanly, and manliness as manifested in bodily form and bodily performance was fundamental to the forms of masculinities promoted within this site. But, as Lawrence-Lightfoot argues 'academic documents – even those that focus on issues of broad public concern – are read by a small audience of people in the same disciplinary field, who often share similar conceptual frameworks and rhetoric'.[8]

How, then, might we construct and communicate histories of men teachers and teaching to a wider and more diverse audience if we believe that the primary purpose of research is to enlarge understanding and advance knowledge? How might we reconfigure the relationship between research texts and their readers/receivers with a view to extending the places and spaces where the outcomes of scholarly inquiries might be disseminated and debated? What practices and processes might we adopt to ensure that research in this field does more than merely inform? What role, if any, can the visual and the practice of art-making play in this process? How might doing and representing research, in, with and through art reconfigure the text we have come to know as the research text? These are some of the questions that I was interested in exploring and addressing when I searched for other ways of making visible that which I came to observe, understand and know from closely reading these teaching practice report books. My questions were grounded in a larger debate about the role and purposes of the arts in research. Within educational research and indeed within the academy there is a growing awareness and recognition of how and what research practices based in the arts can disclose about educational settings and situations. For example, as early as 1993 Elliot Eisner, in his Presidential Address at the American Educational Research Association's annual conference, put forth a call for research that was evocative, and that examined the qualities of education rather than reported on testable facts or results. In a subsequent article he asked what could alternate forms of data representation offer for expanding knowledge and deepening understanding about the worlds that we wish to better comprehend. He answered his question claiming that 'alternate forms of data representation promise to increase the variety of questions that we can ask about the educational situations we study ... we can expect new ways of seeing things, new settings for their display, and new problems to tackle ... put another way, our capacity to wonder is stimulated by the possibilities the new forms of representation suggest'.[9]

However, as I have argued elsewhere, in the process of conceptualizing or doing research, researchers rarely look towards, or at the work of artists, their practices and processes of art-making and their methods of representing and giving visual form to concepts and ideas.[10] Rather, researchers look towards the practices, processes and understandings generated by other researchers, scholars and theoreticians in their field. I have argued that while art can be viewed as a product, it is also a process, a set of ideas, a way of knowing, an encounter with others, and therefore has the potential to inform and guide the design and dissemination of research.[11] Socially and politically engaged artists have always been concerned with drawing attention to social, cultural and political agendas and issues. The work and work practices of such artists attend to making the familiar strange and the strange familiar, as well as making visible that which is hidden but present.

In order to illustrate my point, I could draw on the work and work practices of many contemporary artists, but one artist whose work is particularly useful in this regard is Paul Seawright. Much of Seawright's work engages with the Troubles in Northern Ireland. In a series in which he photographed the unsentimental interiors of police stations and security installations there is an effort to draw attention to and make visible one of the many by-products of the Troubles, by-products that we do not tend to think about, because they are not visible. These are by-products that we do not always recognize because we do not see them; by-products that we do not acknowledge, because we do not know about them. In this work he documents and draws attention to these exaggerated environments which were commonplace throughout Northern Ireland during the Troubles. These were the spaces where policemen and soldiers spent their working lives. In recording these environments Seawright shows that they were brutal and brutalizing spaces that were never seen by many civilians. This work deals with issues and themes of exclusion, imprisonment and surveillance. His work functions as metaphors for deep-seated philosophical polarization in Irish political culture during this time, as does the work of Tracey Moffat which engages with issues of race, sexuality, identity and family. In a recent show in the Guggenheim New York, called *Family Pictures*, Moffat presented a series of work titled *Scarred for Life*, showing children or adolescents, both aboriginal and white, in suburban settings. Each piece records and speaks to a different trauma inflicted by parents or older siblings. Printed as photolithographs in muted colours on cream paper and accompanied by short neutral but descriptive captions, Moffat uses actors to stage these documentary photographs. Jennifer Blessing argues that this "series of deliberately ambiguous and open ended mini-narratives ... evokes the fragmented nature of memory and, as implied in the title, the way which injuries from our childhood years remain with us throughout our adult lives'.[12]

It is true to say that artists have always been in pursuit of giving visual forms to ideas. As noted above, their work is both product and process and has the potential to offer new and different ways of thinking about how we inquire, conduct and represent research finding and build understanding and meaning making. In this present inquiry on masculinizing practices in teacher training, practices and processes of contemporary art offered ways to represent that which I witnessed over and over again in these teaching practice texts – the presentation of particular models of masculinity, the legitimating of certain ways of being and acting like a man, as well as the instability of the masculinities that were constructed, classified, resisted, naturalized and embodied through repeated and stylized acts of performance, pre/formances and post/formances. It provided a way of presenting the many narratives that were happening simultaneously, and to represent the tensions and contradictions in and across these narratives of being and acting in 'manly' ways.

Drawing on the data and textual findings, and cognizant of the potential contribution for understanding that art-making and art products offer, I created an installation comprising four projection screens one positioned on each of the four walls in a blacked out gallery space, and opposite one another and surrounding the viewer (see Figures 1, 2, 3 and 4). Projected onto these four 6ft by 8ft screens are images of college and school interiors, photographs taken from the archive and altered in small ways in order to direct attention to certain parts of the image and direct attention away from other parts. These images come and go. They alternate and change so that at any one time the viewer may be surrounded by the same image, projected on all four screens. Equally, at any given time the viewer may be confronted with four different images. Using slide projectors, I project onto these images extracts taken from the Teaching Practice Reports or the College Rule book; extracts that construct, story, and go in some way to shape these men; words, descriptors, phrases that articulate, legitimate or make deviant particular ways of managing and experiencing one's teacher body. The extracts come and go, always being replaced by another. Words, descriptors, phrases such as 'a nervous and fidgety individual, very earnest but a trifle peculiar, strikes one as being old womanish. Suffers from scruples in relation to points of little importance.' While the installation addresses and extends findings, themes and patterns that emerged in the textual analysis, it offers an additional set of reading and interpretative possibilities. It provides for a range of narratives to be presented simultaneously and contiguously: narratives that speak of the concerted effort of college authorities to construct teaching bodies, form particular types of men, impart Catholic teaching (especially with regard to the body), and disavow homosexual practice among other things. It allows for narratives that describe how the college engaged in a body-building project while men practised teaching. Narratives that encouraged and directed men to act and speak in particular ways: 'Took some time to get this young man to speak and act in a manly fashion'.

Drawing on the close and critical reading of these report books and college photographs which incorporated aspects and techniques of image-based analysis,[13] video ethnography,[14] and photo-elicitation,[15] the installation presents a different narrative structure from that which we are very familiar with in research insofar as it breaks the pattern of a linear narrative, and formulates discontinuous, partial stories. It offers a way to rethink research texts and the relationship between them and their readers. Installed in a gallery, it also speaks to a different audience in a place vastly different from scholarly conferences or publications. It offers opportunities for making visible in visual and three-dimensional form tensions in representation and construction. It brings together images and text in an effort to offer space for interpretation and meaning-making. However, the installation does not simply present images and text, separately, simultaneously and contiguously. Rather the installation is about relationships and conversations between these two active meaning-makers: image and text; the subject and the object; the viewer and the viewed; the student teacher and the professor of method. This installation speaks *of* and *to* ways of seeing. It is about acts of perception, objectification, subjectivity, signification, construction, and meaning-making through looking. While the viewer is being presented with ways in which others saw, pictured and constructed these men teachers and their environs, the installation too requires the viewer (the participant) to engage in processes of identification, objectification and signification, remembering through looking while simultaneously being distanced by the ethnographic aspect of these images and projections.

Similar to the published paper, the installation (*Safe Distance*) is a record of recursive, reflexive and reflective analyses and reanalyses. Images have been selected and choices made. These photographs are in themselves a product of selection. These are selected sights, selected

Figure 1. *Safe Distance,* 2006, Dónal O Donoghue. Installation with text.

Figure 2. *Safe Distance,* 2006, Dónal O Donoghue. Installation with text.

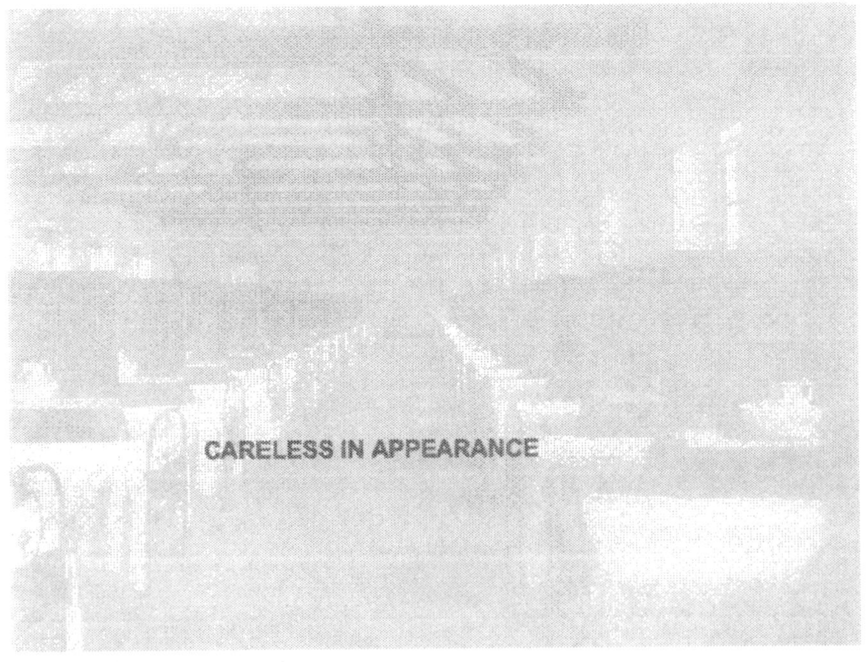

Figure 3. *Safe Distance,* 2006, Dónal O Donoghue. Installation with text.

places from an infinite number of other sights of other spaces. Images of men standing, looking, walking, thinking, feeling, acting, wondering, performing. Images of the spaces and places where these men were formed and form; places and spaces that constitute masculinities and are constituted by particular understandings of masculinities. I focus on positions and positioning, points of connection and points of departure, lines that demarcate and lines that reunite, shapes that lead and mislead, points of entry and exit, boundaries. I attend to surfaces, textures, forms, light, shadows, presences and absences, colours, details. I include some and discard others; I crop; I trim; I position; I join; I create; I make patterns (visual and textual); I add text; I take text away; I position text in images, sometimes beside an image, other times under, over, above or below an image. And I do this to make visible the masculinization practices and processes in practice classrooms.

This installation provides a place and a means for 'learning to perceive differently': I view this work as text, as a tangle of texts, as a text that is being written, rewritten, read and reread, a text that integrates knowing, doing and making. It attends to absences, to the things that are not said, and it makes visible the many things that are said but in ways that are revealing. It, too, is a text to be interrogated. This installation tells the story of projection and construction. The very act of projection (using a slide projector, I project these words, descriptors and phrases, images in their own right, onto images) speaks of an identity that is constructed out of, and through projection. This is not an embodied identity. It is one generated from projections – carefully selected and collated projections. Are these projected identities, projected constructions, projected imaginings and classifications? Does this work speak of disembodied identities, identities that are constructed outside and beyond the person or identities that others construct? Is this work about the possibilities of living different identities or of living a particular identity that generates another? Is the viewer drawn into this piece of work and becomes part of the work? Is s/he positioned in the work, not outside, or looking in from the outside, but right in the middle of the work? Does s/he move from viewer to participant? *Safe Distance* requires the viewer to be a participant, to view and make connections, to place himself/herself in the work, in the centre, physically emplaced and indeed embodied. It is by looking and seeing that establishes the viewer's relation to the piece. The piece is about opening spaces for understanding, for questing and questioning, looking and re-looking. The kind of reading and understanding that

Figure 4. *Safe Distance,* 2006, Dónal O Donoghue. Installation with text.

might be secured from this art work is influenced in great part by the means through which I have selected to make and present *Safe Distance*. The meaning of the work is thus constituted by and in the form, medium and mode of representation.

The installation offers opportunities for telling and retelling. It speaks simultaneously to acts of construction, reconstruction and co-construction. It is participative and requires participation. It requires the engaged participation of the viewer to search for a story, to seek it out, and co-create it from the images and text projections. The work is never complete in itself. Rather it offers spaces for response, for the construction of meaning and understanding, for connection, disconnection and reconnection.

The changing images, the changing text, the unpredictability of what will happen next, what the juxtapositions will be and how text and image will appear, connect, disconnect, speak to, and of the instability of identity. It too makes visible how identities are constructed, classified, resisted, naturalized and embodied through repeated and stylized acts of performance, pre/formances and post/formances. The Professor of Method's comments are inscribed in the bodies and performance of these men. In the installation they become part of the images, sometimes appearing right across and in front of the image (on the skin of the image), and other times they are written in the image (in the body of the image). The only constant is that they are constantly shifting and changing and unsettling our perceptions, our knowing.

The representation of the data in this manner requires active engagement, continuous movement in and through the artwork both conceptually and physically. As James Olthuis observes, being in the presence of creative works necessitates that all participants (the producers, receivers, meaning-makers) are always in the process of 'becoming'.[16] In creating and showing this installation there was a desire to create spaces to linger in, liminal spaces, spaces to encounter.

UNCOVERING FEMINIZING PRACTICES AND THE SOCIAL CONSTRUCTION AND REGULATION OF FEMININITIES IN A SINGLE-SEX FEMALE TEACHER TRAINING COLLEGE

Historians, as Sean Farrell Moran observes, find nontextual evidence 'uncertain' as they are 'committed to the study of written documentary evidence from which they construct narratives'.[17] Photographs nonetheless are of particular interest to the historian. They are evidence of actuality; that, as Barthes suggests, '*the thing has been there*'.[18] They offer up visual connections with the past and bring an absence into the present. They produce, as Rousmaniere, Lawn and Grosvenor have stated, a '"trace" of human activity which can be deciphered'.[19] As signifiers of hard truth, however, they are unreliable. They can perpetuate stereotypes. They can sentimentalize and romanticize. They can reinforce mythologies that define and compartmentalize people. They can present 'a type, a popular perception ... locked in time'.[20] But using photographs as a primary source allows for what Kracaeur calls the redemption of physical reality.[21] The images provide petrified, concrete collections for the historian to order and to clarify possible patterns of intelligibility. Wigoder compares the archive of photographs to an orphanage 'lying in hundreds of boxes and waiting to be sorted. In this jumble of homeless images, one can suddenly find a new order that enables reality to be examined critically'.[22] It is in the finding of this new order that the historian can make sense of the archive.

While the photographic image, Szarkowski suggests, survives the subject and becomes the remembered reality,[23] the images themselves are but fragments of the past. Severed from the broader context of the era the images are merely snapshots of a particular space in time devoid of memories or of knowledge and representing only the appearance of the subject. The historian can, however, use the photographic archive to unlock memories and illuminate particular eras. Evoking Proust's 'memoire involontaire'[24] and Kracaeur's historical subjectivity, the historian can construct the broader context of the past to suggest memories and stories by piecing together the images with other fragments of the past.[25] In this way despite the materiality of images as objects of history, these two-dimensional, cultural artefacts 'at' which we look, it is possible to regard the photographs as a portal through which we can enter and look 'around' – 'to step inside the image... [to] disrupt a traditional narrative of history' and to create, as Rousmaniere states, a 'disjuncture' and one which 'allows [for] the creation of new meaning'.[26]

The interrogation of the photographic archive is therefore not just about seeing the past but about constructing a complex and multi-layered narrative. It requires an engagement with Benjamin's notion of photography's 'optical unconscious' in order to release meanings that were not always apparent at the moment of capture or encapsulation.[27] These meanings and perceptions can be attended to and emphasized by the manner of their representation – through montage and what Rousmaniere calls the 'jumbling together [of] images from different sites and histories'; through the juxtaposition of text with image as in Carrie May Weems' Hampton Project; or in the juxtaposition of past with present such as Victor Burgin's Minnesota Abstract 1989.[28]

In this work I utilize techniques of montage, overlayering and juxtaposition. I scrutinize and deconstruct a series of photographs of women who were training to be primary school teachers in a Catholic single-sex training college in Ireland between the years 1902–30. Created as semi-public documents, these images stand as a record of the presence of these women and of their environment and emplacement. I have overlaid the college photographs with text from the teaching practice reports and with comments made by supervisors who observed the students' practice of teaching in the practicing schools. Excerpts from articles on The Lady Teacher's Own page in the *Irish School Weekly* which was published by the Irish National Teachers' Organisation (INTO), as well as excepts from the Mary Immaculate College annuals written by the students themselves, are juxtaposed with the images. These methods allow for the creation of

Figure 5. *Class*. Image with text.

new and composite images which highlight and amplify the cultural context and milieu in which these women were socialized and through which they operated. By juxtaposing the text with the image I hope to restore an individuality and vitality to the frozen images of groups of women teachers and to elude the objectification of the camera.[29] By creating a series of multilayered, composite images I create a kind of visual palimpsest – where images and text are superimposed onto each other, presenting interwoven historical narratives. This palimpsest belies the notion of the one coherent narrative and suggests that there is not one narrative but many. This in turn leads away from the notion of these women teachers as stereotypes locked into a static and unchanging version of the past.

The central image and representation of women in these images is primarily one of refinement. It requires, as Penny Tinkler has pointed out in her study of the representation of women smokers, attention to the finer details of appearance and is a key signifier of feminine respectability.[30] This is particularly evident in the clothing of the body which is in itself an identifier of social class. Clothing is also, as Burman and Turbin have pointed out, 'one of the most consistently gendered aspects of material and visual culture'.[31] The clothed and fashioned body is at once

Figure 6. *Calling 1*. Photo section.

Figure 7. *Calling 2*. Photo section.

a marker of taste and class and a signifier of personal identity, although clothing can be used to regulate and discipline bodies and act as a marker of social inclusion and exclusion.[32] A 'tone' pervades these image and text pieces and an ambience of quality is created. We are aware of flowers and of lace in these photographs, of the importance of the presentation of the body to convey status and respectability. This sense of status is evident also in the prominent display of books as symbols of these women's occupation. The use of an occupational tool is a common element in early photographic portraits, according to Marsha Peters, and signifies a 'consciousness, pride and occupational identification'.[33] Interestingly, they are only used in the early photographs when the teaching profession was in transition from being a predominantly male profession to becoming a predominantly female profession between 1900 and 1910.

Whether the women themselves chose to portray themselves as teaching professionals or whether it was a photographic norm is unclear. John Berger claims that the normalizing gaze is male: '*men act and women appear.* Men look at women and women watch themselves being looked at ... and the surveyor of woman in herself is male'.[34] This could be taken to mean that these women were fashioned and shaped but were passive in this formation and would appear to lend credence to the concept of women as receivers of the dominant social and cultural setting and location. Women were placed in their sphere. And yet photography allows for and facilitates a construction or a performance by these women. Barthes remarks on the ability of the referent in the photograph to construct and to fashion the product: 'in front of the lens I am at the same time: the one I think I am, the one I want others to think I am, the one the photographer thinks I am'.[35] Because the photograph can be seen not only by others but also by oneself it suggests as Laikwan Pang claims 'a will to power in terms of presenting one's body and identity according to one's wishes'.[36] What the women themselves chose to wear indicates their own sense of position in society: recognition in themselves of their sense of status and standing both to themselves and to the wider community. What is certain is that they were conscious of their appearance in these photographs. In the College Annuals the taking of the photographs is listed prominently in the college diaries and remarked upon by the students:

> October 5th – we assume an optimistic expression of countenance – to have our photographs taken!

10,000 6d. POWDER LEAF BOOKS FREE.

Oatine Powder Leaves are put up in dainty booklets containing 200 leaves. They will be found most useful to all ladies, for, being small and neatly packed, they are easily carried in the purse or pocket. All that is necessary is to tear out a leaf, rubbing it over the face. The paper will then absorb and remove all oiliness, perspiration, and dust from the skin and leave in their place a delicate deposit of powder. The Powder Leaves are supplied in three tints and are delicately perfumed. To introduce this dainty toilet requisite the proprietors will give one of these 6d. Powder Leaf booklets, absolutely free, to all who send for one of the Oatine Shampoo Powders, the price of which is 2d., and send a further 1d. for postage. Address, The Oatine Company, 289B Oatine Buildings, Borough, London, S.E.

Figure 8. *Veneer 1*. Image with text.

Figure 9. *Veneer 2*. Image with text.

> October 27th – Mirrors practically inaccessible. Reason – Photographs after dinner.[37]

While the teaching practice reports rarely comment on the women's clothing and appearance (other than to occasionally state that the student was 'presentable') focusing instead on the women's manner, voice or stance, the images suggest a conscious deliberation and calculation on the part of the women themselves to appear in certain ways consistent with a bourgeois identity.

And yet this image overlaid with text (Figure 9) is suggestive of veneer, of a finish which marks and stamps and reinforces the identity of the group and makes of them a cohesive and interrelated body of women. Middle-class women did not necessarily form the body of entrants into the college. While the social backgrounds of the women in these reports are unclear, the majority in the period studied were aged 20 and had some experience either as pupil-teachers or as monitresses in the schools. There were some older women aged 25 and 29 who had been Junior Assistant Mistresses before commencing their course of training. The fact that they were mature females with experience suggests that these women belonged, for the most part, to the lower middle class, which was expanding in turn of the century Ireland, and also that they were the daughters of small and middling farmers in rural areas. The college was therefore cultivating an air of gentility about these students that would be commensurate with their status as trained lady teachers when they re-entered the world of work. The photographic process and resulting images echo this 'becoming' as Benjamin asserts: 'The procedure itself caused the models to live, not out of the instant, but *into* it; during the long exposure they grew as it were into the image.'[38]

While the production of a feminine appearance was a testament to social standing and taste, the female teacher always had to remember her place and to be wary of immodesty in appearance. In the following image there appears to be a creeping rigidity of manner, of dress, a hardening of attitudes and an insularity which borders on intolerance in the images which reflect the era of the Modest Dress and Deportment Crusade.[39] The cheerful faces belie the unyielding atmosphere of this era as the students sought not only to behave as role models for the children in their charge and to induct them into the ways of the Crusade, but to actively disapprove of all manner of 'modern' dress fashion or of anything that might reflect poorly on their image as pure, demure, upstanding and feminine. In the first

Figure 10. *Chain of Command*. Image with text.

issue of the *Mary Immaculate Training College Annual* in 1927 an article entitled 'Wanted – A New Woman' set out the reasons for and rules of the MDDC. It stated that while a return to 'ridiculous' Victorian fashions was out of the question, describing them as inconvenient and unhygienic, 'modern' fashions were 'mannish' and 'indecent'. What was required, according to the students, was a 'Crusade in the interests of womanly modesty' which 'while aiming at stamping out what is mannish and immodest, not only allows but encourages girls to dress tastefully and becomingly and thereby win the admiration and respect of all'.[40] The propriety and seemliness of a woman's behaviour was also evident in her deportment. Cigarette smoking was 'mannish', 'opposed to womanly delicacy' and 'harmful to health' and while it was acknowledged by the Crusaders as a hard habit to break once acquired, no teacher should ever smoke in public.[41]

Neither should she adopt immodest poses, talk loudly or laugh boisterously in public, utter coarse or irreverent exclamations, drink alcohol at dances or entertainments, attend improper cinema shows, plays or all night dances, or partake in immodest or suggestive dances or sea-bathing.[42] Thus the public teacher persona was one of refinement and poise, of composure and self control, a woman whose person and character could not be questioned as it was so clearly and obviously beyond reproach. This was critical in the case of their religious beliefs. Wearing and displaying the symbols of their Catholicism, particularly the Child of Mary medals, the essence of religious fervour is evident in Figure 10. Peters suggests that the very action of taking a portrait legitimized the group's existence and made the occasion of its gathering an official memory.[43] Here, the sense of group cohesiveness is strengthened and fused with religious overtones and meaning. In this image the students position themselves clearly – on the side of light as opposed to darkness, on the side of order as opposed to anarchy, at the feet of God – as women, as women teachers, as Catholic women teachers.

When we look at the photographs of these women we see group after group of well turned out ladies. Our impression of these women is always as an assemblage, as a unit and this can cause us to classify, categorize and bracket them together as a unified and integrated whole. This cohesion and unity of organization is petrified by the camera, fixed as a monument. The safety of group cohesion is punctured by Figures 11 and 12.

These images remind us of Benjamin's 'tiny spark of accident, the here and now' and are as visceral as Barthes' 'punctum' – the small unintended detail that is powerful enough to disrupt from within and that imbues every photograph and every archive with 'suggestive absences and lurking presences'.[44] The bonds of intimacy between women in the late nineteenth and early twentieth centuries were always more overt than those between men[45] and it is unclear from either the photographs or from a close reading of the textual documents whether this intimacy involved same-sex relationships such as those outlined by Edwards in the English context or by Blount in the American.[46] There are many references in the Annuals to the notion of the students as a family. In fact, one of the reasons given for the institution of the Annual in the first instance was 'with a view to keeping this big family in touch with one another and with their college'.[47] There is only one reference in the Annuals during this period to the possibility of particular friendships and they were represented as antithetical to the ideal of the family-spirit:

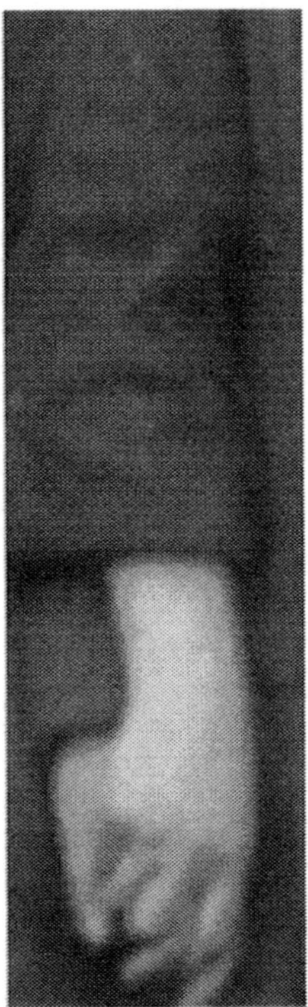

Figure 11. *Student body 1*. Photo section.

Figure 12. *Student body 2*. Photo section.

> Arrived in college, my heart rebelled at first against the small rules and regulations; but I was not long there before I saw that these were all part of the wonderful organisation, and that each, no matter how petty, was necessary for the well-being and happiness of the students as a body, and tended to promote that family spirit amongst them which is so characteristic of the college, where cliques and private parties are looked upon as bad form.[48]

It is the photograph, however, that encapsulates that space between representation and reality and allows the viewer an access to the past by releasing that which might have gone unnoticed. Taken together, the image and text transform the image so as to open up possibilities of seeing in an altered manner. What can the photograph tell us about these women that would have lain hidden or concealed? Does the text contradict the photograph? What, therefore, is the reality of these women's lives? Far from grouping these women teachers together, the juxtaposition of text and image suggests the possibility of exploding the silences that surround the intimacy of women's lives and control of the body. The women captured in these frozen images are imbued with an individualism which is contrary to the unthinking incorporation of them as an assembly or a crowd. The depiction of a stable body of women is disrupted and we need to look again at what we think we know.

What we see from these composite images then is evidence of the socialization of women into ideas of femininity as defined by values such as refinement, modesty and grace. Viewed in their reciprocity these images and texts indicate a way of being, of a regime for the women who inhabited that space in time and in actuality. We are also made aware of the boundaries of that 'normative regime' the challenging of which does not always manifest itself in resistance but in fact as participatory agency so that conceptions of femininity are continually being reworked in practice.

CONCLUSION

Both of these studies consider the training colleges as key sites of gender regulation and construction. Both present a narrative of how historical subjects functioned within systems of power. But using visual methodologies and art practice has a powerful provocative effect on the data. The essential role of the visual is to create a nexus between the fragmented realities of the past, to re/collect events and objects and to look *into* the world of the past rather than look *at* it. Using the visual as a primary source compels the viewer to participate in this looking and questing, to actively engage with what went before and to be present in that time. In this way the images we see whether as installation or as photographs are not just historical objects confined to a sepia-coloured past but repositories of memory which can open up new ways of interpreting reality and cause us to re-examine and re-evaluate our conceptions and notions of an era and of the forces and dynamics which were at work therein.

It is not the visual archive itself however that allows this exposure of an era. The manner of presentation or, in this case, *re*/presentation of both visual and textual data obliges us to attend to what we see and think we know and to open up possibilities for contesting and complicating those 'truths'. It enables us, as Jolicoeur suggests, to trouble the archive 'by collecting, disassembling and recollecting, in different ways, what was once immobilized for preservation' and by questioning 'the authorized epistemologies by the act of remembering'.[49] There is a subjectivity in this representation, an ordering which draws attention to key issues and themes of gender construction. This new order allows for the exploration of that which may have gone unnoticed and gives to the viewer an altered perspective. In making visible the multiple experiences of the lives of these men and women we eschew nostalgia and memorialization. Rather we open up a new territory for investigation, to look again at the construction of gender roles and their shifting meanings through time.

NOTES

1. F. Cullen, 'Art History: Using the Visual', in L.M. Geary and Margaret Kelleher (eds), *Nineteenth-Century Ireland – A Guide to Recent Research* (Dublin: University College, Dublin Press, 2005), p.160.
2. Ibid., p.161.
3. M. Ball, *Looking in: The Art of Viewing* (Amsterdam: G + B Arts International imprint, 2001), p.24.
4. Apart from being located on the college campus and providing a space for student teachers to practice teaching, Practicing Schools were similar in most respects to national schools in Ireland at the time.
5. J. Beynon, *Masculinities and Culture* (Buckingham: Open University Press, 2002), p.144.
6. D.H.G. Morgan, *Discovering Men* (London: Routledge, 1992), p.50 as cited by Beynon.
7. See D. O Donoghue, '"Speak and act in a manly fashion": The Role of the Body in the Construction of Men and Masculinity in Primary Teacher Education in Ireland', in A. Cleary (ed.), *Masculinities, Irish Journal of Sociology: special issue*, Masculinities, 14, 2 (2005), pp.231–52; and D. O Donoghue, 'Teaching Bodies who Teach: Men's Bodies and the Reconstruction of Male Teacher Identity in Ireland', in S. Springgay and D. Freedman (eds), *Curriculum and the Cultural Body* (New York: Peter Lang, 2007), pp.91–113.
8. S. Lawrence-Lightfoot, 'A View of the Whole: Origins and Purposes', in S. Lawrence-Lightfoot and J. Hoffmann Davis, *The Art and Science of Portraiture* (San Francisco: Jossey-Bass Publishers, 1997), pp.1–16.

9. E.W. Eisner, 'The Promise and Perils of Alternative Forms of Data Representation', *Educational Researcher*, 26, 6 (1997), p.8.
10. D. O Donoghue, '"That stayed with me until I was an adult": Making Visible the Experiences of Men who Teach', in R.L. Irwin, C. Leggo, K. Grauer, P. Gouzouasis and S. Springgay (eds), *Being with A/r/tography* (Rotterdam: Sense Publishing, 2007), pp.109–24.
11. Ibid.
12. J. Blessing, *Family Pictures* (New York: Guggenheim, 2005), p.100.
13. See C. Burnett, *Jeff Wall* (London: Tate Publishing, 2005); I. Heywood and B. Sandywell, *Interpreting Visual Culture: Explorations in the Hermeneutics of the Visual* (London: Routledge, 1999); L. Sanders-Bustle, *Image, Inquiry, and Transformative Practice: Engaging Learners in Creative and Critical Inquiry through Visual Representation* (New York: Peter Lang, 2003); G. Sullivan, *Art Practice as Research: Inquiry in the Visual Arts* (London: Sage, 2005); J. Wagner, 'Visible Materials, Visualised Theory and Images of Social Research', *Visual Studies*, 21, 1 (2006), pp.55–69.
14. See M. Müller, *The Memo Book: Films, Videos, and Installations by Matthias Müller* (Toronto, Ontario: YYZ Books, 2005); S. Pink, *Doing Visual Ethnography: Images, Media and Representation in Research* (London and Thousand Oaks, CA: Sage Publications, 2001).
15. See J. Collier and M. Collier, *Visual Anthropology: Photography as a Research Method* (Revised and expanded edition) (Albuquerque: University of New Mexico Press, 1986); D. Harper, 'On the Authority of the Image: Visual Methods at the Crossroads', in N.K. Denzin and Y.S. Lincoln (eds), *Collecting and Interpreting Qualitative Materials* (Thousand Oaks, CA: Sage Publications, 1994), pp.130–49; Jon Prosser and D. Schwartz, 'Photographs within the Sociological Research Process', in J. Prosser (ed.), *Image Based Research: A Sourcebook for Qualitative Researchers* (London: Falmer, 1998); D. O Donoghue, '"James always hangs out here": Making Space for Place in Studying Masculinities in Schools', *Visual Studies*, 22, 1 Special Issue, *The Visible Curriculum* (2007) , pp.62–73.
16. J.H. Olthuis, 'Otherwise than Violence: Toward a Hermeneutics of Connection', in L. Zuidervaart and H. Luttifkhuizen (eds), *The Arts, Community and Cultural Democracy* (New York: St Martin's Press, 2000), pp.137–64.
17. S.F. Moran, 'Images, Icons and the Practice of Irish History', in L.W. McBride (ed.), *Images, Icons and the Irish Nationalist Imagination* (Dublin: Four Courts Press, 1999), p.166.
18. R. Barthes, *Camera Lucida – Reflections on Photography* (London: Hill and Wang 1982), p.76.
19. I. Grosvenor, M. Lawn and K. Rousmaniere, 'Imaging Past Schooling: the Necessity for Montage', *The Review of Education/Pedagogy/Cultural Studies*, 22, 1 (2000), pp.71–85.
20. See B.T. Menlove, 'The Outside Looking in: Photographs of Native Americans', *Points West Online*, Summer 2000, http://www.bbhc.org/pointswestPWArticle.cfm?ArticleID =75,accessed 13/03/06.
21. S. Kracauer, *Theory of Film* (New York: Oxford University Press, 1965), p.300, quoted in D.N. Rodowick, 'The Last Things before the Last: Kracauer and History', *New German Critique*, 41, Special Issue on the Critiques of the Enlightenment (Spring–Summer 1987), pp.109–39.
22. M. Wigoder, 'History begins at Home – Photography and Memory in the Writings of Siefried Kracauer and Roland Barthes', *History and Memory*, 13, 1 (2001), pp.19–59, p.29.
23. Quoted in M. Peters and B. Mergen, 'Doing the Rest: the Uses of Photographs in American Studies', *American Quarterly*, 29, 3 (1977), pp.280–303.
24. A concept explored in Marcel's Proust's novel, *A la Recherche du Temps Perdu* in which memories of the past are evoked unconsciously in the person by sights or smells, for example.
25. See Rodowick, 'The Last Things before the Last', p.123.
26. K. Rousmaniere, 'Questioning the Visual in the History of Education', *History of Education*, 30, 2 (2001), pp.109–16.
27. Ibid. See also W. Benjamin, 'A Short History of Photography', in A. Trachtenberg (ed.), *Classical Essays in Photography* (New Haven, CT: Leetes Island Books, 1980), p.203.
28. Rousmaniere, 'Questioning the Visual in the History of Education', pp.109–16; V.

Patterson, *Carrie May Weems, The Hampton Project* (Massachusetts: Aperture in association with Williams College Museum of Art, Williamstown, 2000); L. Taylor (ed.), *Visualizing Theory, Selected Essays from VAR, 1990–1994* (New York and London: Routledge, 1994), Foreword, p.xviii.

29. See J. Leonard, 'Not Losing her Memory: Stories in Photographs, Words and Collage', *Modern Fiction Studies*, 40, 3 (1994), pp.657–85.
30. P. Tinkler, 'Refinement and Respectable Consumption: the Acceptable Face of Women's Smoking in Britain, 1918–1970', *Gender and History*, 15, 2 (August 2003), pp.342–60.
31. B. Burman and C. Turbin, 'Introduction: Material Strategies Engendered', *Gender and History*, 14, 3 (November 2002), pp.371–81.
32. See I. Dussel, 'When Appearances are not Deceptive: A Comparative History of School Uniforms in Argentina and the United States (19th–20th centuries)', *Paedagogica Historica*, 41, 1–2 (2005), pp.179–95; N. Enstad, 'Fashioning Political Identities: Cultural Studies and the Historical Construction of Political Subjects', *American Quarterly*, 50, 4 (1998), pp.745–82.
33. Peters and Mergen, 'Doing the Rest: the Uses of Photographs in American Studies', p.297.
34. J. Berger, *Ways of Seeing* (London: Viking Press, 1972), pp.46–7.
35. Barthes, *Camera Lucida*, p.13.
36. L. Pang, 'Photography, Performance, and the making of Female Images in Modern China', *Journal of Women's History*, 17, 4 (2005), pp.56–85, p.66.
37. *Mary Immaculate Training College Annual*, Vol.1, 1927, p.43; Vol.3, 1929, p.56.
38. Benjamin, 'A Short History of Photography', p.204.
39. In 1927 the students in Mary Immaculate College Limerick founded the Mary Immaculate College Modest Dress and Deportment Crusade (MDDC) which urged Catholic women, especially teachers and their girl pupils, to eschew 'modern, mannish fashions', to dress tastefully and modestly and to emulate the Virgin Mary. See Ú. Ní Bhroiméil, 'Images and icons: female teachers' representations of self and self-control in 1920s Ireland', *History of Education Review*, 37, 1 (2008), pp.4–14.
40. *Mary Immaculate Training College Annual*, Vol.1, 1927, pp.35–6.
41. *Mary Immaculate Training College Annual,* Vol.2, 1928, p.17.
42. *Mary Immaculate Training College Annual,*Vol.2, 1928, pp.17–18.
43. Peters and Mergen, 'Doing the Rest: the Uses of Photographs in American Studies', p.295.
44. Benjamin, 'A Short History of Photography', p.202; Barthes, *Camera Lucida*, p.42: 'occasionally a "detail" attracts me. I feel that its mere presence changes my reading, that I am looking at a new photograph, marked in my eyes with a higher value. This "detail" is the punctum'; D. McCance, 'Introduction', *Mosaic: A Journal for the Interdisciplinary Study of Literature*, 37, 4 (2004), pp.v–xii.
45. See C. Smith Rosenberg, 'The Female World of Love and Ritual: Relations between Women in Nineteenth-Century America', *Signs: Journal of Women in Culture and Society*, 1, 1 (1975), pp.1–29; L. Moore, '"Something more tender still than friendship": Romantic Friendship in Early Nineteenth-Century England', *Feminist Studies*, 18, 3 (Autumn 1992), pp.499–520. See also M. McGarry, 'Female Worlds', *Journal of Women's History*, 12, 3 (2000), pp.9–12 for an interesting reference to *marianismo* and female relationships.
46. See E. Edwards, *Women in Teacher Training Colleges, 1900–1960 : A Culture of Femininity* (London: Routledge, 2001); J. Blount, 'From Exemplar to Deviant: Same-Sex Relationships among Women Superintendents, 1909–1976', *Educational Studies* 35, 2 (2004), pp.103–22.
47. *Mary Immaculate Training College Annual*, Foreword, Vol.1, 1927.
48. *Mary Immaculate Training College Annual*, Vol.IV, 1930. p.56.
49. J. Perrault and P. Levin, 'The Camera made me do it: Female Identity and Troubling Archives', *Mosaic: A Journal for the Interdisciplinary Study of Literature*, 37, 4 (2004), pp.127-47.

CHAPTER ELEVEN

Affect and the History of Women, Gender and Masculinity

KATHERINE O'DONNELL

> But history, real solemn history, I cannot be interested in ... I read it a little as a duty; but it tells me nothing that does not either vex or weary me. The quarrels of popes and kings, with wars and pestilences in every page; the men all so good for nothing, and hardly any women at all – it is very tiresome: and yet I often think it odd that it should be so dull, for a great deal of it must be invention. The speeches that are put into the heroes' mouths, their thoughts and designs – the chief of all this must be invention, and invention is what delights me in other books.[1]
>
> Catherine Morland, Jane Austen's *Northanger Abbey*

Historians begin their projects with the problem of discovering what actually happened in a particular historical period, and so they search for primary sources that are as close to a record of the events under investigation, with the aim of making an interpretation of these sources in order to understand what truly happened in the past. The initial problematic for literary scholars is a literary text or texts and they work to understand the mentality of the individual and culture that shaped this text and on how that work has been interpreted and received. If they ask questions about reality they enquire into how that reality was understood by that person or in that culture, or how an aesthetic 'realism' was achieved. Any curiosity they may have about reality has an *a priori* scepticism to the idea that an objective account of reality can be recovered beyond the dominant fiction. Literary scholars work with the largely unspoken assumption that all narratives, even those, or rather particularly those that lay claim to truth and reality, are inspired by the self-serving interests of individuals or groups. The fact that those of us who work in literature departments often read history writing in this manner can lead to a certain disciplinary chill between us and the historians.[2]

Further distinctions between the two disciplines can be seen by tracing the history of the development of the subject areas within the Academy. In the early modern period European intellectual life was invigorated by an argument that became known as the Battle of the Books.[3] This debate took place between those who considered that the writings of Classical Greece and Rome could not be improved on but at best creatively imitated (the Ancients), and those who wanted to progress human thought by building on the foundations of the Classics through a methodological rigour (the Moderns). The split resulted in the arts of rhetoric and oratory, with their allied linguistic skills of exegesis and persuasion, remaining on the side of the Ancients, while the Moderns developed the scientific study of material phenomenon. The study of history was never entirely resolved to the camp of the Moderns, though the discipline firmly proclaims that its scientific methods (such as proof through corroboration by source material) enable the claim that the fact-finding is impartial and objective. Yet the medium of history, however much abjected as untrustworthy, is literary – historians must write persuasively.

In literary studies, the raw material, the phenomena or data if you will, is the writing that works to create 'the suspension of disbelief', to quote the poet Coleridge: literature is bracketed as a special case that sets it apart from all other texts.[4] There is a psychological typology shared by those of us who have ended up working in literature departments: as school children we would have responded inordinately strongly to what the poet Keats heard from the Grecian urn: 'Beauty is truth, truth beauty,—that is all/Ye know on earth, and all ye need to know.'[5] We privilege literary texts then as having a particular claim to truth, paradoxically by their very artificiality, in that precisely as literature consciously seeks and forms a relationship with an audience through resonating on emotional even more than rational levels, literature therefore might be considered more truthful accounts of what humanity is, how it performs – of what it really is to be human.[6]

The texts we venerate as classical or canonical are those that are regarded as maintaining a connection with audiences, having meaning and significance across time periods. Literary scholars are not averse to drawing on psychoanalysis to analyze the effect of texts on an audience, psychoanalysis works with the presumption that we are all in varying degrees unaware or unconscious of aspects of our emotions or on how they are stirred. Literary scholars and psychoanalysts deal in realms of the suggested or suggestive, the subliminal and symbolic: realms not readily considered by the historian looking for hard evidence. In some respects then the work of literary scholars might be considered a-historical or even anti-historical except that we recognize that various forms of relationships and knowledge (ontologies and epistemologies if you will) are practices that produce affects and that the significance, the meaning in the expression of affect, depends on the specificities of its historical context.[7]

The terms affect and emotion are often used interchangeably. However, in precise terms affect is the sense of an ongoing emotional preference or attachment, a predisposition that informs the individual about those experiences that it values more than others.[8] Affect then is that realm of feeling that describes our innate value preferences in our experience of emotional connection: our gut reactions and the kinds of experience and particular forms of connection that we seek.[9] The seventeenth-century Dutch philosopher, Baruch Spinoza, was one of the earliest and most influential theorists of affect which he discussed in volume III of his work, *Ethics*. Spinoza's affect relates to our innate ability to affect and be affected, a quality he defines as being integral to that fundamental essential drive we have to 'preserve in our being'. Spinoza's affect is any change in the power and force of that drive. As Brian Massumi explains it: 'It is a pre-personal intensity corresponding to the passage from one experiential state of the body to another and implying an augmentation or diminution in that body's capacity to act ... Spinoza's *affection* is each such state considered as an encounter between the affected body and a second, affecting, body'.[10]

Literary scholars concern themselves less with cracking the semantic codes of the past (although they inevitably do this work as well) than with analyzing, historically contextualizing, how practices, habits and beliefs shape the quality of our lives through the emotional resonance they seem to inspire. The impulse behind this work is the assumption that personal integrity and nothing less than human happiness depends on not living in a passive acquiescence to received codes and ideologies but living in critical relation to those codes and ideologies, particularly those that evoke terror or represent beauty, that are pleasurable or painful. There is a fascinating debate in the realms of psychology as to whether affect or cognition is primary in the formation and change of attitudes.[11]

Literary scholars sidestep this debate to examine the aesthetic techniques deployed in the conceptual and emotional effects of the work and the moral implications of the work's reception. The largely unarticulated belief that forms the basis for work in the field is that in analyzing our appreciation of creative literary works that create strong emotional identifications and reactions, we can develop both an appreciation and a critique of received wisdom so that we might evolve knowledge practices and create affects that are nourishing to ourselves, our loved ones and our communities. By the end of the twentieth century the value of the study of literature and its related arts (a 'liberal education') was at best being deemed irrelevant in the atmosphere of the overwhelmingly dominant discourses of an expanding global capitalism and the successful coup by right-wing conservatives in the 'culture wars' of the USA (where 'liberal' was swiftly and successfully redefined as 'anti-family values').

Literary scholars' belief seemed unsupportable: that the study of literature led to the development of more tolerant individuals with enhanced capacities for enjoyment and pleasure; providing leaders for an expansive, liberal democracy. There was certainly no quantitative measure to support the literary scholar's understanding of affect as a practice that might be developed and nourished, although recent neuro-scientific experiments that map brain functioning, specifically the brain's 'plasticity', seem to offer intriguing possibilities in this regard.[12] Cognitive scientists have shown that in the brain's anatomy the neuronal circuits that support emotions are inseparable from those that support cognition.[13] Even if we take affect to be a pre-personal hardwiring, neuroscience demonstrates that emotions appear in the context of action and thought, and Keats' declaration that the only knowledge we need is that Beauty and Truth are the same register seems less fanciful than might be supposed. The assumption that personal and social morality is dependent on an ongoing reflective and responsive understanding of norms is the *raison d'être* of much academic work in the Humanities. This is the common ground that historical and literary studies often share.

Within the academy the boundaries of feminist literary studies and feminist history writing intersect to create a large, shared, interdisciplinary territory where the disciplinary lines often share the same contours. Feminist literary scholars are regularly in the business of archival research bringing to light 'lost' work, or rather work that may have been extremely popular, even critically well-received, but has been consistently ignored by the Academy (this is particularly the case for those of us who work on Irish women authors).[14] Much feminist literary scholarship might be termed 'New Historicist' in that it is concerned with understanding literature within the historical context in which it was created and in giving the same quality of attention to other documents and written sources from the period. Feminist historians tend to differ from their non-feminist colleagues in being more creative in their approach to sourcing archival material, using oral histories, personal testimonies, popular media, visual art, records of the built environment or landscape, and in making detailed close-readings of this material while being sceptical of official records. Feminist literary scholars may be more willing than feminist historians to use the perspectives of psychological or cultural theory, but the central hallmark of all feminist theorizing and research is a self-reflective awareness of the researcher's standpoint position in terms of their class, ethnic and other socio-economic, political and cultural experiences. They seek to make evident the implications of their standpoint and how their perspective might facilitate and limit the generation of their research. In common with other feminist scholars, both feminist literary scholars and feminist historians foreground the political, cultural and social implications of what is being researched with attention to power differentials in terms not only of gender, but frequently attention is also given to power differences in the dynamics of class and race relations.

I have argued that the focus on affect is a distinguishing characteristic of academic literary studies but the examination of affect has animated, if not actually instigated, history writing by feminists: it is now over thirty years since Carroll Smith Rosenberg's 'The Female World of Love and Ritual: Relations between Women in Nineteenth-Century America', which was the lead article in the very first issue of renowned feminist journal, *Signs*.[15] In this article, Smith-Rosenberg asserts that the cultural and social framework of the late eighteenth and nineteenth centuries made possible close, intimate, same-sex friendships between women. Further, the author contends that examining the correspondence and diaries that were never meant for publication gives valuable insight into the emotional lives and world of nineteenth-century women. She argues that American society during this period maintained such strict gender roles that women often did not develop close relationships with men even after marriage. Within this gender segregation, however, women developed intimate relationships with each other that were wholly acceptable within the constraints of Victorian society. Inside this intimate world women could share confidences, joys, sorrows and the experiences of marriage, birth and death that were their predominant rituals.

From the time a daughter was born, her days would be spent almost exclusively with women. The relationship between mother and daughter formed the first introduction women had to the traditional domestic roles they would occupy. The extended family of sisters, cousins and aunts and the onset of education with other young women further defined the close friendships and the primacy of connections between women. Smith-Rosenberg notes that the relationships between these women were physical as well as emotional. Women often wrote of physical contact, or their longing for renewed physical contact in terms of hugging, kissing and long embraces. Not unusual, the bonds forged between these nineteenth-century women retained an intensity throughout their lives. They freely spoke of their love for each other and knew that they could rely on one another for emotional support. Because of the strict gender-roles of the culture, marriage brought an enormous adjustment for women as well as men. Therefore, it is not surprising that women experienced a further intensification of already close friendships after marriage. Smith-Rosenberg concludes the article by suggesting that within the cultural framework of the nineteenth century, there was a tolerance of close emotional bonding between women. Further, the author believes that rather than trying to label sexual impulses as 'normal' or 'abnormal', we should rather see these impulses as a spectrum with gradations that are influenced by cultural norms and their indictments and inducements.

Smith-Rosenberg's article was a foundational article in what has come to be called the field of women's history, and its methods and focus have been the staple fare of that field since then. Women's history is acutely conscious of the ethical implications of focusing on 'extraordinary women' and is interested in recovering the experience of what it was like to live an 'ordinary woman's life'. There remains a strong interest in the private sphere, feminine occupations, networks and education and in the archives of diaries and letters. While female bonds remain a central concern there is still a reluctance to describe passionate love and bodily desire between women as lesbian. This reluctance stems from concerns generated by our current contemporary context. There seems to be an impulse not to stigmatize this desire, as the term lesbian is overwhelmingly used to denigrate women, in particular to denigrate feminist women, regardless of evidence of happy adjustment to heterosexuality: in this sense it is also an imprecise term and there may be a fear of its contagious powers to impugn the character of the historian herself. Perhaps fear of imprecision or contagion has led these historians to require a standard of proof that is rarely recorded: incontrovertible evidence, clinical and precise, of genital sexual intercourse. There is also the embarrassment about the extent of the archive of expressions of love and passion between women: how are we to understand this vast trove?

In her large tome, *Surpassing the Love of Men*, Lillian Faderman provided brief chronicles, over 496 pages, of numerous women who expressed their passionate love and physically-felt desire for other women from the seventeenth to the nineteenth centuries in America and England.[16] She elected to use the term 'Romantic Friends' in describing these relationships as sexually chaste. Faderman believed that these genteel ladies would have been sexually ignorant, presuming that sexual knowledge, recognizable as such in the twentieth century, must be a prerequisite for the performance of sexual intercourse. There is a dominant trope in women's history of declarations of ignorance and even (most unusual for academics) a personal inability to evaluate when it comes to the proposition that there could be both kind-hearted love and sexual desire between two women.[17]

Terry Castle eschews this approach of regarding the lesbian as a ghost effect, a barely visible but persistently haunting presence in Western culture, or a 'recent invention', to argue that there is an abundance of corporeal manifestations of lesbian subjects, acts and affects, throughout our history.[18] Adrienne Rich proposed the concept of a lesbian continuum, where all love between women, including love between daughters and mothers, sisters and friends might be regarded as lesbian and could find its place on this scale. Rich's evocative concept succeeded in irritating a wide gamut of feminists, particularly self-defined lesbians who felt that their sexual identity was rendered indistinct and invisible, and this concept has not been widely applied by historians.[19]

On the whole, Smith-Rosenberg's sophisticated call for women's history to set aside contemporary ideas of normal and abnormal when analyzing same-sex love has not been widely answered.[20] However, gender history, that is history writing that focuses on the relations between masculinity and femininity, has been much better placed to analyze same-sex love and desire, understanding that same-sex bonds are prohibited or encouraged in terms of how they are understood within the matrix of gender relations.[21]

Gender is sometimes used in a shorthand way to refer to 'issues concerning women'; however, this is to misunderstand the term as gender is a relational term that describes how masculinity and femininity, male and female are contingent terms, continually constructed, contested and negotiated in relation to each other. Gender designates a historically-bound social performance, inflected by class, race and other dynamics of power differentials. While women's history takes the subject of women as its focus and ground, gender is a term that is designed to problematize the categories of men and women and the easy assumption of a straightforward essential nature that these categories might infer. What is proper to men and women is constantly being enunciated, performed, resisted, subverted, imposed and negotiated in every culture, and this is the fluctuating dynamic which is the focus of gender history. Feminists have pioneered work on gender formation since Simone de Beauvoir's declaration that 'one is not born but rather becomes a woman'.[22] A classic text is that of Gayle Rubin's 1975 landmark essay 'The Traffic in Women', which argues that the development of the public sphere depended upon the primacy of men's same-sex bonds.[23] As Eve Kosofsky Sedgwick terms it, 'male homosocial desire' coalesces through the men's exchange and mutual domination over women.[24] One does not have to be a feminist to see that the largely all-male preserves of professional sport and religious rituals demonstrate how cultures eroticise male relations while making women the object in a system of exchange.

Sedgwick, a feminist literary scholar, broke new ground in her book, *Epistemology of the Closet* when she moved from the argument that the erotics of male bonding are integral to the maintenance of patriarchal power systems to point out that this homosocial world depends on the paranoid abjection of male homosexuals and homosexuality. She declared that 'virtually any aspect of modern Western culture, must be, not merely incomplete, but damaged in its central substance to the degree that it does not incorporate a critical analysis of modern homo/heterosexual definition'. She went on to argue that the ways in which male homosexuality functions in our culture is not a minority interest but is an issue of concern to all those interested in power and the psyche. According to Sedgwick, homo/heterosexual definition has become the site of angry argument because of a lasting incoherence 'between seeing homo/heterosexual definition on the one hand as an issue of active importance primarily for a small, distinct, relatively fixed homosexual minority ... and seeing it on the other hand as an issue of continuing, determinative importance in the lives of people across the spectrum of sexualities'. These opposing perspectives are described by Sedgwick as a 'minoritizing versus a universalizing' view of sexual definition.[25] Sedgwick has been one of the foremost theorists and historiographers of masculinity and male same-sex erotic bonds and in her axiomatic statement that we reject a 'minoritizing' view of sexual definition she might be read as responding to Smith-Rosenberg's caution against applying contemporary understandings of normal and abnormal to historical expressions of affect.

Since the publication of *The Epistemology of the Closet* there has been a proliferation of studies on the history of masculinity and male-male love and sexual desire. While women's history might be considered a sub-discipline or distinct field of studies within the larger field of historical studies, there is no concomitant sub-section of 'men's history' for the simple reason that the vast bulk of history writing still focuses on men's lives and deeds. Histories of masculinity and histories of male homosexual love and desire are not necessarily reducible to each other but both are heavily indebted to women's history with its focus on affect and to the work of feminist theorists of gender. Gender theory has been vital in charting how different models of masculinity have been constructed and negotiated in relation to the feminine, and how men react to perceived challenges to their manhood,[26] but to my mind it is the recent focus on affect that is producing some of the most interesting history writing on masculinity.

Michael O'Rourke and I edited two collections of essays in recent years on the topic of love, sex, intimacy and friendship between men in the time period 1550–1800.[27] Critical reception of these collections has focused on how the authors make affect central to their enquiries; to quote David Halperin, the essays look beyond 'the practices or classifications of sex to the ways of being and relating that such a history [of sexuality] discloses ... the various studies assembled here all testify to a new surge of interest on the part of scholars of male sexuality in the history of affect'.[28] As George Haggerty notes: 'Love has often been ignored in histories of [male] sexuality, in part because it is the most elusive of the four-letter words and in part because it has not been understood as central to the question of sexuality itself.'[29] Goran Stanivukovic writes, 'it might be better to talk about the kind of desire between men that we now call homoeroticism, or even queer, not within the context of power, violence, and domination, but within the context of emotions, love and friendship where desire and passion are not clearly demarcated or reduced to one meaning'.[30]

In pre-modern and early-modern Europe, expressions of passionate love between men were to be found in abundance. The bodily expression of this love seems perversely to have been enabled by that shadowy figure of the sodomite, a man whose predilection for sex with men might seem to be a precursor to the modern male homosexual. Following Michel Foucault and Alan Bray, most historians of this period point to the fact that there were scarcely any prosecutions for sodomy and those few prosecutions that did take place regard the sodomite as a discursive construct, a symbol of the political traitor, heretic, foreigner or corruptor of domestic order, rather than a desiring individual.[31] Foucault famously describes the sodomite as 'that utterly confused category' and in his last work, *The Friend*, published in 2003, Bray concurs with the assertion that 'one cannot write a history of "sodomites"'.[32] There was no name for passionate love and desire between men such as the love that Shakespeare expressed in his sonnets, other than 'friendship'; the sexual terminology of the day such as pederasty and sodomy denoted sin, corruption and inequality whereas expressions of love between men generally celebrated this love as leading to a higher self.

Bray has explored how rites and expressions of such male friendships such as the kiss of peace, or taking communion together in a Catholic mass, sending personal passionate letters, sharing of food and beds and raunchy jokes and co-burial memorials are testimony to the particular kinship of such friendships and how 'the language of "sodomy" could be suspended from the physical intimacies between men that were all-pervasive in the culture of sixteenth- and seventeenth-century England'.[33] Thus the vague imprecise abstraction of the sodomite sublime (perversely) legislated the practice of sworn friendships, which were so rich in signification and reference and were constantly reiterated, affirmed and verified, were honoured as central to public life. Over the course of the eighteenth century, with the spread of capitalism, the development of urban centres and the rise of the middle-class there was a shift in the society of eighteenth-century Britain which transitioned from this older regime of social order based on what Foucault termed 'alliance' which had subordinated all men, women, and boys to higher ranked males, to one founded in sexuality, through which men and women have since embodied their claims to personal and political privacy.[34]

The traditional formulations of same-sex friendships with their socially recognized kinship and ethical functions were understood as being less significant to familial and heterosexual bonds. Over the course of the century such passionate friendships were understood as potentially inimical to these now socially-vital bonds. In the eighteenth century then we can see the ground shift under passionate male friendships. The early-modern seventeenth century looks strange to us, with the license allowed to eroticism between men, but as the modern-age of the eighteenth century progresses we begin to recognize how this passion is increasingly denied a public function or open expression. It becomes not normal and more recognizably queer. Sodomy is seen to transgress social and gender roles, and the perpetrator and his haunts and practices become more clearly defined by the processes of criminal law: investigation, arrest, arraignment and punishment. He is later specified by medical pathology, and as ever receives the condemnation of the churches.

Feminist scholars in every discipline have shown how affect is not an individual matter but that groups generate and transmit affect: girls, women and femininity being the abjected object of patriarchal culture and societies. A key argument of feminist scholarship has been that these sexist regimes (however 'natural' their forms and expressions purport to be), are man-made, socially-constructed, and therefore open to deconstruction and reconstruction under more equitable principles. In tandem with this argument, feminism is internationalist in that it is critical of the ideologies of nation states and calls on women to consider themselves as a global, oppressed, revolutionary class. Through these somewhat ambivalent charges of collectivity and deconstruction we can see how feminism became one of the central discourses that acted as a harbinger of post-modernity: where the subject is understood to be in constant re-formation in dialogue with social contexts and forces. The permafrost of modernity is at last beginning to melt, to paraphrase Alan Bray,[35] with the decline of that society focused on the symbolic and material primacy of the nuclear family. It is a truism of history writing that each period reformulates past ages in terms of current debates and contemporary concerns. Our historical vision may now be able to reveal a future vision for the ethical development of loving commitments within kinship structures and communities of shared-interest that are non-biological. Feminist history writing (whether by literary scholars or historians) has been at the forefront in outlining various webs of relationality, voluntary kinship, interlocking webs of obligation, forms of ethical commitment, the vital bonds of friendship, all the matter and effects of affect which may be about to take on a new salience and a new importance for postmodern human subjects.

NOTES

1. Jane Austen, *Northanger Abbey* (Oxford: Oxford University Press, The World's Classics Series, reissue 1990 [1803]), p. 84.
2. Historiography, the study of history writing, has been dominated by literary scholars, one of the most influential being Hayden White, who in *Metahistory: The Historical Imagination in Nineteenth-Century Europe* (Baltimore, MD: The John Hopkins University Press, 1973) argued that histories are determined by literary tropes. In *The Content of the Form* (Baltimore, MD: The John Hopkins University Press, 1990 [1987]) he argued that 'A true narrative account ... is less a product of the historian's poetic talents, as the narrative account of imaginary events is conceived to be, than it is a necessary result of proper application of historical "method"'(p.27) and 'plot is not a structural component of fictional or mythical stories alone; it is crucial to the historical representations of events as well'(p.51). See also Louis O. Mink, 'Narrative Form as a Cognitive Instrument', in David H. Canary and Henry Kozicki (eds), *The Writing of History: Literary Form and Historical Understanding* (Madison, WI: University of Wisconsin Press, 1978), pp.129–49; Paul Ricoeur, *History and Truth*, trans. Charles A. Kelbley (Evanston, IL: Northwestern University Press, 1965 [1955]); and Paul Ricoeur, *Time and Narrative* (*Temps et récit*), 3 vols. trans. Kathleen McLaughlin and David Pellauer (Chicago, IL: University of Chicago Press, 1984, 1985, 1988 [1983, 1984, 1985]).
3. Joseph M. Levine, *The Battle of the Books: History and Literature in the Augustan* Age (Ithaca, NY: Cornell University Press, 1991). See in particular pp.267–413.
4. Samuel Taylor Coleridge, *Biographia Literaria or Biographical Sketches of My Literary Life* [1817] Chapter XIV.

   > During the first year that Mr. Wordsworth and I were neighbours, our conversations turned frequently on the two cardinal points of poetry, the power of exciting the sympathy of the reader by a faithful adherence to the truth of nature, and the power of giving the interest of novelty by the modifying colours of imagination ... In this idea originated the plan of the *Lyrical Ballads*; in which it was agreed, that my endeavours should be directed to persons and characters supernatural, or at least romantic, yet so as to transfer from our inward nature a human interest and a semblance of truth sufficient to procure for these shadows of imagination that willing suspension of disbelief for the moment.

   Opinions, edited by James Engell and W. Jackson (London: Routledge, Kegan Paul, 1983 [1817]), p.93.
5. John Keats, 'Ode on a Grecian Urn', lines 49–50. Sir Arthur Thomas Quiller-Couch, *The Oxford Book of English Verse* (Oxford: Clarendon, 1919 [c.1901]; Bartleby.com, 1999) www.bartleby.com/101/. Accessed 21 March 2007.
6. Much literary work deals explicitly with the past and with memory as acts of forgetting, remembering, even dismembering. The *tour de force* of this literary exploration is to be found in the work of Marcel Proust. The narrator of this multi-volume, lifetime work, *In Search of Lost Time* marks its genesis from the enlightened insight into time and the realization of being that was inspired on the occasion of tasting a dessert confection:

   > the sound of the spoon on the plate, the uneven flagstones, the taste of the madeleine, had something in common, which I was experiencing in the present moment and at the same time in a moment far away, so that the past was made to encroach upon the present and make me uncertain about which of the two I was in; the truth was that the being within me who was enjoying this impression was enjoying it because of something shared between a day in the past and the present moment, something extra-temporal, and this being appeared only when, through one of these moments of identity between the present and the past, it was able to find itself in the only milieu in which it could live and enjoy the essence of things, that is to say outside of time. This explained why my anxieties on the subject of my death had ceased the moment when I unconsciously recognized the taste of the little madeleine since at that very moment the being that I had been was an extra-temporal being, and consequently unconcerned with the vicissitudes of the future. It lived only through the essence of things, and was unable to grasp this in the present, where, as the imagination does not come into play, the senses were incapable of providing it; even the future towards which action tends surrenders it to us. This being had only ever come to me, only ever manifested itself to me on the occa-

sions, outside of action and immediate pleasure, when the miracle of an analogy had made me escape from the present. It alone had the power to make me find the old days again, the lost time, in the face of which the efforts of my memory and my intellect always failed.

Marcel Proust, *Finding Time Again* [*Le Temps retrouvé*, 1927] *In Search of Lost Time* Vol. VI trans. Ian Paterson (London: Allan Lane/Penguin Books, 2002) pp.179–80.

7. There has been a wealth of feminist-inflected work on affect recently; see: Sara Ahmed, *The Cultural Politics of Emotion* (New York: Routledge, 2004); Lauren Berlant, *Intimacy* (Chicago, IL: Chicago University Press, 2000) and *The Culture and Politics of an Emotion* (New York: Routledge, 2004); Teresa Brennan, *The Transmission of Affect* (Ithaca, NY: Cornell University Press, 2004); Sally R. Munt, *Queer Attachments: The Cultural Politics of Shame* (Aldershot: Ashgate, 2007); Sianne Ngai, *Ugly Feelings* (Cambridge, MA: Harvard University Press, 2007); Denise Riley, *Impersonal Passion: Language as Affect* (Durham, NC: Duke University Press, 2005); Kathleen Stewart, *Ordinary Affects* (Durham, NC: Duke University Press, 2007); Rei Terada, *Feeling in Theory: Emotion After the 'Death of the Subject'* (Cambridge, MA: Harvard University Press, 2003) and Patricia Ticineto Clough and Jean Halley (eds) *The Affective Turn: Theorizing the Social* (Durham, NC: Duke University Press, 2007).
8. 'Feelings are *personal* and *biographical*, emotions are *social*, and affects are *prepersonal*.' Eric Shouse, 'Feeling, Emotion, Affect', *M/C Journal*, 8, 6 (2005), para. 2. http://journal.media-culture.org.au/0512/03-shouse.php. Accessed 31 March 2007. C. Daniel Batson, Laura L. Shaw and Kathryn C. Oleson, 'Differentiating Affect, Mood and Emotion: Toward Functionally Based Conceptual Distinctions', *Personality and Social Psychology Review*, 13 (1992), 294–326. Batson and colleagues made their distinctions based on functional differences, like changes in value state (affect) beliefs about future affective states (mood), and the existence of a specific goal (emotion). 'Reserve the term "emotion" for the personalised content, and affect for the continuation. Emotion is contextual. Affect is situational ... Impersonal affect is the connecting thread of experience. It is the invisible glue that holds the world together.' Brian Massumi, *Parables for the Virtual: Movement, Affect, Sensation* (Durham, NC: Duke University Press, 2002), p.217.
9. Silvan S. Tomkins is one of the most influential theorists of affect in the twentieth century. Building on the work of Charles Darwin in *The Expression of the Emotions in Man and Animals* (London: Harper Collins, 1998 [1872]), Tomkins understood affect as the sum of a set of discreet physiological responses that stimulates a distinctive qualitative experience which causes the organism to care about what is happening. See E. Virginia Demos (ed.), *Exploring Affect: The Selected Writings of Silvan S. Tomkins* (Cambridge: Cambridge University Press, 1995).
10. Brian Massumi, 'Notes on the Translation and Acknowledgements', in Gilles Deleuze and Felix Guattari, *A Thousand Plateaus* (Minneapolis, MN: University of Minnesota Press, 1987), p.xvi. Among the most recent philosophical writing on affect is that of Deleuze. According to Deleuze an affect is an intensive neuronal response to external stimulus. Qualitative, not quantitative, it involves the body's power to absorb an external action and react internally. Typical of his radical post-humanism, affects, according to Deleuze, are not simple affections, as they are independent from their subject. In his later work (from about 1981 onward), Deleuze sharply distinguishes art, philosophy and science as three distinct disciplines, each analyzing reality in different ways. Artists create affects and percepts, 'blocks of space-time', new qualitative combinations of sensation and feeling (what Deleuze calls 'percepts' and 'affects'), whereas science creates quantitative theories based on fixed points of reference such as the speed of light or absolute zero (which Deleuze calls 'functives') and philosophy creates concepts.
11. Some scholars, such as the influential Stanford-based social psychologist, Robert B. Zajonc, argue that affect is primary in that it is the first thing to evolutionarily distinguish animals from plants. He argues that affective reactions are unavoidable and involuntary, that affect relies on energy whereas thinking relies on information. People do most things based on affection and justify their choices later with cognition: 'Feeling and Thinking: Preferences Need No Inferences', *American Psychologist*, 35, 2 (1980), pp.151–75; 'On the Primacy of Affect', *American Psychologist*, 39, 2 (1984), pp.117–23. See Jan De Houwer and Dirk Hermans (eds), 'Automatic Affective Processing', *Cognition and Emotion*, Special Issue 15, 2 (2001), pp.113–14. For those who are at the forefront of arguing that cognition comes

first in attitude development, see Alice H. Eagly and Shelly Chaiken, *The Psychology of Attitudes* (Orlando, FL: Harcourt Brace Jovanovich, Inc., 1993). For an engaging overview of debates and agreements within the field of 'affective science' see, Paul Ekman and Richard J. Davidson (eds.), *The Nature of Emotion: Fundamental Questions* (Oxford: Oxford University Press, 1994, Series in Affective Science).

12. For an overview of the literature on the brain's capacity (its 'plasticity') to expand, retrain and develop in 'enriched environments', that is, an environment where the subjects (including rodents) are encouraged to enjoy greater aesthetic pleasure, see Gerd Kemperman and Fred Gage, 'New Nerve Cells for the Adult Brain', *Scientific American* (May 1999), pp.48–53. See also A. Lutz, L.L Greischar, N.B. Rawlings, M. Ricard and R.J. Davidson, 'Long-Term Meditators Self-Induce High-Amplitude Gamma Synchrony During Mental Practice', *Proceedings of the National Academy of Sciences*, 101, 46 (16 November 2004), pp.16369–73.
13. See R.J. Davidson and W. Irwin, 'The Functional Neuroanatomy of Emotion and Affective Style', *Trends in Cognitive Science*, 3 (1999), pp.11–21; R.J. Davidson, 'Cognitive Neuroscience Needs Affective Neuroscience (and Vice Versa)', *Cognition and Emotion*, 42 (2000), pp.89–92; E.T. Rolls, *The Brain and Emotion* (New York: Oxford University Press, 1999).
14. Angela Bourke, Siobhán Kilfeather, Maria Luddy, Margaret Mac Curtain, Gerardine Meaney, Máirín Ní Dhonnchada, Mary O'Dowd and Clair Wills (eds), *The Field Day Anthology of Irish Literature: Irish Women's Writing and Traditions: Vol. IV/V* (New York: New York University Press, 2002).
15. Carroll Smith Rosenberg, 'The Female World of Love and Ritual: Relations Between Women in Nineteenth-Century America', *Signs*, 1 (1975/76), pp.1–29; reprinted in Nancy F. Cott and Elizabeth H. Pleck, *A Heritage of Her Own: Toward a New Social History of American Women* (New York: Simon and Schuster, 1979), pp.311–42. See also Lelia J. Rupp (ed.), 'Women's History in the New Millennium: Carroll Smith-Rosenberg's "The Female World of Love and Ritual"' after Twenty-Five Years', *Journal of Women's History*, 12, 3 (Autumn 2000).
16. Lillian Faderman, *Surpassing the Love of Men. Romantic Friendship and Love Between Women from the Renaissance to the Present* (London: The Women's Press, 1985 [1981]).
17. For example, see Elizabeth Mavor, *Ladies of Llangollen* (Harmondsworth: Penguin Books, 1983 [1971]) in her biography of the eighteenth-century Irish women, Lady Eleanor Butler and Sarah Ponsonby, who on their second attempt succeeded in their elopement to North Wales writes:

    > I have preferred the terms of romantic friendship (a once flourishing but now lost relationship) as more liberal and inclusive and better suited to the diffuse feminine nature. Edenic it seems such friendships could be before they were biologically and thus prejudicially defined. Depending as they did upon time and leisure, they were aristocratic, they were idealistic, blissfully free, allowing for a dimension of sympathy between women that would not now be possible outside an avowedly lesbian connection. Indeed, much that we could now associate solely with a sexual attachment was contained in romantic friendship: tenderness, loyalty, sensibility, shared beds, shared tastes, coquetry, even passion. (p.xvii.)

    Mavor's title for Chapter 5 which discusses the wide-scale phenomenon of 'romantic friendship' refers to a quote from Mrs Piozzi who in 1795 wrote: ''tis now grown common to suspect Impossibilities – (such as I think 'em) whenever two Ladies live too much together'. Mavor and Piozzi both share an ability to deny that sexual pleasure and love can be simultaneously found between women (and so safeguard their own social standing) and that those (lesbian) women who do admit that sexual pleasure and love can be expressed between women cannot claim a kinship with 'romantic friendships' of former eras.
18. Terry Castle, *Apparitional Lesbian: Female Homosexuality and Modern Culture* (New York: Columbia University Press, 1993). For her discussion on 'recent invention' see pp.8–10.
19. Adrienne Rich (ed.), 'Compulsory Heterosexuality and Lesbian Existence' [1980], in *Blood Bread and Poetry: Selected Prose 1979–1985* (New York: Norton, 1986) pp.23–75. For an on-line version of the essay see: http://www.terry.uga.edu/~dawndba/4500compulsoryhet.htm. Accessed 4 March 2007.
20. To give some recent examples from Irish feminist history writing: in the introduction to

their edited collection *Female Activists: Irish Women and Change, 1900–1960* (Dublin: The Woodfield Press, 2000), Mary Cullen and Maria Luddy coyly caution against 'reading too much' into the character of life-long, loving, committed female couples (p.4). Rosemary Cullen Owens, *Louie Bennett* (Cork: Cork University Press, 2001, Radical Irish Lives Series) is an excellent study on Bennett (1870–1956) who was one of the most prominent women in Irish public life in the twentieth century. She was a suffrage and peace activist and a leading trade unionist for forty-six years, yet she was 41 before she embarked on this public life. Cullen Owens asks, 'What was the spark that fuelled this development on the part of one whose background and early life showed no indication of what was to come? Why at the age of forty-one did she turn her life about so dramatically and enter the public arena?' (p.118). Following these questions Cullen Owens discusses family rumours that Bennett had been disappointed in love affairs with unavailable men. Yet the answer to the questions posed at the book's conclusion has already been answered on p.12: if her friendship with the brilliant and politically-active Helen Chenevix did not inspire her first entry to public life (when they were jointly appointed honorary secretaries of the newly formed Irish Women's Suffrage Federation in August 1911) the committed love from Chenevix sustained Bennett's political activity for the next forty-plus years: '[Helen Chenevix] would become a lifelong friend and companion of Bennett, sharing her commitment to a wide range of social issues during the next forty years.' (p.12) Margaret Ó hÓgartaigh's, *Kathleen Lynn: Patriot, Irishwoman, Doctor* (Dublin: Irish Academic Press, 2006) does not mention the word lesbian while declaring 'there is no evidence of sexual activity between Lynn and ffrench-Mullen', (p.4). Ó hÓgartaigh does not discuss Marie Mulholland's *The Politics and Relationships of Kathleen Lynn* (Dublin: The Woodfield Press, 2002) nor does she even cite it in her extensive bibliography of secondary sources. Mulholland reads the thirty-plus year relationship between Lynn and her 'dearest MffM' (Ó hÓgartaigh, p.3) as a long-term lesbian love relationship; see, in particular, pp.16–19 and pp.38–41.

21. See, for example, two very different studies in terms of era and sources but both excellent exponents of sensitive readings of the deployment of gender relations in the ontology and epistemology of female same-sex desire: Laura Doan, *Fashioning Sapphism: The Origins of Modern Lesbian English Culture* (New York: Columbia University Press, 2001) and Valerie Traub, *The Renaissance of Lesbianism in Early Modern England* (Cambridge: Cambridge University Press, 2002).
22. Simone de Beauvoir, *The Second Sex* (*Le deuxième sexe*) (Paris: Gallimard, 1947): 'One is not born but rather becomes a woman' is the opening sentence from Part IV The Formative Years, Chapter XII: Childhood (New York: Vintage Reissue Edition, 1989) p.267.
23. Gayle Rubin, 'The Traffic of Women: Notes on the Political Economy of Sex', in Rayna R. Reiter (ed.), *Toward an Anthropology of Women* (New York: Monthly Review Press, 1975), pp.157–210.
24. Eve Kosofsky Sedgwick, *Between Men: English Literature and Male Homosocial Desire* (New York: Columbia University Press, 1985). In a later book Sedgwick summarized her central argument in *Between Men* as an attempt 'to demonstrate the immanence of men's same-sex bonds, and their prohibitive structuration, to male-female bonds in nineteenth-century English literature ... [The book] focused on the oppressive effects on women and men of a cultural system in which male-male desire became widely intelligible primarily by being routed through triangular desire involving a woman'. *Epistemology of the Closet* (Berkeley, CA: University of California Press, 1990), p.15. Sedgwick in more recent years has worked explicitly in affect studies, co-editing (with Adam Frank and Irving E. Alexander), a Reader of Silvan Tomkins' work: *Shame and Its Sisters* (Durham, NC: Duke University Press, 1995) and authoring: *Touching Feeling: Affect, Pedagogy, Performativity* (Durham, NC: Duke University Press, 2003).
25. Sedgwick, *Epistemology of the Closet*, pp.1–2.
26. To choose two recent examples: James Gilbert, *Men in the Middle: Searching for Masculinity in the 1950s* (Chicago, IL: The University of Chicago Press, 2005) examines the 'crisis of masculinity' in American culture in the 1950s in relation to the perceived feminizing effects of suburbanization, consumerism and mass culture. This crisis and cultural era he sees ending in the publication in 1963 of Betty Friedan's *The Feminine Mystique* and her radical critique of the effect of this culture on its women: 'the problem that has no name'. Martin W. Huang, *Negotiating Masculinities in Late Imperial China* (Honolulu: University of Hawaii Press, 2006) sees two common strategies for constructing and nego-

tiating masculinity in this period: the 'strategy of analogy' and the 'strategy of differentiation' in relation to femininity.

27. Katherine O'Donnell and Michael O'Rourke (eds), *Love, Sex, Intimacy and Friendship Between Men, 1550*–1800 (Basingstoke: Palgrave Macmillan, 2003); Katherine O'Donnell and Michael O'Rourke (eds), *Queer Masculinities, 1550–1800: Siting Same-Sex Desire in the Early Modern World* (Basingstoke: Palgrave Macmillan, 2005).
28. David M. Halperin, 'Among Men: History, Sexuality and the Return of Affect', in O'Donnell and O'Rourke (eds), *Love, Sex, Intimacy and Friendship Between Men, 1550–1800*, p.1.
29. George E. Haggerty, 'Male Love and Friendship in the Eighteenth Century', in O'Donnell and O'Rourke (eds), *Love, Sex, Intimacy and Friendship Between Men, 1550–1800*, p.69.
30. Goran V. Stanivukovic, 'Between Men in Early Modern England', in O'Donnell and O'Rourke (eds), *Queer Masculinities, 1550–1800: Siting Same-Sex Desire in the Early Modern World*, pp.248–9.
31. Michel Foucault, *The History of Sexuality* Vol. I. *An Introduction*, trans. and ed. Robert Hurley (New York: Pantheon, 1978). Alan Bray, *Homosexuality in Renaissance England* (London: Gay Men's Press, 1982), pp.13–80.
32. Foucault, *The History of Sexuality*, p.101. Alan Bray, *The Friend* (Chicago, IL and London: University of Chicago Press, 2003)), p.275.
33. Bray, *The Friend*, p.275.
34. Foucault, *The History of Sexuality*, p.106.
35. Bray, *The Friend*, p.306.

CHAPTER TWELVE

Nimrods and Amazons: The Gendering of British Big Game Hunting in Africa, 1880–1914

ANGELA DOWDELL

In *Hunters Three*, an 1895 novel by Thomas Knox, three young men hunting in Africa meet with two English women pursuing elephants. That ladies would be hunting with only hired hands for an escort was 'enough to take any man's breath away', but the men quickly recovered and set to debating the more important issues: namely, how might they make the acquaintance of these independent women and what should they call them? Was an 'amazon [*sic*] of the African woods' a hunter or a 'huntress'? Citing the precedent of female doctors, Jack Delafield argued that, 'In sport, as in science, there's no distinction of sex', and since 'Hunting big game ... is entitled to be called a science', she's 'a hunter as much as you or I'.[1] This unisex categorization of the women, it should be noted, did not negate their appeal; by the conclusion of the novel, the three men had made them no less than four offers of marriage, two of which were accepted.

Knox's declaration on the sex-less nature of big game hunting stands at odds with the established histories of hunting, science and the Victorian period in general. Numerous studies have explored the ways in which women's participation in sporting and scientific pursuits was differentiated from that of men, and in most cases, dismissed, curtailed or barred.[2] With reference to hunting, existing studies have shown that while a few women did participate in safaris, the sport overwhelmingly expressed and validated Britain's masculine and imperial prowess. In his groundbreaking work, *The Empire of Nature*, John MacKenzie illustrated that hunting symbolized the patriarchal authority of elite whites and furthered their domination of the colonial landscape.[3] Subsequent studies have argued that big game hunters reified the gender, race and class hierarchies that were so crucial to the British cultural framework. Hunting provided a venue in which soldiers and upper-class men could demonstrate the martial, homosocial masculinity valorized at home and in the colonies.[4] At its most extreme, hunting was seen by members of the middle-class 'radical' right as a tool 'to hold back the lapping waves of gender and class emancipation in order to reassert a "pure" form of masculinity – privileged, controlled and in control'.[5] The trophies hunters brought back reduced the complexity of the colonial landscape into archetypal specimens and inscribed social patriarchal norms into nature by privileging the male form. They also provided clear signs of imperial domination, a function that was underscored by their prominent display in natural history museums throughout the British Isles. Scholars in a number of disciplines have argued that the stark display cabinets and parades of specimens favoured by museums in this period – and which can be still seen in the Museum of Natural History in Dublin today – glorified the Whiggish belief in progress and the advancement of (Western) knowledge.[6]

This essay does not argue against these assessments. There can be little doubt that hunting advanced the imperial project materially and symbolically by extracting resources and producing images of British men exerting their dominance over colonized subjects and landscapes. These arguments, however, do not account for women hunters, who did exist outside of fiction, if in limited numbers. Their presence in this symbolically loaded field raises a number of questions, not the least of which is how the cultural image of the 'mighty hunter', that paragon of masculine virility, allowed for the participation and successes of the 'weaker' sex. The two articles that do examine British women hunters in this period conclude that their involvement did not challenge existing gender norms. In the context of colonial India, Mary Procida argued that their participation served to uphold the patriarchal hierarchies, while in a more general analysis of women's hunting activities in England, India and Africa, Callum McKenzie asserted that their numbers were too nominal to overcome the preconception that hunting was a man's sport.[7] This study, on the other hand, approaches the issue from a different angle by arguing that precisely because this was a man's world, the actions and portrayals of even a few female hunters were deeply significant to the cultural import of big game hunting and the masculinity it supported.

Moreover, despite nearly every study of British hunting in the last twenty years having been attentive to issues of masculinity, their lack of attention to women hunters has produced a fundamentally limited historiography of the sport, as this chapter will demonstrate.

This re-evaluation of women's participation is all the more important in light of the popular histories being written about the safari institution. In general, these works have been painstakingly researched, drawing on a wealth of published works, privately held papers, and personal interviews. Several of the authors, however, are hunters themselves, and that personal identification coupled with their desire to entertain their readers has produced a series of narratives that glorify the 'adventure, danger, and romance' of African hunting and serve to reinscribe a number of troubling stereotypes.[8] Taking contemporary hunters' writings at face value, these histories relate incident after incident in which European hunters coolly dispatch a dangerous animal while their 'terrified' African or South Asian counterparts take refuge up trees, huddle in shelters, or simply run.[9]

Interestingly, these authors have incorporated 'huntresses' into their narratives, and while acknowledging that women hunters were the exception rather than the rule, they have tended to describe women as 'quite at home in this masculine institution'.[10] Generally, the aim of these accounts was to resurrect rather than analyze the place of women in the practice of African big game hunting, and the narratives can border on hagiography, though the tendency to emphasize the most colourful stories can produce an element of caricature as well. As little else is known about her, the often repeated story of 'Lady Nesta Fitzgerald, the daughter of an Irish aristocrat, [who] entered the annals of unorthodox conduct' by reportedly riding her horse into the central hotel in Nairobi and indulging 'in some ad hoc target practice' at the bar, does more to paint British East Africa as a frontier in the 'wild west' mould than it does to contextualize the experience of women hunters or their place in metropolitan or colonial culture.[11] Until scholars reconsider the place of women in safaris, however, these narratives will remain, as one reviewer claimed, the 'authoritative' voice on the subject.[12]

By considering the attitudes of, and towards, women hunters, Procida's and McKenzie's examinations bridged a critical gender gap in the scholarly history of hunting. Both restricted their analysis, however, to how women's participation was thought of in relation to the patriarchal system of Victorian culture. This volume, however, asks more. In addition to analyzing women's actions and their gendered roles, gender history aims to integrate their potentially differentiated experiences into the analysis of general historical topics. In this instance, that means asking how women hunters might inform our understanding of the broader cultural resonance of big game hunting. It involves expanding our analysis past how women hunters challenged or were positioned in relation to gender norms and considering what women's experiences and perspectives can tell us about the many notions bound up with safari hunting. What do these women's narratives reveal about contemporary perceptions of Africans, nature, science or the 'sport' of killing? Incorporating the participation of, and reactions to, women thus throws a masculine institution like big game hunting into relief, bringing new features to the forefront and rectifying the hypermasculine focus. Currently, scholars view big game hunting as a quintessential example of the contemporary reification of British patriarchal masculinity, but the inclusion of women suggests that in certain respects masculinity was secondary or even ancillary to the cultural resonance and import of big game hunting.[13]

Recognizing that masculinity and femininity are not constructed solely in relation to each other, but vis-à-vis other races, classes, generations and/or cultures, our analysis must also assess what other categories hunters' manliness was constructed with and against.[14] These considerations are not absent from the current historiography on hunting. John MacKenzie's work demonstrated that the gentleman's hunting code, which stipulated what constituted 'good' kills, was constructed in part to exclude lower class white males and racial others from the symbolic power of hunting.[15] There is still much work to be done in this area, and the ability of women to enjoy hunting without disrupting its cultural capacity to fortify and represent manliness opens up a rich space for deconstructing the 'mighty hunter' ideal. Those characteristics which were easily attributed to both men and women hunters should be considered for how they differentiated British hunters from images of (allegedly) emasculated 'Others'. Such an analysis has the potential to place the feminine within the gendered matrix of race, class and national character that was reified through the idealization of hunters' hypermasculinity.

With this chapter, I intend to take a small step towards these goals by returning to Jack Delafield's declaration and considering women as hunters, gendered but equal to their male counterparts. By looking, first, at their participation in hunting and then at the qualified support they received from male hunters, the British public and the institutions that facilitated the big game industry, I will argue that though marginal in numbers, women hunters were not marginalized in their own time. After establishing that these women were operating within the boundaries of hunting and British culture, I will consider just one of the more striking insights afforded by studying them as hunters: the perceived absence of sexual danger on the African frontier. In contrast to their counterparts in the settler communities of southern Africa, women on safari neither feared, nor were represented as being in danger of, sexual advances from African men. This absence of black peril anxieties illustrates the distinctive connotations of the safari in Victorian and Edwardian culture and highlights the profound insights that can be obscured when only one aspect of the gender equation is considered. This is only a small piece of a broader project, but I wish to suggest that during this period, the safari addressed fears about the effects of 'over-civilization' as much as it did Britain's masculinity, and it was within the subtext of civilization that women's performance was accepted and their sexual safety presumed, as both further verified the ascendancy of civilized culture over wild nature.

One of the reasons scholars have overlooked women hunters is that many travelled with their husbands, but this did not preclude them from being active participants in their own right. In one hunter's experience, ladies were as 'enthusiastic in their praise of the independence and exhilaration' of camp-life as men were, and he had 'yet to meet the woman who, after one trip to the wild, has not been anxious to repeat the experiment'.[16] Cullen Gouldsbury noted that he and his wife, Beryl, travelled well together because they shared a '*penchant* for shooting things'.[17] Lady Sarah Wilson, Winston Churchill's aunt, thought part of the 'charm of the veldt' was 'hearing the roar of the lions at night, and following their "spoor" by day'.[18] In fact, some may have enjoyed it more than their husbands. Helena Mary Molyneux, the Countess of Sefton, made several safaris with her husband, but she also went twice without him.[19] The Duchess d'Aosta hunted with the Honourable Susan Hicks Beach rather than with her husband, and a few unmarried women made their way out, accompanied by another woman or solely by their hired assistants.[20]

Further, these women did not just enjoy hunting, they succeeded. While most women lacked the opportunities men had for honing their shooting skills, safaris generally lasted for months, and even those who went out inexperienced could return accomplished hunters with respectable 'bags'. Moreover, given the opportunity, women could and did outperform men, a fact that was often relatively well received. It seems with some level of pride that Gouldsbury recorded that his wife had bested him and another hunter one afternoon, having stalked and killed three 'puku rams and a fine fat doe' 'in really first-class style'.[21] On rare occasions, the proficiency of women even converted their critics to a more enthusiastic point of view. Before setting out on safari with her cousin Cecily, Agnes Herbert overheard a fellow hunter, referred to only as 'The Leader of the Opposition Hunt', warning his companion, Ralph, to stop paying the 'girls' so much attention, as they would try 'to tack on to our show. And I won't have it, for they'll be duffers, of course.'[22] Ultimately, however, it was the women's safari that was 'much the most successful'; a fact that 'the Opposition' acknowledged in a failed bid to combine their caravan with the women's 'show'. Ralph had more luck in his attempt to 'tack on' to Cecily; she accepted his offer of marriage during a subsequent hunting trip the two parties made in Alaska.[23]

That even a few 'Dianas' were enthusiastically taking part in colonial big game hunting and being welcomed by some male hunters is an interesting consideration, but to what extent were such women integrated into the broader hunting culture? While acknowledging that female hunters found support in some quarters, Callum McKenzie argued that women's position was that of 'outsiders' in a sport that was 'essentially an introduction into, and a demonstration of, masculinity'.[24] Drawing primarily on statements made in contemporary editorials and articles, McKenzie demonstrated that many sportsmen strongly discouraged women's participation in big game and fox hunting.[25] His analysis covers a broad period, however, stretching from the 1850s through to the 1920s; he acknowledges that by the late Victorian and Edwardian periods there was a more moderate tone to the opposition and a growing level of acceptance towards women hunters within the hunting community.[26] Indeed, by the late Victorian period, women were beginning to assume leadership roles in the British hunting community. Though it was still uncommon in the interwar years, several women assumed the Mastership of harriers as early as the 1890s, and in 1902, a Mrs Hughes took control of the Neuadd-fawr pack of foxhounds, with Edith Somerville taking the reins of the West Carbury pack in County Cork the following season.[27]

To be sure, resistance to women's participation continued, and many sportsmen frankly expressed their doubts about the ability of women to hunt successfully. Such sentiments were not reserved for abstract discussions either, and could become quite personal, as demonstrated in a response sent by Hildegarde Hinde to Charles E. Fagan, the Assistant Secretary of the Natural History Museum in London:

> I couldn't help being rather insulted – perhaps *grieved* would be the better word – at your doubting whether I killed my animals at 300 yards. Of course I do – what would be the good of shooting if I didn't? I have quite a nice collection of heads and skins of my own shooting and I must confess to being rather proud of them. I do love to see a big beast roll over and know I have killed him.[28]

Fagan's initial letter is not included with this correspondence, but it is clear that he openly questioned Hinde about her accomplishments. That he did so as a representative of the Museum in what was most likely professional correspondence is all the more telling of the social barriers women confronted both in terms of accessing hunting activities and in being recognized for their skill.[29] Nonetheless, classifying them as 'outsiders' over-emphasizes the disapproval they faced and dismisses the many counter-examples of support and acceptance women found within the hunting community. As Hinde's letter shows, she engaged in hunting frequently enough to be quite skilled, suggesting that her husband was tolerant, if not encouraging, of her interest.

Hinde was not alone in this respect either; many husbands were pleased by their wife's abilities and interest. With his daughter's curiosity in mind, Reginald Loder kept a journal of the two consecutive safaris that he and his wife Margaret made together in 1910–11.[30] He believed that the most dangerous animals were not suitable game for 'a lady', a proscriptive that did not stop his wife from pursuing them when she chose, but his general pleasure in her interest and ability is evident in his summation of the safaris: 'Maggie has surprised me in what she has been able to do day after day if she wished to. She has shot quite a good bag during this Safari. Few ladies have ever been on two Safaris lasting continuously just three months. I trust she will look back upon the time spent on Safari with some little pleasure.'[31]

The ornamental role many women played in marriages during this period makes it dangerous to rely too heavily on the tolerance or approval husbands had for the hunting prowess of their wives. There may have been more than a touch of self-congratulation in comments such as those made by Loder above. The appreciation of women's hunting abilities was not limited to husbands, however. While the sources on this matter are more limited, it seems that many third-party male hunters, that is, men on whom a woman's performance could not be said to reflect, could view a woman's performance much as they would any male hunter. It was an uncle, 'one of the greatest shikaris of his day', who taught Herbert and her cousin Cecily to shoot, and when they announced their intention of going on safari in Africa, he expressed doubts about their physical ability 'to see the trip through', but gave them his best guns and helped plan their trip. Herbert attributed her confidence in part to his 'great trust in [their] powers'.[32] Hugh Frasier made two hunting safaris with Helena Molyneux and her husband, Oswald. When 'Nellie' got the first kill on one trip, Frasier recorded in the communal diary that she had spotted, stalked and taken a 'fine shot' at a Dik Dik 70 yards away. His description, including the remark, 'The first blood of the trip!! vast [*sic*] excitement except Nellie who was as cool as possible', gave no indication that he was patronizing or resentful of her having out-performed him.[33] Indeed, throughout their safaris, it seems the three hunters shared shooting opportunities, successes and fortunes with relatively little regard for the gender of the hunter.[34]

This is not to say that there truly was, as Jack Delafield argued, 'no distinction of sex' in big game hunting.[35] Women routinely faced obstacles unknown to the male hunter, and it is no coincidence that so many of the women who hunted big game in Africa prior to the First World War were titled. To some degree this probably reflects a bias of the archive. Despite never publishing anything herself, Lady Margaret Loder, daughter of the Earl of Listowel and a prominent figure in Anglo-Irish Society, left ample evidence of her time in Africa, whereas nothing is known about a number of other women beyond the fact that they were accompanying their husbands on hunting expeditions.[36] That said, many upper-middle-class men had the option of making their way to Africa in some professional capacity and then indulging in hunting while there. Women, on the other hand, had to either travel with their husbands or have an annual income that could accommodate the hefty expenditure required for a lengthy safari. So while there may have been more middle-class women hunting than is indicated by contemporary publications, by-and-large, only the most privileged women were able to embark on an African hunting expedition.

What is more interesting, however, is that the achievements of respectable ladies in the hunting fields of Africa, a proving ground of British masculinity, generated surprisingly little defensive posturing on the part of male hunters. While the approval of husbands suggests otherwise, it is worth considering whether women hunters were, in a social or public sense, neutered or even made masculine by their activities. Such an interpretation is not without precedent. Research into contemporary female explorers has suggested that women became 'public "white men"' when they used their race and nationality to claim a position of authority in colonial or foreign lands. This was a temporary identification, however, seemingly limited to their relations with Africans. Through a number of stratagems women travellers insured that they were still viewed as feminine within British society.[37]

The same can be said of women hunters, and moreover, while it could be argued that they were *functioning* as 'public white men' in relation to the Africans they encountered, this was not true of their interactions with other Europeans in Africa. One indication of this is the number of men who viewed female British hunters as attractive marriage prospects. An editorial Callum McKenzie quoted in his study warned women that proficiency at even small arms shooting 'deters rather than attracts serious suitors', because it was the mark of someone with a strong character, a trait which might prove 'uncomfortable' for a future husband.[38] This priggish warning, printed in 1872, does not seem to have held true, however, for the women who travelled to Africa in the early twentieth century to pursue their sport. For a single woman, skill and fortitude in hunting may have actually increased her appeal in the eyes of her male counterparts. Though the number of marriage proposals Thomas Knox wrote into *Hunters Three* bordered on ludicrous, it was in no way unrealistic for an unwed woman hunting in Africa, whether she was single, divorced or widowed, to be courted by a male hunter she met in the 'bush'. As mentioned above, Ralph proposed to Cecily while they were hunting in Alaska, and Herbert strongly implied that she and 'the Leader' developed a romantic attachment.[39] Marguerite Roby set off into the Congo wearing men's breeches, hunting and commanding her caravan with gusto, yet, by her own account, she was considered quite attractive by those she met:

> Indeed, whether on account of my fatal beauty or merely because of the lack of white women in Central Africa I know not, but the fact remains that I could have become a Mormon without the slightest difficulty during this expedition of mine. Yes, in all modesty I can confess that I was responsible for a regular District messenger service of porters, whose sole duty it was to pursue me through the bush, bearing epistles of an amatory nature from officials residing at posts through which I had passed.[40]

The 'lack of white women in Central Africa' may have heightened Roby's allure in the eyes of the men she encountered, but so too might her desire to hunt and her willingness to travel under rough conditions. Roby's suitors may have seen a pleasant potential for companionship in a wife who shared their interests or have been attracted by the very fact that she transgressed the typical boundaries of feminine behaviour. At the very least, her hunting certainly did not deter them.

Tramping through the African wilderness, chasing wild game, and braving all the touted perils of Africa including disease, insurrection and a climate purported to wreak havoc on one's complexion, women hunters definitively pushed at the boundaries of feminine behaviour. This did not translate, however, into their being portrayed as masculine, or indeed, anything less than ladylike within British society. Travelling on the imperial frontier, hunters may have felt quite removed from that society, but this was a period of deep interest in Africa, and hunting was a particularly popular element of *fin-de-siècle* metropolitan culture. The British public avidly consumed a wide array of hunting products, including published narratives, trophies, fashion accessories and natural history specimens.[41] Newspapers throughout the British Isles carried articles on game hunting and reviewed hunters' books, though the topic seems to have received more coverage in England, Ireland and southern Scotland than it did in Wales or the Highlands.[42] So while hunters waxed poetic about their voluntary seclusion in 'darkest' Africa, it must be remembered that they did so to an attentive public and never ventured far from metropolitan culture.

The relative scarcity of women hunters made their actions all the more newsworthy. When Molyneux, the Countess of Sefton, shot her first lion in 1908, it was reported in a news blurb entitled 'A Lady Lion Hunter', which described her as 'the adventurous Society sportswoman'. The portrait which accompanied the text showed Molyneux in a formal gown ornamented by a modest strand of pearls, her femininity emphasized by the fillet crochet-like design that surrounded the picture.[43] Years later, when King George V visited the Seftons at their home, an article covering the trip included a section entitled 'Lady Sefton's Trophies', which noted that she was 'a mighty hunter of big game … Lady Sefton has shot, I believe, lions, tigers, and elephants. She does not care to go out on the moors to bring down grouse.'[44]

Women's accomplishments were not just Society news, either. The few who published their accounts received notice in the sporting, scientific and general press. Herbert's book, *Two Dianas in Somaliland*, which recounted her and Cecily's four-and-a-half month safari, was critically acclaimed by reviewers throughout the empire.[45] The book did not receive unqualified approval, however. One reader returned her copy to Herbert because she 'didn't like so much killing'. This was noted, though, in Herbert's next work, *Two Dianas in Alaska*, as a tongue-in-cheek warning to readers that if they agreed that the 'taking of life' was 'unwomanly' and 'books on sport and adventure' were for 'the sterner sex', they should stop reading at once, because she and Cecily, 'went to Alaska to shoot, and – we shot'.[46] The continued success of Herbert's works suggests that there were plenty of readers who did not object to the gentler sex indulging their passion for shooting big game.

In addition to the recognition women hunters received from male hunters and a broader segment of the British public, they also had the benefit of practical assistance from the network of merchants and officials who facilitated and promoted safari hunting. The less contentious acceptance of ladies target shooting insured a supply of guns designed for women, and there are indications that women could practice at shooting ranges in Britain before going out on safari.[47] Once in Africa, women could employ an outfitter, who arranged, for a price, to have an entire caravan organized and waiting upon a hunter's arrival. These firms seem to have been no less willing to take commissions from women than men. On a page describing the services of the Grand Hotel Mombasa's 'Safari Department', the promotional travel guide *'Verb. Sap.' on Going to East Africa* included thumbnail drawings of a man and of a woman, each holding a rifle.[48]

As for the support of officials, Herbert and Cecily not only secured permits to hunt in British East Africa, but through the aid of 'that much maligned, useful, impossible to do without passport to everything worth having known as "influence"', they received access to districts off-limits to most hunters. Influence is indeed a powerful tool, but it would have been all too easy for the officials involved to deny such potent 'open sesames' had they been opposed to or doubted the abilities of women hunters.[49] In fact, influence was trumped by precisely those types of doubts when HRH the Duchess d'Aosta's application to hunt elephants in Uganda was denied on the grounds that it was too dangerous.[50] This rejection cannot be read as a summary of d'Aosta's hunting experiences, however. She was able to hunt in North-Eastern Rhodesia, and successfully killed a bull elephant. Further illustrating the endorsement she found in other quarters, a well-known hunter, James Dunbar-Brunton, reproduced a photograph of her kneeling beside the elephant, rifle in hand, in his book, *Big Game Hunting in Central Africa*. He also dedicated the book to her.[51]

The mixture of chauvinism and approval d'Aosta encountered typifies the place of women in hunting culture; excluded from certain arenas they found everything from tolerance in some to admiration in others. It is these latter elements that have been dismissed within the current historiography, obscuring the potentially enlightening ability of women to be feminine hunters without negating hunting's ability to prove Britain's masculine and imperial prowess. The recognition some men granted women hunters coupled with the positive reception they found in British culture suggests that their performance was not perceived as a challenge to men or the status quo.

Mary Procida has argued that in the context of the British Raj, the 'perceived demands of Imperialism' led the colonial patriarchy to sanction and encourage British women's involvement in masculine activities like big game hunting. Viewed through the lens of imperial domination, women's participation infringed neither their femininity nor the masculinity of their counterparts.[52] Procida's conclusions are suggestive, and I suspect they may be in part also applicable to the African setting. It seems that women hunters, as a category, were acting within rather than challenging the patriarchal system, which accounts for the manner in which men showcased their wives' performances and single female hunters were not disadvantaged in the marriage market. The 'perceived demands of imperialism', however, were at times quite different in Africa, and big game hunters operating there were never as removed from metropolitan culture and gender identities as those Procida considered within the British Raj. More work is needed, but the reception women hunters received suggests that African safari hunting addressed imperial and metropolitan needs above and beyond that of asserting Britain's potential for manliness and martial proficiency.

This sketch of women's involvement in big game hunting and the reception they received from male hunters and the broader British public is, thus, just the beginnings of a much needed study. Hopefully it has served to establish, however, that women hunters were acting from within the contemporary culture of hunting, and their experiences and perspectives constitute a valid source for examining the cultural resonance of safari hunting and the masculinity embodied by the 'mighty hunter' ideal. My intent for the rest of this chapter is to explore just one example of the unique insights that analyzing women hunters can bring to the historiography of hunting. By examining these women's experiences less for what they reveal about gender relations in the metropolitan or colonial setting, and more for what they expose about the safari institution and *its* role as a cultural trope, I hope to demonstrate the intellectual gains made possible by including narratives by and about women in the analysis of a masculine institution.

In their quest for big game, hunters had to travel beyond the settled landscapes of the colonies, to the 'Interior' of Africa, where civilization, by their estimation, had not yet encroached upon the natural world. Despite a popular fixation with the 'savage native' of this Interior, it was a basic assumption among hunters that the men they hired as their gunbearers, guides and carriers would not threaten or harm them. This sense of security says much about the extent of European influence in Africa and has been read as further evidence of the safari's symbolic expression of imperialism. Focusing on women hunters, however, reveals that this sense of security extended into the sexual sphere. The logistics and choices made on safaris often placed women alone with men, both European and African. This was still a socially progressive act in and of itself, particularly for the middle-class women who ventured out on safari, but the extent to which all parties seemed safe from the accusation of sexual impropriety provides a productive space for reconsidering what it meant to be a British big game hunter in the African frontier.

It is well recognized in imperial historiography that colonial spaces, particularly on frontiers and prior to any systematic settlement, offered British men the opportunity to engage in transgressive sexual practices, and it is not surprising that no concerns were raised about male hunters' interactions with African women. Such was not the case with British women, however. Access to their bodies was stringently policed as a potent symbol of the power and authority of white rule. The presumption, then, that women hunters were in no danger of attack or seduction, and that the voluntary choice to be, or to leave one's wife, alone with African men was entirely reasonable, is one of the more striking elements to emerge out of hunting narratives. It is also an indication of how far removed contemporaries viewed the African Interior and safari relations from the standards which governed metropolitan and colonial society.

It must first be understood that un-chaperoned male-female interactions were so *de rigueur* on safaris that no-one thought to remark upon them. When pursuing game, hunters typically separated, each going out with one or more assistants. Thus, most women were alone with one or more men, out of the sight or hearing of anyone else in their party, potentially every day. It does not seem to have mattered if the men were European or African, hired assistants or other hunters, or how long they were gone. Agnes Herbert openly acknowledged a 'most amusing' moment when she and her Somali headman, Clarence, 'got benighted in the jungle, and didn't get home until morning'. She acknowledged that the incident sounded 'like the plot for a fashionable problem novel', but there are no other indications that their night was, or could potentially have been, looked at askance. Herbert related that she and Clarence slept in shifts, so the other could keep guard, until an attack by a hyena made sleep impossible. They then spent the rest of the night talking. Upon returning to camp the next day, they found Cecily unconcerned, because she had faith in Clarence's ability to keep Herbert safe.[53]

Travelling without European companions, Marguerite Roby spent all of her time alone with African men, again with no apparent censure or fear of sexual assault, even though she at times feared for her life. Towards the end of her journey in the Congo, Roby spent a harrowing few days in constant battle with her carriers. She had forced them to work for her, and they resisted many of the tasks she assigned them, in response to which she repeatedly threatened and brutally beat them. Finally, when the men refused to put up her tent one night and insisted on sleeping in a clearing with her, she shot at their shins, forcing them to retreat into the surrounding forest, leaving her alone with Thomas, the one servant she trusted. That she published this account of sleeping alone with Thomas is a clear indication that she believed it would not tarnish her reputation, but her violent refusal to sleep in close proximity to the carriers is more ambiguous. She was likely responding, as she claimed, to their none-too-veiled threat that she might not reach her destination, but she may also have been fearful of, or covertly raising the spectre of, rape. In the days that followed, however, she continued to read their every action as an attempt on her life, not her body. More tellingly, the authorities to whom she reported these events did not seem to perceive the situation as an attempted assault on white womanhood either. The men's punishment, a flogging for each and one month's hard labour, was (regrettably) not uncommon for serious disputes between hunters and their carriers in the Congo.[54]

In an even more striking example, Phyllis Mary Coryndon recorded telling a colonial official of her interactions with an unknown African man while on a safari with her husband, a former professional hunter.[55] Most days, the Coryndons hunted together in the mornings, but then he would go back out in the afternoons, taking their servants with him and leaving her alone in camp. One afternoon, while sitting alone, she was startled to hear a man's voice behind her. Coryndon turned around to find 'a big native dressed in full war paint – that is in the skin God gave him, plus shield, spears, Knob Kerry, and feathers in his hair!' He was looking for work, and by her account, she 'gladly accepted his offer' and 'rewarded my warrior with half a pot of marmalade. He was delighted and came daily to help me with my household duties – *after the men folk had left camp*'.[56] After returning to 'civilization', Coryndon told this story to an official, who quickly asked her for more information, explaining that the man was potentially a wanted murderer. She 'hastily replied all natives looked alike', and she would not know him again. The official looked at her 'steadily for a minute, smiled and asked no more awkward questions'.[57]

The issues of complicity raised in this story are tantalizing, but for the purpose of this discussion it is evident that Coryndon believed that the large, virtually naked man and her encouragement of his visits presented no threat to herself or her reputation. Moreover, the official involved seemed remarkably comfortable with the idea of a respectable white woman shielding an African man from the law. Putting it into its contemporary context, this event took place in the Swaziland Protectorate, and though it is unclear precisely when, it was probably shortly after 1909 and no later than 1917, when Coryndon's husband accepted the Governorship of Uganda.[58] Although there was no black peril panic particular to Swaziland, the protectorate was surrounded on three sides by South Africa, the site of panics in 1906–08 and 1911–12.[59] The virulent nature of these outbreaks kept the fear of interracial sex 'at the forefront of everyone's mind', yet, as with Marguerite Roby and Agnes Herbert, the relations between Coryndon and the unknown 'warrior' seem to have gone unquestioned.[60] This is not to say that one would expect Coryndon's account to have set off a panic, but the apparent lack of concern is remarkable, especially as the tenuous acquaintance she developed with the man led her to circumvent colonial authority on his behalf, *with* the seeming collusion of the official involved.

It might be suggested that hunters' class and race positioned them beyond reproach, but this was not true of South African or Rhodesian colonial society. Recent scholarship has shown that black peril panics arose out of a number of political, social and economic anxieties, including a perceived loss of patriarchal control over white, middle- and upper-class women.[61] This was a period of deep concern for British masculinity.[62] Devastating statistics on the health effects of urban poverty had led Britain to question the vitality of its fighting forces and the potential consequences of 'over-civilization'.[63] The emergence of the New Woman, who pursued an independent life away from the domestic duties of a wife and mother, along with the increased momentum of the women's suffrage movement, also added to the stress placed on men to prove their masculinity and their ability to rule.[64]

In the colonial context, where control was tightly bound to race, and (respectable) white women served as the markers of social and moral superiority, these shifts in gender relations took on added significance and fuelled even greater concerns.[65] Therefore, as white male control became strained, attention turned to policing the behaviour and attitudes of white women, particularly in regard to their interactions with African men. Though all social contact was viewed as potentially dangerous, the relations between women and their domestic servants who, due to the colonial labour situation, were generally male, came under particular scrutiny.[66] While the concept of separate spheres was no more a reality in the colonies than in the metropole, the ideal still identified the home as a private reserve that sustained the prestige and moral centre of white, middle-class superiority.[67] Male servants' access to this symbolic space and the supposedly feminine tasks they performed there, marked them in the eyes of an apprehensive colonial society as both dangerous and potentially perverse.[68] During moments of black peril hysteria, women were criticized for being too familiar with their African servants, because it was believed such behaviour could erode the social barriers between the races, and thus increase the potential for revolt, symbolized by the rape or seduction of white women.[69]

This focus of black peril panics on the intimacy of the domestic sphere and its potential for familiarity between African men and white women makes the absence of such worries in the safari setting all the more perplexing, as the relationships between hunters and their assistants mirrored those of the domestic world. Camping on safari put hunters and their African staff in physical proximity every night, and African men performed very domestic tasks, such as setting up tents, cooking food and cleaning up. Many hunters also appointed one of the men as a personal servant, who performed more intimate tasks.

Though these were rarely delineated, in the case of female hunters, such duties must have involved privileged access to a woman's body. In a striking example, Loder noted matter-of-factly that his wife's personal servant had taken to dressing her hair quite well.[70] It is likely that Roby was referring to similar tasks when she praised her servant, Thomas, for his knowledge of 'waiting on a lady'.[71] When she was extremely ill, Thomas was comfortable enough with Roby and her habits to take down her hair in an effort to make her more comfortable and reduce her fever.[72] While the act itself is one any compassionate person would do for another and reflected precisely the kind of 'devotion' Europeans expected to receive from African servants, it is the ability of women to record, and in this instance, publish such interactions with no defensive justifications or fear of misinterpretation that emphasizes the difference perceived between relations in the settler and safari spaces of colonial Africa.

The lack of sexual anxiety in safari interactions presents an intriguing challenge for the historiography of hunting. It is likely that this divergence reflects the dynamics of southern African colonial communities as much as it does those of the safari; the economic and political factors linked to black peril panics simply were not a part of big game hunting culture or practice. That such pervasive and irrational fears did not transfer onto the safari, however, also indicates that an aspect inherent in contemporary big game hunting disassociated this activity from the dynamics of colonial society, making the rhetoric of black peril irrelevant to this space. Imperial authority relied on an artificial distinction between Europeans and colonial subjects, but the blurred nature of race and class categories in settler societies made this a 'brittle system which was constantly being eroded from within'.[73] Faced with such ambiguities, white, male identity was established not only by one's appearance or heritage, but also by the performance of proscribed behaviours that differentiated the properly civilized from the primitive subject. Policing the boundaries between ruler and ruled in South Africa thus remained a constant struggle, and the rhetoric of sexual assault served as a powerful weapon for re-asserting the cultural beliefs that justified white, male authority.[74]

I would like to suggest that in contrast to the precarious class and race categories found in settled colonial spaces, the manner in which hunting culture situated hunters vis-à-vis their African servants constructed a dynamic in which the social boundary between Briton and African seemed assured. My work to this end continues, but my findings indicate that big game hunting gained much of its contemporary appeal by depicting hunters as embodiments of civilization in a landscape defined as the archetype of 'savage' nature. Read through this lens, women's participation supported the imperial hierarchy between civilized and primitive; in fact, their successes and bodily security underlined the social distance between the two worlds in a way male hunters could not.

This is only a tentative conclusion, however, and the very absence of concerns makes it difficult to locate evidence that directly supports or refutes it. The two direct references I have found, however, both link women's security on safaris to the 'un-civilised' state of the frontier landscape, which, in contemporary terms, meant that it was populated by Africans who had not yet been 'tainted' by civilization. Writing in 1911, Owen Letcher argued that a man could send his wife from Ft. Jameson to a post in the 'furthermost confines of Awembaland' 'with a headman or "capitao" and a body of raw porters, and I am quite sure no harm would befall her. But such a thing would be impossible in our civilized South Africa.'[75] Similarly, when he left his wife during their safari in North-Eastern Rhodesia, Cullen Gouldsbury stated that it 'affords rather an interesting insight into the character of the Plateau native that a woman may be left by herself [with African servants] at night, out in the bush ... with no fear for anything ... In civilised South Africa the thing would be impossible; here, in the wilds of Central Africa, it calls for no more than a passing qualm.'[76] The fact that both men even raised the issue undermined their claims that an attack was entirely impossible, but significantly, both also attributed a woman's safety on safari to the rawness of the African 'wilds'. As they saw it, the social boundary between hunters and Africans in the 'savage' interior was assured in a manner unknown in 'civilized South Africa'.

This glimpse into the sexual politics of the safari is an eloquent example of the gaps that have been created in the historiography by examining hunting from the writings and actions of the majority gender. Only by including the experiences, perspectives and contemporary reception of women hunters can we begin to build a gendered understanding of the sport and its resonance in British culture. I hope that the speculative nature of the foregoing paragraphs has underlined not only the need for such research but also its potential to generate significant intellectual insights. Indeed, for a masculinized pursuit like safari hunting, narratives by and about women participants provide an invaluable context for examining the values it evoked and reified. Recalling that hegemonic masculinity is never constructed solely against femininity, but also in opposition to images of subordinate masculinities, we can use women's experiences to consider which elements of the hunter's idealized manliness were as much about being white, British, and/or modern as they were about being a virile, un-effeminate man. The safari symbolized imperial and male prowess, but it also allowed for the participation and representation of women as feminine hunters. Until we have accounted for that, our understanding will remain masculine, but not gendered.

NOTES

1. Thomas W. Knox, *Hunters Three: Sport and Adventure in South Africa* (New York: E.P. Dutton and Company, 1895), pp.14, 17, 19–20.
2. Examples relevant to this paper include: Julie Early, 'Unescorted in Africa: Victorian Women Ethnographers Toiling in the Fields of Sensational Science', *Journal of American Culture*, 18,4 (1995), pp.67–75; Jeanne Kay Guelke and Karen M. Morin, 'Gender, Nature, Empire: Women Naturalists in Nineteenth-Century British Travel Literature', *Transactions of the Institute of British Geographers*, 26,3 (2001), pp.306–26; Kathleen E. McCrone, *Sport and the Physical Emancipation of English Women, 1870–1914* (London: Routledge, 1988).
3. John M. MacKenzie, *The Empire of Nature: Hunting, Conservation, and British Imperialism* (Manchester: Manchester University Press, 1988).
4. J.A. Mangan and Callum McKenzie, '"Pig Sticking is the Greatest Fun": Martial Conditioning on the Hunting Fields of Empire', in J.A. Mangan (ed.), *Militarism, Sport, Europe: War without Weapons* (London: Frank Cass, 2003), pp.97–119.
5. J.A. Mangan and Callum McKenzie, 'Radical Conservatives: Middle-Class Masculinity, the Shikar Club and Big-Game Hunting', in J.A. Mangan (ed.), *Reformers, Sport, Modernizers – Middle-Class Revolutionaries* (London: Frank Cass, 2001), p.203.
6. See Paul S. Landau, 'Empires of the Visual: Photography and Colonial Administration in Africa', in Paul S. Landau and Deborah D. Kaspin (eds), *Images and Empires: Visuality in Colonial and Postcolonial Africa* (Berkeley, CA: University of California Press, 2002), pp.141–71; Harriet Ritvo, *The Animal Estate: the English and Other Creatures in the Victorian Age* (Cambridge and London: Harvard University Press, 1987), pp.243–88; Carla Yanni, *Nature's Museums: Victorian Science and the Architecture of Display* (London: The Athlone Press, 1999), pp.150–3. During this period, the more scenic diorama models that dominated museums in the twentieth century were still a controversial idea. Some museums did adopt them however, and Donna Haraway has argued that these displays similarly reified masculine privilege but also reflected and attempted to 'arrest' the growing fears about decay and decadence. Donna Haraway, 'Teddy Bear Patriarchy: Taxidermy in the Garden of Eden, New York City, 1908–36', in Nicholas B. Dirks, Geoff Eley and Sherry B. Ortner (eds), *Culture/Power/History: a Reader in Contemporary Social Theory* (Princeton, NJ: Princeton University Press, 1994), p.87. Finally, it should be noted that while the National Museum of Ireland – Natural History does maintain a similar system of display, it is, in part, as a museum to a museum. In 2008, the museum website still explained that the giraffe installed in January 2003 had died from natural causes and had lived in a wildlife park, whereas its predecessor had been shot by Colonel Plunkett in 1899. National Museum of Ireland, '*Spoticus*, at The Museum of Natural History', (Dublin: National Museum of Ireland, nd) http://www.museum.ie/naturalhistory/spoticus.asp. Accessed 10 March 2008.
7. Mary Procida, 'Good Sports and Right Sorts: Guns, Gender, and Imperialism in British India', *Journal of British Studies*, 40, 4 (2001), pp.454–88; Callum McKenzie, '"Sadly Neglected" – Hunting and Gendered Identities: A Study in Gender Construction', *The International Journal of the History of Sport*, 22, 4 (2004), pp.545–62.
8. Brian Herne, *White Hunters: The Golden Age of African Safaris* (New York: Henry Holt Owl Books, 2001), back cover.

9. See, for example, Herne, *White Hunters*, pp.18, 24–5, 29–30; Fiona Capstick, *The Diana Files: The Huntress-traveller through History* (Johannesburg: Rowland Ward Publishing, 2004), p.198.
10. Kenneth M. Cameron, *Into Africa: The Story of the East African Safari* (London: Constable, 1990), p.63. It should be noted that this text is largely an exception to the rule among the popular histories of safari hunting. Cameron, a writer and former university professor, approaches contemporary accounts with a critical eye and is one of the few to address the brutality of hunting expeditions.
11. Capstick, *The Diana Files*, pp.200–1; Herne, *White Hunters*, p.19.
12. Elizabeth Bukowski, 'Bookmarks', Review of *White Hunters*, by Brian Herne, *Wall Street Journal*, 9 July 1999, Eastern Edition, http://www.proquest.com/. Accessed 11 March 2008.
13. For an example of the scholarly equation between big game hunting and the performance of masculinity, see John Tosh, *Manliness and Masculinities in Nineteenth-Century Britain: Essays on Gender, Family and Empire* (Harlow: Pearson Education Limited, 2005), pp.199–200.
14. For an excellent discussion of the potential binary pitfalls of gender analysis, see Afsaneh Najmabadi, 'Beyond the Americas: Are Gender and Sexuality Useful Categories of Historical Analysis?', *Journal of Women's History*, 18,1 (2006), pp.11–21.
15. MacKenzie, *Empire of Nature: Hunting, Conservation, and British Imperialism*, pp.121–2.
16. A.E. Leatham, *Sport in Five Continents* (Edinburgh: William Blackwood and Sons, 1912), pp.8–9.
17. Cullen Gouldsbury, *An African Year* (London: John Arnold, 1912), p.13. The italics were in the original.
18. Sarah Wilson, *South African Memories: Social, Warlike, and Sporting, from diaries written at the time* (London: Edward Arnold, 1909), p.vii.
19. Liverpool Records Office, Sefton Family Papers, Lady Helena Mary Molyneux Travel Diaries and Albums (hereafter referred to as LRO), 920 SEF 5.
20. The Duchess d'Aosta née Princess Hélène of France was not British, but her companion Susan Hicks Beach was. Both were also well-known to British hunting society, as is discussed below. Quex Park Archive, Birchington, Kent, 'Duchess as Elephant Hunter', *Daily Mail*, 19 March 1908, 'Newscuttings: on various Travellers (not Maj. Powell-Cotton) 1903–1906', PCQ 65, p.27.
21. Gouldsbury, *An African Year*, p.312.
22. Agnes Herbert, *Two Dianas in Somaliland* (London: John Lane, the Bodley Head, 1908), p.19.
23. Ibid., p.269; Agnes Herbert and 'a Shikári', *Two Dianas in Alaska* (London: John Lane, the Bodley Head, 1909), pp.315–16.
24. McKenzie, '"Sadly Neglected" – Hunting and Gendered Identities', p.548.
25. Ibid., pp.548, 553–5.
26. Ibid., p.556.
27. 'Hunting', *The Times*, 10 March 1906, http://infotrac.galegroup.com. Accessed 11 March 2008. Emma Griffin reports that, with the exception of those who finished a season after their husbands' deaths, no women served as master of foxhounds in Britain in the nineteenth century, but there were six by the beginning of the First World War and twelve by the end of it. Emma Griffin, *Blood Sport: Hunting in Britain since 1066* (New Haven, CT: Yale University Press, 2007), pp.168, 178.
28. Hildegarde Hinde to Mr Fagan, 18 August 1899, Natural History Museum, DF 232/5/229, emphasis in the original.
29. Hildegarde Hinde was not unknown to museum officials. She and her husband, S.L. Hinde, donated specimens to the museum annually while they were in Africa. Throughout that time, H. Hinde was the primary correspondent with the museum.
30. Royal Geographical Society Library, Reginald B. Loder MSS, Journals of Hunting Expeditions, Vol.I, British East African Journal, 1910–11, p.74.
31. Ibid, pp.45, 210.
32. Their uncle was no longer hunting due to an injury he received while pursuing lions. His assistance included arranging for his former Somali headman to manage his nieces' safari. The guns he gave them were nice enough that two hunters they met turned 'green with envy' at the sight of them and attempted to buy them on the spot. Herbert, *Two Dianas in Somaliland*, pp.3, 5, 32–3.

33. LRO SEF 920/5/1c, entry for 25 December 1907.
34. Ibid.
35. Knox, *Hunters Three*, pp.19–20.
36. See 'Major Reginald Loder'. *The Times*, 29 October 1931, http://infotrac.galegroup.com/ itw/. Accessed 11 March 2008. For references to these more anonymous women, see Capstick, *The Diana Files*, p.42.
37. Katherine Frank, 'Voyages Out: Nineteenth-Century Women Travelers in Africa', in Janet Sharistanian (ed.), *Gender, Ideology, and Action: Historical Perspectives on Women's Public Lives* (New York: Greenwood Press, 1986), pp.67–93, p.72; Frank's term has since been employed in Monica Anderson, *Women and the Politics of Travel, 1870–1914* (Madison & Teaneck, NJ: Fairleigh Dickinson University Press, 2000), p.52.
38. 'Sport and Matrimony', *The Field*, 39 (January 1872), p.49, quoted in McKenzie, '"Sadly Neglected" – Hunting and Gendered Identities', p.548.
39. *Two Dianas in Alaska* ends with 'the Leader' standing in Herbert's hotel room door, 'smiling, smiling'. Herbert, *Two Dianas in Alaska*, p.316.
40. Marguerite Roby, *My Adventures in the Congo* (London: Edward Arnold, 1911), p.62.
41. For examples of the decorations and ornaments commonly made from animal parts, see P.A. Morris, *Edward Gerrard & Sons: A Taxidermy Memoir* (Ascot: M.P.M., 2004), pp.62–76. The unfinished five volume catalogue of ungulates (hoofed animals) in the Natural History Museum is indicative of the immensity of their collection. Richard Lydekker, *Catalogue of the Ungulate Mammals in the British Museum (Natural History),* 5 vols (London: Printed by Order of the Trustees, 1913–16).
42. For examples, see, 'Court and Fashion', *The Belfast News-Letter*, 16 February 1899, http://find.galegroup.com/bncn/. Accessed 19 February 2008; 'Christmas Shopping in the City', *Freeman's Journal and Daily Commercial Advertiser*, 9 December 1899, http://find.galegroup.com/bncn/. Accessed 10 March 2008; 'Big Game Hunting', *The Leeds Mercury*, 6 January 1894, http://find.galegroup.com/bncn/. Accessed 31 October 2007; 'Miscellaneous Books', Review of *East Africa and Its Big Game*, by John Willoughby, *Glasgow Herald*, 26, November 1889, http://find.galegroup.com/bncn/. Accessed 11 March 2008.
43. LRO 920 SEF 5/14; LRO, 'Lady Lion Hunter', Helena Mary Molyneux Newscuttings, c.1898–1939, 920 SEF 10/4.
44. LRO, unknown article, Helena Mary Molyneux Newscuttings, c.1898–1939, 920 SEF 10/4.
45. John Lane, 'Two Dianas in Somaliland Advertisement', in Herbert and a Shikári, *Two Dianas in Alaska,* pp.1–4.
46. Herbert and a Shikári, *Two Dianas in Alaska*, p.1.
47. For examples see, William Kyans, Advertisement, *The Field,* 22 March 1890, p.xi; Charles Lancaster, & Co, Advertisement, *The Field,* 6 June 1914, p.xi.
48. *'Verb. Sap.' on Going to East Africa, British Central Africa, Uganda, and Zanzibar, and Big Game Shooting in East Africa*, 1906 edn, 'Verb. Sap.' Series, 2 (London: J. Bale & Co, 1906), p.35.
49. Herbert, *Two Dianas in Somaliland,* pp.5–6.
50. Quex Park Archive, Birchington, Kent, 'Duchess as Elephant Hunter', PCQ 65, p.27.
51. Dunbar-Brunton did not have any pictures of his own and instead used those of six other hunters and the British South Africa Company to 'decorate' his book. The picture of d'Aosta was taken by Susan Hicks Beach, who supplied Dunbar-Brunton with two reels of photographs of 'carnivorae which she shot in Africa'. James Dunbar-Brunton, *Big Game Hunting in Central Africa* (London: Andrew Melrose, 1912), pp.viii, 236.
52. Mary Procida, 'Good Sports and Right Sorts', pp.455, 461.
53. Herbert, *Two Dianas in Somaliland,* pp.85–92.
54. Roby, *My Adventures in the Congo*, pp.186–93.
55. Coryndon was married to R.T. Coryndon, then Resident Commissioner of Swaziland. He was from a respected Cape family and went on to a prominent career as a colonial official. In 1919, he was promoted to the rank of KCMG, from which position his and Lady Coryndon's titles derived. Christopher P. Youé, 'Coryndon, Sir Robert Thorne (1870–1925)', *Oxford Dictionary of National Biography*, Oxford University Press, September 2004; online edn, May 2006, http://www.oxforddnb.com.proxy.lib.umich.edu/view/article/32578. Accessed 19 January 2007.

56. Bodleian, Rhodes House, Papers of Sir Robert Thorne Coryndon, Lady Coryndon MSS, Camping Holidays, Mss Afr s.633, File 4, ff 79, p.9. Emphasis in the original.
57. Ibid, ff. 79–80, pp.9–10.
58. The Coryndons married in 1909, and she described the safari as essential for restoring their good humour in the 'early days of makeshift on a small salary'. Lady Coryndon MSS, ff.70.
59. See Gareth Cornwell, 'George Webb Hardy's *The Black Peril* and the Social Meaning of "Black Peril" in Early Twentieth-Century South Africa', *Journal of Southern African History*, 22, 3 (September 1996), p.442. The Union of South Africa was not formed until 1910. The term as used in this paper refers to the area eventually encompassed by the Union.
60. Diana Jeater, *Marriage, Perversion, and Power: The Construction of Moral Discourse in Southern Rhodesia, 1894–1930* (Oxford: Clarendon Press, 1993), p.188.
61. See Jeater, *Marriage, Perversion, and Power*, pp.186–9; Jack McCulloch, *Black Peril, White Virtue: Sexual Crime in Southern Rhodesia, 1902–1935* (Bloomington, IN: Indiana University Press, 2000); Simon Dagut, 'Gender, Colonial "Women's History" and the Construction of Social Distance: Middle-Class British Women in Later Nineteenth-Century South Africa', *Journal of Southern African Studies*, 26, 3 (September 2000), pp.555–72; Jeremy C. Martens, 'Settler Homes, Manhood and "Houseboys" an Analysis of Natal's Rape Scare of 1886', *Journal of Southern African Studies*, 28, 2 (June 2002), pp.379–400.
62. For a discussion of the changing markers of masculinity in this period see John Tosh, *A Man's Place: Masculinity and the Middle Class Home in Victorian England* (London and New Haven, CT: Yale University Press, 1999), pp.145–97.
63. During recruitment for the Boer War, approximately 70 per cent of volunteers were found unfit for service. In large urban areas the figures were even more worrisome: in Manchester, of 11,000 volunteers only 1,200 were accepted as 'fit in all respects'. Joanna Bourke, *Dismembering the Male: Men's Bodies, Britain, and the Great War* (Chicago, IL: University of Chicago Press, 1996), p.13.
64. For a succinct discussion of the effects of these movements on perceptions of masculinity, see Tosh, *A Man's Place*, pp.152–3.
65. In a particularly interesting example of the potential cross-over of colonial class and race categories, Timothy Keegan argues that white prostitutes convicted of having sexual relations with Africans were dealt with leniently in South African courts because the women's status, in the eyes of colonial society, made them only nominally white and not part of the ruling class. Timothy Keegan, 'Gender, Degeneration and Sexual Danger: Imagining Race and Class in South Africa, ca.1912', *Journal of Southern African History*, 27, 3 (2001), pp.464–5. For a counter example of this argument, see John Pape, 'Black and White: The "Perils of Sex" in Colonial Zimbabwe', *Journal of Southern African Studies*, 16, 4 (December 1990), p.703.
66. Jeater, *Marriage, Perversion, and Power*, pp.92–3, 187–9; Pape, 'Black and White', p.701.
67. The defining work on the separate spheres ideology is Catherine Hall and Leonore Davidoff, *Family Fortunes: Men and Women of the English Middle Class, 1780–1850* (Chicago, IL: University of Chicago Press, 1987). For a discussion on its implications in the colonial setting, see Dagut, 'Gender, Colonial "Women's History" and the Construction of Social Distance', pp.560–3. The term 'prestige' as used here is drawn from McCulloch, *Black Peril, White Virtue*, p.191.
68. Jeater, *Marriage, Perversion, and Power*, p.186; Marten, 'Settler Homes, Manhood and "Houseboys" an Analysis of Natal's Rape Scare of 1886', pp.381–2.
69. Marten, 'Settler Homes, Manhood and "Houseboys" an Analysis of Natal's Rape Scare of 1886', pp.379, 397–8; W. Bazeley, *Report of the Departmental Committee on Native Female Domestic Labour*, 1932, p.43, quoted in Pape, 'Black and White', p.699.
70. RGS Library, Loder MSS, British East African Journal, p.20a.
71. Roby, *My Adventures in the Congo*, p.13.
72. Ibid., p.137.
73. McCulloch, *Black Peril, White Virtue*, p.193.
74. Ibid., pp.191-4.
75. Owen Letcher, *Big Game Hunting in North-Eastern Rhodesia* (London: John Long, 1911), p.231.
76. Gouldsbury, *An African Year*, p.71.

CHAPTER THIRTEEN

What a City Ought to Be and Do: Gender and Urbanism in Chicago, Dublin and Toronto

MAUREEN FLANAGAN

There is no specifically agreed upon definition of the concept of urbanism among scholars of cities. In general, however, it encompasses the cultural meanings of a city: that is, an identifiable urban culture manifested through lifestyle, politics, and social structures and decisions, that describe and define what it means to be urban.[1] In this chapter, I focus on the cultural/political ideas that urban residents embrace as to what a city ought to be and do. An integral element of this urbanism, I argue, is how gendered ideas have been applied to the construction of cities, the result of which has been built environments segregating the productive and reproductive spaces of life. Such segregation, in turn, has specific differentiated effects on the uses of, and access to, public space, urban resources and institutions for women and men.

Applying a gender analysis to the historical development of cities is a fairly recent scholarly approach in urban history. Doing so requires a definition of gender that recognizes the specificity of cities as both place and space. In this case, the most appropriate definition to be applied is that of gender as a social construction that in cities has resulted in a ranking of 'values and behaviors ... so that those associated with men are normally given greater value'; a situation that has been historically embedded in urban institutions in ways that structure access to urban resources 'generating male privilege and domination and female subordination'.[2] In other words, every city is constructed as a gender regime: a 'distinctive relationship between its political, economic, and familial systems that constructs its gender regime, its particular version of patriarchy'.[3]

Yet, I do not wish this depiction of the role that gender ideas have played in urban growth to be read as yet another example of women's victimization.[4] The historical fact is that the physical structure of the three cities examined in this chapter, which I conceptualize as belonging to an Anglo-Atlantic world, has been decided by those who hold political and economic power and wish to keep it. Women, generally, have not held such positions; therefore they have been unable to exert equal power over many public decisions. In the absence of such power, reinforced by male ideas that they wanted cities shaped to promote their economic desires and social privileges, gendered ideals became powerful tools through which men have constructed cities.

One way to test such a broad, and potentially contentious, hypothesis is to compare cities across time, space and context. For my study here, I am comparing these three cities across the last century in order to identify these commonalities of urbanism. As an urban historian whose work heretofore has dealt primarily with North America, I am here attempting to broaden my own perspective to comprehend the ways in which shared sets of gendered ideals have shaped the urban built environment in this Anglo-Atlantic world; that is, those areas that share aspects of cultural norms imposed by the English colonial experience. While each of the three countries considered in this essay dealt differently with this experience vis-à-vis its specific context, all three believed that there were four fundamental components to building and maintaining a successful city in the late-nineteenth, early-twentieth century: a capitalist economic system that guaranteed accumulation of capital and property; democratic governing institutions; envisioning the city as a legal and financial corporation; and patriarchal control. The built environments of the three cities were thus constructed in this time period to reflect these ideals. While London and other English and Scottish cities could be included, for purposes of brevity they will not be considered here.

My starting point, rather paradoxically for a historian, is a 1994 conference that the Organization for Economic Co-operation and Development (OECD) held in Paris and titled *Women in the City: Housing, Services and the Urban Environment*. The proposal for the conference boldly stated that 'A major aim of this Conference is to accord higher visibility to women's "vision of the city" ... in order to take more into account their views and contributions to urban society'.[5] The conference's sessions and presentations all highlighted the idea that women have a particular *vision* of the city.

Women social scientists in Canada, the United States and Europe are currently arguing this proposition in their work. These scholars assert that those of us who study cities, or indeed wish to understand contemporary urban life, must accept several propositions: that 'women experience cities differently ... because of the gender asymmetries that are embedded in distinct institutions and local institutional relations'; that 'planning and policy making have historically been the province of white, upper-middle-class men, and the decisions that have been made reflect the interests and experiences of this group'; and, that urban space and the built environment must be acknowledged as social constructs that reflect 'the dominant thinking about women and families'. Social scientists concerned with the issue of gender and cities, look at the city as it is today and, thus, quite simply assert that the city is gendered because it has been 'historically designed by men and for men'.[6]

As a historian interested in these issues, however, my focus is on investigating the historical contexts and processes by which these ideas were embedded into the places and spaces of the city earlier in time. I want to demonstrate here how the observations of contemporary social science inquiry, as well as the issues raised at the OECD conference, can be useful for investigating and understanding the historical formation of a modern gendered urban built environment. My analysis here does not pretend to be definitive, but rather suggestive of the possibilities for re-envisioning cities as gendered spaces. It is an attempt to rethink the city along the lines proposed by Canadian urban geographer Suzanne MacKenzie:

> [I]n order to understand the importance of changing gender roles to the constitution and change of city form and urban process, we must examine the city from the perspective of the relationship between production and reproduction ... [we must look at cities as] concrete but mutable systems which provide resources for production and reproduction.[7]

ORIGINS OF A MODERN GENDERED VISION OF THE CITY

In their introduction to a volume of essays on European planning, *Gender and the Built Environment: Emancipation in Planning, Housing and Mobility in Europe*, the editors assert the necessity of a 'gender aware approach to the built environment' for the contemporary city. For the contemporary city, they make two arguments that have historical resonance: first, that contemporary cities must be rethought and redesigned within an integral approach 'in which housing, living environment, level of provisions and facilities, transportation and employment are dealt with as a whole'; and, second, that cities must be understood as 'a place where people spend their lives'.[8]

In the early twentieth century, Canadian and US cities closely resembled each other in several important ways. In both countries, industrialization had brought rapid urban growth, conspicuous poverty, miserable housing and a lack of adequate sanitation facilities among other problems that moved many urban residents to think strategically about how to effect reform. At the same time, both countries were adopting shared ideas of urban (town) planning that aimed to produce a comprehensive approach to relieving cities of such conditions and advancing the economic prospects of these cities. Moreover, new proponents of such planning were investigating, proposing and sharing urban reform plans for cities in the United States, Canada, England and Ireland. As Scottish-born Thomas Adams succinctly expressed this phenomenon in his speech to the Third National Conference on City Planning, held in the United States:

> Before entering upon the discussion of this afternoon, I should like to make one or two observations, on my own behalf, in expressing the pleasure it gives me as a British citizen to be present here at this American gathering, and to take part in discussing this great town planning movement. It is ... a world-wide movement, which is finding its expression in many activities among the English-speaking peoples on both sides of the Atlantic.[9]

As part of that Anglo-Atlantic world, Dublin experienced similar appalling urban conditions, and was the site of considerable interest in reforming and planning the city on the part of these same men. American planners John Nolen and Henry Long, for example, gave lectures on planning Dublin in 1914, while English and Scottish planners Raymond Unwin and Patrick Geddes submitted to the Dublin Corporation a comprehensive report on their investigation of housing conditions in the city, complete with plans and diagrams for replanning much of central Dublin.[10]

The gender component of ideas and decisions made about the built environment invites comparison, furthermore, because, some differences in municipal government structures and powers notwithstanding, male political power allowed implementation of specifically gendered ideas about a city and life within it that intended to keep women under the control of men. This was true for the past and remains true for the present. In her extensive examination of the issue of gender and the built environment in English cities, historian Helen Meller has abundantly demonstrated that an underlying historical problem is that women's ideas about the built environment have always been 'people centred'; that is, they were interested in how people experienced living in the city. With very rare exceptions, the men controlling cities and the emerging profession of urban planning were, instead, concerned to plan an 'ideal' city within a model 'that put women, children, and the family first under a benign patriarchy'.[11]

One telling example of this for Dublin appeared during the early civil war years. Seanad Éireann had passed a resolution withholding £400,000 in housing funds from Dublin Corporation because it was paying partial support to families of Corporation employees who were jailed for their participation in the revolt. Some members tried to rescind the resolution, arguing that the dreadful housing conditions of the poor in the city were causing a terrible mortality rate. 'Surely', argued member Thomas Farren, 'it is not fair to visit the sins that rightly belong to the sixteen members of the Corporation [those being jailed] on the unfortunate people who are rotting in the filthy slums of the city?' The President rejected this argument with the following statement:

> It may be that the families of these men have suffered for the sins that have been committed by the bread-winners. That is, unfortunately, one of the disadvantages of sin ... The time comes when fathers, as well as Governments, have got to correct any delinquencies of their children, or subjects, or citizens.[12]

The motion to rescind was then rejected.

While many women were increasingly able to express their own vision of the city and its needs in the early twentieth century, men felt little obligation to listen if they disagreed with women.[13] What male planners, politicians and businessmen proposed was to reorder and control urban growth by embedding the separation of the public world of the city (the productive domain) from the private world of the home (the reproductive domain) in a new vision of the physical and spatial arrangements of the urban environment. No matter how much freedom western women have gained, no matter how much control they have been able to exert over their own lives – personal, professional, familial – public power, the ability to wield it, and the results of that power still constrain how women are able to live in, and negotiate their way through, the city.

My starting point for explaining the twentieth-century historical context of my thesis is actually poetry, specifically three poems by the prolific American poet Carl Sandburg. Many of the hundreds of poems published by Sandburg celebrated the masculine vigour of the industrial city. While his poetry acknowledged the city's problems, it did so in a specifically gendered way, a sensibility that is best exemplified in what is perhaps his most famous poem, *Chicago*, published in 1916. For Sandburg, Chicago was the

> Hog Butcher for the World,
> Tool Maker, Stacker of Wheat
> Player with Railroads and the Nation's Freight Handler;
> Stormy, husky, brawling,
> City of the Big Shoulders

The city's problems – those lacking vigour and strength – were specifically cast as female:

> They tell me you are wicked and I believe them, for I
> have seen your painted women under the gas lamps
> luring the farm boys.[14]
> And they tell me you are brutal and my reply is: On the
> faces of women and children I have seen the marks
> of wanton hunger.

Yet, as Sandburg continues, the weakness and frailty of painted women and hungry women and children pale in comparison with male strength:

> Come and show me another city with lifted head singing
> so proud to be alive and coarse and strong and
> cunning.

In every stanza following this one above, Chicago in simile and metaphor is male: It is 'fierce as a dog' and 'cunning as a savage'. It is 'laughing the stormy, husky, brawling laughter of Youth, half-naked, sweating, proud'.

In his poem *Streets Too Old*, the simile for the weakness of an old city (perhaps in contrast to the newness and vigour of Chicago) extends to old women:

> How old, how old, how old we are –
> the walls went on saying,
> Street walls leaning toward each other like old women of the people,
> like old midwives tired and only doing what must be done.[15]

Finally, his poem *Windy City* captures his vision of the city as separated into vigorous productive spaces as opposed to the softness of its reproductive ones. A long poem of hundreds of lines in ten stanzas barely mentions the latter except to speak of 'monotonous houses' and to add 'I am the woman, the home, the family' – the city as woman specifically meant the soft, controlled, reproductive sphere.

In a more prosaic form, Horatio Hocken, the mayor of Toronto, expressed his view of women's weakness, and lack of control, as a danger to the city. 'There can be nothing more dreadful in a large community', he declared, 'than to have feeble-minded women running at large'.[16] If one steps back to consider this statement, one sees two ways to understand it. The first is the standard one that appears in the analysis of this time period in burgeoning industrial cities: fear of disorder and lack of control over transgressive groups or individuals. The second, and I believe correct, way to understand it, is to ask why feeble-minded *women*? Why not just the feeble-minded? The gender of the feeble-minded was obviously the key point. Having such women 'running at large' was more disruptive of the male-centred public spaces of production than having feeble-minded men doing so.

Sandburg's urban vision and Hocken's fear of feeble-minded women can be placed into their broader historical context by turning to the argument made by Elizabeth Wilson at the OECD conference that by the late nineteenth century increasing '[U]rbanization [had] loosened the patriarchal, familial control of women', and thereby threatened to disrupt the prevailing order of society. The need for factory labour and the impoverishment of many in the working classes necessitated that women either leave the home to work outside of it, or that the home take in lodgers for extra income. Increasing numbers of women went out of the home, were left at home without male supervision, or brought 'strangers' into the household. Thus, Wilson argued, new forms proposed for ordering the urban built environment arose in tandem with women crossing the older boundaries between the public and the private that presumably had been constructed to keep western women out of the public spaces of the city and prevent them from transgressing their purely reproductive functions. 'Utopias, model villages, garden cities and town planning', according to Wilson, 'represented one answer to the threat of female independence'.[17]

In all three countries, this gendered ideal played out early in the twentieth century as Canadian and US cities underwent significant reform movements, and Ireland struggled to confront Dublin's massive poverty and housing issues as it sought to transform Dublin into a worthy capital city. What a city ought to be and do was then arranged for the century to come.

For many men in the early twentieth century in Canada and the United States, the city was the 'workshop', the economic world, and needed to be well-ordered and controlled. In 1917, W.F. Burditt, Chair of the St John, New Brunswick Town Planning Committee, articulated the separation of the residence (home) and the workshop when he advocated that the city

> be planned as a whole, functioning the different parts to the needs of the whole community: one part should be for work and service, another for rest and still another for recreation. It follows that the effective planning of a city involves the proper choice of sites for the different parts; industrial establishments should be located on land best suited to industrial purposes, while the residential portion, the rest-room of the city, should be protected from the noisy intrusion of the workshop.[18]

A newspaper editor in Berlin (now Kitchener), Ontario, Canada used another functional metaphor: 'The city was like a watch; wheels within wheels. The factories were the great wheel, industry the mainspring; the Council the balance wheel, and the Board of Trade the hair-spring.'[19]

Planning ideas at the time by-and-large envisioned a well-ordered city as one in which the productive (economic) sphere was top priority and clearly separated from the reproductive sphere. Many planning proposals, thus, totally neglected attention to living spaces in favour of work spaces. The winning plan submitted by architect Wilhelm Bernhard in a competition for planning a new suburban area in Chicago in 1915 is one example. Bernhard's plan stressed giving detailed attention to street layout and traffic flow, to separating business and residential buildings, and to building a community centre for business and civic life. At the 6th National City Planning Conference in Toronto in 1914, the plan singled out for praise was similar in content and intent. This plan was extolled as one of 'handsome curves arranged in every sort of ingenious fashion ... pleasing to the eye, as healthy and park-like as possible while in no way interfering with commercial and other necessities'.[20] The authors of the winning entry in the 1914 Dublin Planning Competition declared that they had 'not hesitated to produce a drastic Town Plan ... to provide for [Dublin's] shipping and industrial development', while they recommended removing almost 60,000 people from their current dwellings to 'extra-urban land', anticipating that their former residences 'will be rebuilt or remodelled for commercial purposes'.[21]

All three plans implicitly separated the city into different spheres. None considered how the emphasis on separating the functions of the city, and moving people to 'extra-urban' land, consigned women to the reproductive world of the home, nor to how such plans might make a homemaker's life more difficult.[22]

Plans, of course, are often hypothetical. Rarely in the early twentieth century were they carried out in their entirety, or even at all. Yet, with or without a specific overall plan to work from, the needs of women who were being housed in outlying areas were rarely considered. In Dublin, for example, new residential development between the world wars was 'conceived of as catering for individuals who would find employment and seek services in the city centre'. Thus, shopping and employment opportunities were scarcely available in residential areas.[23]

When architect Anna P. Schenck of New York, by contrast, submitted a plan to the Chicago City Club, its key element was attention to family needs. She focused on the *content* of the buildings themselves. She proposed buildings of different space and use: various sized apartments to accommodate different sized families, laundry, library and hospital facilities, nurseries and playgrounds were all to be services easily accessible to the people who lived in the buildings.[24] While male architects and planners generally offered plans in which 'community' life would revolve around separate centres to which people had to travel, Schenck's plan integrated daily living needs in planning. While not connected to planning *per se*, the women of the Alexandra College Guild Tenement Company in Dublin operated within a similar understanding of the needs of daily life for families when they focused their efforts on rehabilitating tenement buildings and their internal environment rather than trying to move residents out of their neighbourhoods. In Chicago, settlement house director Mary McDowell tried, unsuccessfully, to find investors for building and maintaining model tenements in her working-class neighbourhood. Her plans had included furnishing showers, laundries and steam dryers in such tenements.[25] By contrast, immediately following the First World War urban planner Thomas Adams had succeeded in crafting a male vision of a new built environment when he created a model community in suburban Ottawa, Canada, that specifically segregated women by putting emphasis on the self-contained individual home. In her analysis of this plan, Jill Delaney emphasized how such a plan depicts the ways in which the 'image of women and their place in the home during this period was also to have a major impact on the conception of appropriate housing form'.[26]

While the Adams plan focused on fashioning an isolated home as a site for women and domesticity, in 1909 New York City settlement house founder Mary Kingsbury Simkhovitch had articulated a more integrated ideal which envisioned the neighbourhood as the site for planning. She called on planning professionals to make the social needs of each neighbourhood their first priority. 'Parks, playgrounds, schools, churches, shopping centers, residences, and good transit facilities', she argued, 'all hang together'. When she and activist Florence Kelley organized the first American National Conference on City Planning that year, they chose the theme 'using planning to deal with social problems'. Kelley and Simkhovitch encountered almost total resistance to their proposal that planning had to be thought out in terms of social needs. Benjamin Marsh, Executive Secretary of the Committee on Congestion of Population in New York, declared that proper planning for 'orderly development of a city by which each section is arranged for the purpose for which it is best and most economically adapted', would solve pressing urban problems.[27]

The emphasis on economics in Marsh's declaration, rather than social needs, exposes a fundamental division in the vision of the city that existed between male and female urban reformers. Female reformers in the US and Canada in the earlier twentieth century viewed the city not as a workshop, but as a home. 'The city and the home', argued Chicago reform activist Anna Nicholes, 'are tied up in the most intimate and important events of life'. A city first and foremost was the place where people lived and wherein they were able 'to rear children to live a joyous life'.[28] Toronto reformer Mary Joplin Clarke contended that a good city had to be one that eradicated bad housing, inadequate food and clothing, unjust labour conditions, and lack of recreational facilities – all 'conditions resulting from unequal distribution of wealth'.[29] In Dublin, Lady Aberdeen and the Women's National Health Association were unable to secure creation of local, neighbourhood-based recreation spaces at a time when there were only two public parks in Dublin. When a Miss Edith MacTier petitioned the Public Health Committee to provide a large recreation hall 'for the respectable young people of the city' the committee informed her that they had no such hall to give.[30]

As concerns about reforming and reordering the urban built environment advanced across the early twentieth century, men used gender as a visual metaphor to express the differences between the unplanned and the planned city. An essay appearing in the professional journal *American City* in 1922 reprinted a cartoon that proponents of planning were using to promote their pro-zoning campaign. Side-by-side were pictures of two women. The one on the left was labelled 'Miss Turvey Town' (as in Topsy Turvy). She was dishevelled and slovenly in her appearance, with ripped stockings, messy hair, and wearing a shapeless dress. Next to her appeared 'Miss Zoned City', perfectly dressed and coiffed. The caption under her picture read:

> While this Fair Town Has Clearly Had,
> Some Plan in Her Formation,
> Her Lythe Young Form For Charm and Grace
> Is Famed Throughout the Nation.

The gendered allusion here to the city as either an orderly or disorderly woman is quite clear.[31]

Women concerned with urban problems, on the other hand, proffered an analogy of the city as a home, not as a site of female order or disorder. For the leader of the Women's Municipal League of Boston in 1912, this meant that the group's work was

Figure 1. The Gendered Vision of the City

> founded on the belief that woman has a special function in developing the welfare of humanity which man cannot perform. This function consists in her power to make, of any place in which she may happen to live, a *home* for all those who come there. Women must now learn to make of their cities great community homes for all the people.[32]

THE GENDERED URBAN EXPERIENCE ARISING FROM THIS GENDERED VISION

What I have argued to this point is that an earlier vision of the city as a space of separate gender functions resulted in one vision – primarily that of men who wielded power – becoming the focus for planning and constructing the urban built environment. Let me add here that there are many more examples of what men and women were arguing in this time period that would support my assertion. At this point, however, I would like to offer some general conclusions, based on a few specific additional examples of how this gendered urban vision, connected as it was to the issue of power and who wielded it, has resulted in early twenty-first century cities wherein there is not only a continuing unequal balance of power between men and women – generally speaking, and I do recognize that class and race also played a part in constructing cities – but also one in which women continue to be disadvantaged in terms of their access to public spaces, institutions and services.

Within that generalization, specific examples demonstrate how deeply embedded this gendered vision of the city is and how it has been reflected in both historical analysis and practical decision-making within cities. Urban scholars, first of all, tend to treat women's urban issues based on assumption without verifiable evidence. In doing so, they tell us much about male scholars' attitudes that have helped shape our notions of urban life and women in it. One good example of this interpretive tendency is from an incident in Chicago in 1913. As the city was continuing to build its rapid transit system, a group of stenographers and businesswomen in Chicago requested that a new transit stop be added because they currently had to descend at a location in that city's so-called 'vice district'. In recounting this episode in a history of transit in the city, one historian simply stated that such a request was due to these middle-class women not wanting to mingle with the lower classes.[33] He failed to acknowledge that these women might have a legitimate concern for their safety in having to walk through such an area to and from work, especially in the early darkness of the winter months. He did not think to examine whether this might be the case for these women. The location of mass transit stops is a legitimate public concern for women who have rarely ever been consulted, or taken seriously when finally consulted, on such an issue.[34]

Beyond the contemporary gender bias this author exhibits in dismissing women's concerns as emanating only from middle-class female sensibilities, there are numerous examples from all three cities that demonstrate how men were determined to exercise patriarchal control over all facets of urban life that might affect women, children and families. In Dublin in 1916, for example, the Women's National Health Association proposed a scheme to co-ordinate its activities with those of the Infant Aid Society and the Public Health Committee of the Dublin Corporation. The Health Committee rejected the women's scheme and instead proposed that it supervise all activities with 'the right to examine the books of the various Clubs [run by the WNHA] whenever it is considered advisable and to have power to attend the usual meetings of the committees controlling the Clubs'. The Corporation, moreover, determined that the two women's organizations had each to accept the appointment of three members of the Public Health Committee to represent the Corporation. For another example, as one study of the Alexandra Guild detailed, the Guild's tenements were subject to considerably more scrutiny than the property of other landlords. As the women of the Guild rather acerbically observed: 'We certainly have no reason to complain of any lack of Corporation inspection ... Their inspectors are ever with us ... We wonder if other people are as highly honored.' The following year, the Public Health Committee even sent a man to represent the Corporation at a Glasgow Conference on Child and Maternity Welfare.[35]

In Chicago, public health concerns of women were similarly subjected to male control and dismissal. Women's organizations in the city promoted a municipal ordinance regulating smoke pollution, but their proposal was dismissed as 'a woman's ordinance' and they were advised that when it came to passing legislation, 'men, experienced men, ought to have the final say, and not women concerned with a little dirt' inside their houses.[36] The specific concerns that women had for the health and welfare of women and children were rarely given top consideration in deciding what should be the priority of designing the built environment. Beginning in 1904, Chicago settlement worker

Mary McDowell began pleading, unsuccessfully, for a public hospital in her neighbourhood, particularly in order to confront contagious diseases among the poor children who lived there. She was consistently told that there was no money for such a hospital. There was only one children's hospital in the city, located many miles north of McDowell's neighbourhood, and largely inaccessible to these children of the city's south side. The city plan that Chicago's businessmen and political leaders were drawing up in these same years gave no thought to such health concerns as it focused on street widenings, railway terminals, bridges and other schemes to enhance the city's business growth. In Dublin, Abercrombie's plan for rebuilding the city had even proposed closing the Dr Mosse (Rotunda) Maternity Hospital at the top of O'Connell Street and turning the area into gardens.[37]

A final element of the built environment I wish to address here that reflected a gendered vision of the city, is that of transit. Transportation schemes have always been central to all plans for the urban built environment. Speakers at the 1994 OECD conference pointed out that globally 'women's use of cities differs from that of men and that current patterns and hours of [transportation] service delivery are incompatible with the transportation needs of many women'.[38]

As the building and provision of public services such as transit systems became defined earlier in the twentieth century as a business enterprise rather than as a public service, technology, cost-benefit analysis and attention to male worker needs for transportation became the driving forces of decision-making. Abercrombie's plan for Dublin paid no attention to women's potential transit needs as they were moved out of the city centre; his primary concern was to ensure that male workers who were to be moved out of the centre would have transportation back to that area, where he presumed most would still go to work. In Toronto, the concern of city reformers in determining how and where to extend mass transit likewise revolved around its viability in bringing 'working men' to their jobs. Focus on the abilities of 'working men' to commute between their jobs and 'new suburban communities' was also conceptualized as the way to better the health of the family.[39]

As Canadian scholar Gerda Wekerle has demonstrated for public transit in Toronto at the end of the twentieth century, this business focus continues to structure women's access to, and safety on, public transit. Despite the fact that all studies show that the majority of the Toronto system's users are women, women's pleas to the Toronto

Transit Commission for the system to be redesigned to 'protect and better serve women' are too often rejected as 'social' concerns that are not relevant to transit. As Wekerle expressed it,

> Those aspects of feminist discourse that were congruent with the prevailing business discourse were adopted; other gender needs were ignored. The discourse on equity which expanded the discussion to rights of access to resources was dismissed as social welfare demands that were not legitimately the concern of a business, albeit a business that is a monopoly with no competitors.[40]

The transportation networks that were put into place earlier in the twentieth century were never designed to recognize that 'women's travel needs frequently require transport outside of peak hours and to alternative destinations from those of men'. As women at the OECD conference charged, decisions of transit service are invariably made 'by planners who use conventional cost-benefit measures ... which place little value on the journeys women make' and bus/subway car designs fail to consider how these vehicles, often designed for male commuter 'straphangers' might not work for women escorting the elderly or children, carrying heavy packages or pushing baby carriages.[41] The depth of anger over this issue was best captured in the heartfelt declaration of one of the participants that failure to consider women's public safety in decisions over the built environment so affects women's ability to participate and function equally in a democratic city that it 'can prove as effective as purdah in restricting women's mobility'.[42] That women across the world feel this gendered nature of the city, both in its historical and contemporary dimensions, was clearly expressed by many of the women attending the OECD conference.

I began by discussing the concept of urbanism and how this can be seen as a set of cultural norms, or a cultural vision, that shape what urban residents believe a city ought to be and do. Chicago, Dublin and Toronto all developed from a shared vision of capitalism, legalism, democracy and patriarchy. This vision was shared by those men who controlled the development in all three cities, as well as by those men who were articulating the original ideas of urban planning. This being the case, one must conclude that the prevailing sense of urbanism in the Anglo-Atlantic world was defined and controlled by only certain groups of city residents who viewed the city primarily as the site of male economic activity. Because these were the men with political, economic, social and professional power, the obvious next conclusion is that urban democracy is a limited concept. Patriarchy automatically consigns women to second-class citizenship in their cities. American scholar Dolores Hayden has recently asked us to ponder the question: 'What would a nonsexist city be like?' In asking this question she reflects on the city as she sees it today, one in which 'dwellings, neighborhoods, and cities designed for homebound women constrain women physically, socially, and economically'.[43] If one reflects on the artificial boundaries that have been steadily constructed between the realms of production and reproduction, on the ways in which a range of public services upon which today's city residents depend have been provided, one can see that these conditions still prevail in all decision-making about urban growth. All of them still work against women's equal access to public space, urban institutions and services. Only when we recognise the historical gendered nature of the urban built environment can we begin to remake an urban vision that focuses on imagining cities first and foremost as places for people to live, and within whose spaces the artificial boundaries between the needs of production and reproduction might be dismantled.

NOTES

1. See Stuart M. Blumin, 'Two Decades of Urban History', *Journal of Urban History*, 21 (November 1994), pp.7–30, esp. pp.9–10 for his definition of urbanism.
2. Lourdes Benería and Martha Roldán, *The Crossroads of Class and Gender: Industrial Homework, Subcontracting, and Household Dynamics in Mexico City* (Chicago, IL: University of Chicago Press, 1987), pp.11–12.
3. Lynn M. Appleton, 'The Gender Regimes of American Cities', in Judith A. Garber and Robyne S. Turner (eds), *Gender in Urban Research* (Thousand Oaks, CA: Sage Publications, 1995), p.47.
4. See the caution against so doing by Elizabeth Wilson, *The Contradictions of Culture: Cities, Culture, Women* (London: Sage Publications, 2001), p.71.
5. OECD Conference on Women in the City, *Women in the City: Housing, Services and the Urban Environment*, 4–6 October 1994 (Paris: OECD, 1995), p.13.
6. Kristine B. Miranne and Alma H. Young (eds), *Gendering the City: Women, Boundaries, and Visions of Urban Life* (Lanham, MD: Rowman and Littlefield, 2000), p.5; Susan S. Fainstein and Lisa J. Servon (eds), *Gender and Planning: A Reader* (New Brunswick, NJ: Rutgers University Press, 2005), p.2; and Lia Karsten, 'Women and Children First', in Liesbeth Ottes, Erica Poventud, Marijke van Schendelen and Gertje Segond von Banchet (eds), *Gender and the Built Environment: Emancipation in Planning, Housing and Mobility in Europe* (Assen: Van Gorcum & Comp., 1995), p.8. For this last assertion, see Jo Beall, 'Participation in the City: Where do Women Fit In?', in Caroline Sweetman (ed.), *Women and Urban Settlement* (Oxford: Oxfam, 1996), p.9.
7. Suzanne MacKenzie, 'Building Women, Building Cities: Toward Gender Sensitive Theory in the Environmental Disciplines', in Caroline Andrew and Beth Moore Milroy (eds), *Life Spaces: Gender, Households, and Employment* (Vancouver: University of British Columbia Press, 1988), p.16. See also Miranne and Young, *Gendering the City* and Jo Little, Linda Peake, and Pat Richardson (eds), *Women in Cities: Gender and the Urban Environment* (New York: New York University Press, 1988).
8. Ottes *et al.*, 'Introduction', *Gender and the Built Environment*, p.xv.

9. Thomas Adams, 'The British Point of View', *Proceedings of the Third National Conference on City Planning* (Boston: National Conference on City Planning, 1911), pp.27–37.
10. For Unwin and Geddes, see their proposal in *Reports and Printed Documents of the Corporation of Dublin*, vol.1, no.78 (1915), pp.709–53. See also Ruth McManus, *Dublin, 1910–1940: Shaping the City and Suburbs* (Dublin: Four Courts Press, 2002), pp.49–50. For overviews of conditions and planning in Dublin, see M.J. Bannon (ed.), *The Emergence of Irish Planning, 1880–1920*, esp. Mary E. Daly, 'Housing Conditions and the Genesis of Housing Reform in Dublin, 1880–1920', pp.77–130. Planning was just beginning to emerge as a 'profession' at this time. Its proponents and practitioners thus had backgrounds in architecture, landscape architecture and sociology among other areas of training.
11. See Helen Meller, 'Gender, Citizenship, and the Making of the Modern Environment', in Elizabeth Darling and Lesley Whitworth (eds), *Women and the Making of Built Space in England, 1870–1950* (Aldershot: Ashgate Publishing, 2007), p.16, and Meller, 'Women and Citizenship: Gender and the Built Environment in British Cities, 1870–1939', in Robert Colls and Richard Rodger (eds), *Cities of Ideas: Civil Society and Urban Governance in Britain, 1800–2000* (Aldershot: Ashgate Publishing, 2004), pp.247–8.
12. Seanad Éireann, *Debates*, vol.1 (7 February 1923). http://historical-debates.oireachtas.ie/en.toc.seanad.html>
13. The municipal housekeeping movement, the playgrounds and recreations movements in both Canada and the United States, for example, brought many aesthetic, as well as other, reforms into the cities. But, without suffrage, women had to depend largely on persuasion. In conceptualizing the urban built environment as a whole and how it should be structured and planned, when there was a conflict between the desires of men in power and those of women, women generally lost. For examples, see Maureen A. Flanagan, 'Gender and Urban Political Reform: The City Club and the Woman's City Club of Chicago in the Progressive Era', *American Historical Review*, 95 (October 1990), pp.1032–50.
14. This poem concords with Elizabeth Wilson's analysis that the prostitute in the industrial city was considered both a sign of uncontrolled women and of male frailty to female temptation. See Wilson, *The Contradictions of Culture*, p.74 and Doreen Massey, *Space, Place, and Gender* (Minneapolis, MN: University of Minnesota, 1994), pp.233 and 258.
15. Carl Sandburg, 'Chicago', in *Chicago Poems*, and 'Streets Too Old', in *Smoke and Steel* (1920), 'Windy City', section 6, in *Slabs of the Sunburnt West* (1922), printed in Rebecca West (ed.), *Selected Poems of Carl Sandburg* (New York: Harcourt, Brace, and World, 1954).
16. Hocken quoted in Paul Rutherford, *Saving the Canadian City: The First Phase, 1880–1920 [An Anthology of Early Articles on Urban Reform]* (Toronto: University of Toronto Press, 1974), p.197.
17. For Wilson, see OECD, 'Culture and Gender Concerns in Spatial Development', *Women in the City*, p.41. See also Elizabeth Wilson, *The Sphinx in the City: Urban Life, the Control of Disorder, and Women* (Berkeley, CA: University of California Press, 1991). For a Canadian planned model community, see Jill Delaney, 'The Garden Suburb of Lindenlea, Ottawa: A Model Project for the First Federal Housing Policy, 1918–1924', *Urban History Review*, 19 (February 1991), pp.151–65. The map printed therein (p.152) depicts just such a segregated vision.
18. Burditt, 'Civic Efficiency and Social Welfare in Planning of Land', in *Saving the Canadian City*, p. 238.
19. Berlin editor quoted in Elizabeth Bloomfield, 'Community Leadership and Decision-Making: Entrepreneurial Elites in Two Ontario Towns, 1870–1930', in Gilbert Stelter and Alan Artibise (eds), *Power and Place: Canadian Urban Development in the North American Context* (Vancouver: University of British Columbia Press, 1986), p.99.
20. Elizabeth Bloomfied, 'Reshaping the Urban Landscape? Town Planning Efforts in Kitchener-Waterloo, 1912–1925', in Gilbert Stelter and Alan Artibise (eds), *Shaping the Urban Landscape: Aspects of the Canadian City-Building Process* (Ottawa: Carleton University Press,1982), pp.256–98, quote pp.279–80.
21. Patrick Abercrombie, Sidney Kelly and Arthur Kelly, *Dublin of the Future: The New Town Plan – Being the Scheme Awarded the First Prize in the International Competition* (prepared 1914, awarded 1916, published Dublin: Civics Institute of Ireland, 1922). See also, McManus, *Dublin, 1910–1940*, pp.56–67.
22. See 'Minutes of Meetings', 18 November 1915, *Committee on Housing Conditions*, City Club of Chicago, Ms Collection, Box 17, folder 3; and 25 May 1916, Box 18, folder 7,

Chicago History Museum and Alfred B. Yeomans, *City Residential Land Development: Studies in Planning, Competitive Plans for Subdividing a Typical Quarter Section of Land in the Outskirts of Chicago* (Chicago: University of Chicago, 1916). For Canada, see Elizabeth Bloomfield, 'Reshaping the Urban Landscape? Town Planning Efforts in Kitchener-Waterloo, 1912–1925', in Stelter and Artibise (eds), *Shaping the Urban Landscape*, p.279.

23. James Killen, 'Transport in Dublin: past, present and future', in F.H.A. Aalen and Kevin Whelan (eds), *Dublin City and County: from Prehistory to Present* (Dublin: Geography Publications, 1992), p.310.
24. 'Minutes of Meetings', 8 March 1915, *Committee on Housing Conditions*, City Club of Chicago, Ms Collection, Box 16, folder 3.
25. Maryann Gialanella Valiulis, 'Toward the "Moral and Material Improvement of the Working Classes": The Founding of the Alexandra College Guild Tenement Company, Dublin, 1898', *The Journal of Urban History*, 22 (March 1997), pp.295–315. These women were following the example of the Hill sisters in England. See, Anne Anderson and Elizabeth Darling, 'The Hill Sisters: Cultural Philanthropy and the Embellishment of Lives in late-Nineteenth Century England', in Darling and Whitworth, *Women and the Making of Built Space*, pp.33–50. For McDowell, see Mary McDowell Manuscript Collection, Chicago History Museum, Box 2, folder 14.
26. Delaney, 'The Garden Suburb of Lindenlea, Ottawa', p.154.
27. Susan Marie Wirka, 'The City Social Movement: Progressive Women Reformers and Early Social Planning', in Mary Corbin Sies and Christopher Silver (eds), *Planning the Twentieth-Century American City* (Baltimore, MD: The Johns Hopkins University Press, 1996), pp.55–75; Simkhovitch quoted on p.73. For Simkhovitch and Kelley, see also Daphne Spain, *How Women Saved the City* (Minneapolis, MN: University of Minnesota Press, 2001), p.71. For Marsh, see Marsh, 'Economic Aspects of City Planning', *Proceedings*, Municipal Engineers of the City of New York, paper 57 (1910), pp.73–87 and Marsh, 'Causes of Congestion in Population', *Proceedings of the Second National Conference on City Planning and Congestion* (May 1910), pp.35–39.
28. Anna Nicholes, 'How Women Can Help in the Administration of a City', *The Woman's Citizen Library*, vol. 9 (Chicago: Chicago Civics Society, 1913), pp.2150–51. For an extended account of Nicholes and her vision, see Maureen A. Flanagan, *Seeing with Their Hearts: Chicago Women and the Vision of the Good City, 1871–1933* (Princeton: Princeton University Press, 2002).
29. For Mary Joplin Clarke, see 'Report of the Standing Committee on Neighbourhood Work', to Canadian Conference of Charities and Correction, 23–25 September 1917, in Rutherford, *Saving the Canadian City*, p.174.
30. See F.H.A. Aalen, 'Health and Housing in Dublin, c.1850–1921', in Aalen and Whelan, *Dublin City and County*, p.299; and *Reports of Dublin Corporation*, vol.2, no.127 (1913), pp.255–56.
31. *American City* (June 1922), p.542.
32. Mrs T.J. Bowlker, 'Woman's Homemaking Function Applied to the Municipality', *The American City*, 6 (June 1912), p.863. See also Philip J. Ethington, 'Recasting Urban Political History: Gender, the Public, the Household, and Political Participation in Boston and San Francisco during the Progressive Era', *Social Science History*, 16 (Summer 1992), pp.305–6; and Maureen A. Flanagan, 'The City Profitable, the City Livable: Environmental Policy, Gender, and Power in Chicago in the 1910s', *The Journal of Urban History*, 22 (January 1996), pp.163–90.
33. See Paul Barrett, *The Automobile and Urban Transit: The Formation of Public Policy in Chicago, 1900–1930* (Philadelphia, PA: Temple University Press, 1983), p.252, n.45.
34. See Laurie Pickup, 'Hard to Get Around: A Study of Women's Travel Mobility', in Little, Peake and Richardson, *Women in Cities*, pp.99–116.
35. Dublin Corporation Reports, vol.2, no. 163 (1916), p.473 and 'Minutes of the Municipal Council of the City of Dublin' (1916); Valiulis, 'The Founding of the Alexandra College Guild Tenement Company', pp.310–11; and 'Minutes of the Municipal Council of the City of Dublin', Public Health Committee, No.216 (1917), p.130.
36. Quoted in David Stradling, *Smokestacks and Progressives: Environmentalists, Engineers, and Air Quality in America, 1881–1951* (Baltimore, MD: The Johns Hopkins University Press, 1999), pp.122–23.

37. See McDowell Collection, Box 2, folder 13; Carl Smith, *The Plan of Chicago: Daniel Burnham and the Remaking of the American City* (Chicago, IL: University of Chicago Press, 2006); and Abercrombie *et al.*, *Dublin of the Future*, p.41.
38. OECD, *Women in the City*, p.28.
39. See Abercrombie *et al.*, *Dublin of the Future*, p.26, for Dublin; G. Frank Beer, 'A Plea for City Planning Organization', in Rutherford, *Saving the Canadian City*, p.230 [Beer was president of the private Toronto Housing Company.]; and John C. Weaver, 'The Modern City Realized: Toronto Civic Affairs, 1880–1915', in Alan Artibise and Gilbert Stelter (eds), *The Usable Urban Past: Planning and Politics in the Modern Canadian City* (Toronto: Macmillan Company of Canada, 1979), p.64.
40. Gerda Wekerle, 'Gender Planning in Public Transit: Institutionalizing Feminist Policies, Changing Discourse, and Practices', in Fainstein and Servon, *Gender and Planning: A Reader*, pp.275, 277, 283 and 291–92. Wekerle outlines how some of the women's requests were implemented, but that changing political administrations subsequently dismantled some of the more 'woman friendly' initiatives and the Toronto Transit Commission removed women from its 'policy agenda'.
41. Quotes are from Carmen Belloni, 'A Woman-friendly City: Policies Concerning the Organisation of Time in Italian Cities', in OECD, *Women in the City*, pp.105 and 108.
42. OECD, *Women in the City*, p.98.
43. Dolores Hayden, 'What Would a Nonsexist City Be Like?: Speculations on Housing, Urban Design, and Human Work', in Fainstein and Servon, *Gender and Planning: A Reader*, p.47.

Index

M

N

O

P

R